Assessing Sector Performance and Inequality in Education

STREAMLINED ANALYSIS WITH ADePT SOFTWARE

Assessing Sector Performance and Inequality in Education

Emilio Porta
Gustavo Arcia
Kevin Macdonald
Sergiy Radyakin
Michael Lokshin

THE WORLD BANK
Washington, D.C.

© 2011 The International Bank for Reconstruction and Development / The World Bank
1818 H Street, NW
Washington, DC 20433
Telephone: 202-473-1000
Internet: www.worldbank.org

All rights reserved

1 2 3 4 14 13 12 11

This volume is a product of the staff of the International Bank for Reconstruction and Development / The World Bank. The findings, interpretations, and conclusions expressed in this volume do not necessarily reflect the views of the Executive Directors of The World Bank or the governments they represent.

The World Bank does not guarantee the accuracy of the data included in this work. The boundaries, colors, denominations, and other information shown on any map in this work do not imply any judgement on the part of The World Bank concerning the legal status of any territory or the endorsement or acceptance of such boundaries.

Rights and Permissions

The material in this publication is copyrighted. Copying and/or transmitting portions or all of this work without permission may be a violation of applicable law. The International Bank for Reconstruction and Development / The World Bank encourages dissemination of its work and will normally grant permission to reproduce portions of the work promptly.

For permission to photocopy or reprint any part of this work, please send a request with complete information to the Copyright Clearance Center Inc., 222 Rosewood Drive, Danvers, MA 01923, USA; telephone: 978-750-8400; fax: 978-750-4470; Internet: www.copyright.com.

All other queries on rights and licenses, including subsidiary rights, should be addressed to the Office of the Publisher, The World Bank, 1818 H Street, NW, Washington, DC 20433, USA; fax: 202-522-2422; e-mail: pubrights@worldbank.org.

ISBN: 978-0-8213-8458-9
eISBN: 978-0-8213-8717-7
DOI: 10.1596/978-0-8213-8458-9

Cover photo: Scott Wallace/World Bank (schoolgirl); ©iStockphoto.com/Olga Altunina (background image)
Cover design: Kim Vilov

Library of Congress Cataloging-in-Publication Data

Assessing sector performance and inequality in education : streamlined analysis with ADePT software / by Emilio Porta . . . [et al.].
   p. cm.
  Includes bibliographical references and index.
  ISBN 978-0-8213-8458-9 — ISBN 978-0-8213-8717-7 (electronic)
  1. Educational indicators—Data processing. 2. Educational equalization—Data processing. I. Porta, Emilio.
  LB2846.A76 2011
  379.2'60285—dc23

2011015

Contents

Foreword xv

Preface xvii

Abbreviations xix

Overview 1

Chapter 1
Introduction to ADePT Edu: Broadening Access to School and Household Data in Education 5

    The Need for Data 5
    Complementing ADePT Edu: Broadening the Availability of
      Education Projections Modules 7
        Education Projections Modules 8
        World Bank Education Projects Database 9
        Public Expenditure Database 9
    ADePT Edu As a Tool for Analyzing Education Inequality ... 9
    Notes 12
    References 12

Contents

Chapter 2
Using Household Survey Data 15

Use of Household Surveys to Analyze Educational Inequality
 and Education Sector Performance 16
Main Household Surveys 17
  The Living Standards Measurement Study 18
  The Demographic and Health Survey 19
  The Multiple Indicator Cluster Survey 22
  Which Survey Is Best for Analyzing Education Inequality?
   A Quick Guide 22
Advantages and Limitations of Using Household Surveys in
 Data Analysis 26
  Enrollment versus Attendance 26
  Level of Education Reported in Household Surveys 27
  Age, Timing, and Duration of Household Surveys 27
  Standard Errors 28
  Poverty Quintiles and Poverty Groups 28
  Missing and Contradictory Values 29
Notes 29
References 30

Chapter 3
Using ADePT Edu: A Step-by-Step Guide 33

System Requirements 33
  Hardware Requirements 33
  Software Requirements 33
Installing ADePT 34
Using ADePT 37
  Starting and Closing ADePT 37
  ADePT's Computation Process 37
  Loading Data 42
  Specifying Variables 44
  Using Compound Fields 51
  Generating Tables and Figures 53
  Choosing a Reporting Option 55
Performing Common Tasks 55
  Generating Tables on a Subsample of Observations 57

Generating Tables with Standard Errors and Tables of
    Frequencies 61
Describing a Complex Survey Design 62
Defining Missing Values 62
Specifying Expressions in Variables Fields 64
Running Simulations 66
Adjusting Settings 67
Changing the Screen and Output Language 67
Selecting the Computational Engine and Output Viewer 69
Working with Projects in ADePT 72
Using ADePT Project Files on a Different Computer 74
Replicating Results 74
Using ADePT in a Batch Mode 75
Updating ADePT 76
Troubleshooting ADePT 78
Resolving Problems Encountered during Installation 78
Using the Debug Mode 78
Notes 80

Chapter 4
Generating and Interpreting Output Tables and Graphs 81

Output Information Tables 83
    The Contents Table 83
    The Notifications Table 83
    Original Data Report 87
School Participation Indicator Tables 88
    Table A1: School Attendance Ratios and Out of School,
        by Level 88
    Table A2: Primary Grade 1 Intake, Over-Age in First Grade,
        and Survival Rate to Grade 5 93
    Table A3: On-Time, Under-Age, and Over-Age in Primary
        Education 95
    Table A4: On-Time, Under-Age, and Over-Age by Single Grade
        of Primary Education, according to Background Characteristics 98
    Table A5: Percentage of the Population That Has Ever
        Attended School, by Age 99
    Table A6: Out-of-School Reasons 99
    Table A7: Typology of Out of School 100

Contents

School Progression Tables 103
    Table B1: Promotion, Repetition, Dropout, and Completion
    Rates by Level, and Transition Rates 103
    Table B2: Promotion, Repetition, and Dropout Rates by
    Single Grade of Primary Education 108
    Table B3: Promotion, Repetition, and Dropout Rates by
    Single Grade of Secondary Education 111
School Attainment Tables 111
    Table C1: School Attainment of Adult Population 111
    Tables C2–C5: Proportion of Adult Population That
    Completed Each Grade 114
    Table C6: Proportion of 10- to 19-Year-Olds Expected to
    Complete Each Grade 114
    Table C7: Inequality in Years of Schooling 114
Education Expenditure Tables 118
    Table D1: Primary Level 119
    Table D2: Secondary Level 119
    Table D3: Postsecondary Level 121
Labor Market Outcome Tables 121
    Table E1: Earning Inequalities 121
    Tables E2, E2a, and E2b: Employment for Youth 123
    Table E3: Employment by Sector 125
    Table E4: Earnings by Education Level 127
    Table E5: Economic Independence 129
    Table E6: Returns to Education 129
ADePT Education Graphs 132
Notes 139
References 140

Chapter 5
Analyzing Education Inequality with ADePT Edu 141

Reporting Education Inequality with ADePT Edu 143
Global Educational Inequality 144
    The Gini Coefficient in Education 144
    Correlation between Inequality in Income and Inequality in
    School Attainment 145

  Correlation between Inequality in School Attendance and
   Inequality in School Attainment 146
  Correlation between School Completion and Inequality in
   School Attainment 148
  Correlation between Extreme Poverty and Inequality in
   School Attainment 149
  How Has Inequality in Educational Attainment Changed
   over Time? 150
  Educational Inequality and Internal Efficiency in the
   Education Sector 152
  Disparity in School Participation 153
  Disparity in School Progression 154
  Disparity in the Number of Years of Schooling 155
 Educational Inequality across Regions 156
  Regional Disparity in School Participation 157
  Regional Disparity in School Progression 164
  Regional Disparity in School Attainment 167
 Concluding Comments 171
 Notes 173
 References 174

Bibliography 177

About the Authors 183

Index 185

Box

 4.1: UNESCO's Method for Estimating the Percentage of
   Children Out of School 101

Figures

 1.1: Percentage of Countries Reporting Data on Education,
   1990–2008 7
 1.2: Global Availability of Data Needed to Estimate MDG
   Indicators for Education, 1990–2008 8
 4.1: Estimates of Percentage of Out-of-School Children, by Type 102

Contents

5.1: The Education Lorenz Curve 145
5.2: Relationship between Gini Coefficient of School Attainment and Gini Coefficient of Income 146
5.3: Relationship between Gini Coefficient of School Attainment and Net Primary School Attendance Ratios 147
5.4: Relationship between Gini Coefficient of School Attainment and Primary Completion Rate 148
5.5: Relationship between Gini Coefficient of School Attainment and Extreme Poverty 149
5.6: Sources of Global Disparity in Educational Attainment among the 26–29 Cohort, 1985–2007 151
5.7: Sources of Global Disparity in School Participation among the 15–19 Cohort, by Education Level 153
5.8: Sources of Global Disparity among Out-of-School Children 154
5.9: Sources of Global Disparity in School Progression among the 15–19 Cohort 155
5.10: Sources of Global Disparity in School Attainment among the 15–19 Cohort 156
5.11: Sources of Global Disparity in Net Primary Attendance Rates, by Region 158
5.12: Net Primary Attendance Ratios in Benin, 2006 158
5.13: Sources of Disparity in Net Secondary Attendance Rates, by Region 159
5.14: Sources of Disparity in Gross Postsecondary Attendance Rates, by Region 161
5.15: Sources of Disparity in Net Intake Rate for First Grade of Primary School, by Region 162
5.16: Sources of Disparity in Children Out of Primary School, by Region 163
5.17: Sources of Disparity in Dropout Rates, by Region 164
5.18: Sources of Disparity in Late Entry among Out-of-School Children, by Region 165
5.19: Sources of Disparity among Out-of-School Children Who Never Attended School, by Region 166
5.20: Sources of Disparity in Primary Completion Rates, by Region 167
5.21: Sources of Disparity in Secondary Completion Rates, by Region 168
5.22: Primary and Secondary Completion Rates in India, 2005 168
5.23: Sources of Disparity in Primary to Secondary Transition Rates, by Region 169

5.24: Sources of Disparity in Total Years of Schooling, by Region 170
5.25: Gini Coefficient of School Attainment, by Region 170

Graphs

4.1: Educational Attainment of 15- to 19-Year-Olds in Nicaragua, by Income Quintile 132
4.2: Enrollment Rates for Boys and Girls 6–14 Years Old in Rural and Urban Areas of Nicaragua 133
4.3: Grade Survival Profiles for 10- to 19-Year-Olds in Nicaragua, by Income Quintile 134
4.4: Enrollment Pyramid for 6- to 24-Year-Olds in Nicaragua, by Income Quintile 135
4.5: Educational Attainment Profiles for Men and Women 30–39 Years Old in Rural and Urban Areas in Nicaragua 136
4.6: Typology of Out of School, by Subpopulation and Level in Nicaragua 136
4.7: Reasons Why Primary School–Age Children Are Out of School in Nicaragua 137
4.8: Lorenz Curve for Years of Schooling in Nicaragua 138
4.9: Age-Earnings Profile by Education Level 138
4.10: Earnings by Years of Schooling and Labor Market Experience in Nicaragua 139

Screenshots

3.1: Accepting the License Agreement 35
3.2: Installing ADePT 36
3.3: Completion of Setup 36
3.4: Starting ADePT Using the Start Menu 38
3.5: Selecting a Module 39
3.6: Guide to the Main Screen 40
3.7: Opening a Dataset 43
3.8: Full Path of the Selected Dataset 43
3.9: Labeling the Dataset 43
3.10: Opening a Stata Data File 44
3.11: Variable Names and Labels 45
3.12: Variable Names in the Main Form 48
3.13: Specifying Variable Names in the Education Tab 48
3.14: Variable Names for the Labor Market Tab 50
3.15: Variable Names for a Loaded Dataset 51

3.16: Disabled Variables in Gray, Active Variables in Bold 51
3.17: Compound Field for Missing Values 52
3.18: Table and Figure Window: Selecting the Education
       Tables to Generate 54
3.19: Record and Stop Button for Creating Tables 55
3.20: Selecting a Level of Reporting 56
3.21: Clearing Contents or Changing Fonts 56
3.22: Using the Global Filter 57
3.23: Setting an If-Condition 58
3.24: Example of an If-Condition 60
3.25: Clearing an If-Condition 61
3.26: Generating Tables with Standard Errors, Frequencies, or Both 62
3.27: Adding Household Weights and Other Parameters 62
3.28: Changing the Code for Missing Values 64
3.29: Creating an Expression to Recode a Variable .65
3.30: Changing the Language 68
3.31: Selecting the Proper Code Page 69
3.32: Appearance of Variable Names When the Code Page Is
       Set Correctly 70
3.33: Appearance of Variable Names When the Code Page Is
       Not Set Correctly 70
3.34: Final Set, Ready to Run 72
3.35: Commands for Working with Project Files 73
3.36: Checking for Updates of ADePT 77
3.37: Debug Mode 79
4.1: ADePT Edu Table of Contents 84
4.2: Error, Warning, and Notification Messages 85
4.3: Examples of Errors and Warnings in ADePT Output 86
4.4: Original Data Report 87
4.5: Table A1: School Attendance Ratios and Out of School,
      by Level 89
4.6: Table A2: Primary Grade 1 Intake, Over-Age in First Grade,
      and Survival Rate to Grade 5 94
4.7: Table A3: On-Time, Under-Age, and Over-Age in
      Primary Education 96
4.8: Table A5: Percentage of the Population That Has Ever
      Attended School, by Age 99
4.9: Table A6: Reasons Why Children Are Out of School 100

4.10: Table A7: Typology of Reasons for Being Out of School
 (UNESCO Method) 101
4.11: Table B1: Rates of Promotion, Repetition, Dropout,
 and Completion 104
4.12: Table B2: Promotion, Repetition, and Dropout Rates by
 Single Grade of Primary Education 109
4.13: Table B3: Promotion, Repetition, and Dropout Rates by
 Single Grade of Secondary Education 112
4.14: Table C1: School Attainment 113
4.15: Table C2: Proportion of 15- to 19-Year-Olds That
 Completed Each Grade 115
4.16: Table C6: Proportion of Population 10–19 Expected to
 Complete Each Grade 116
4.17: Table C7: Inequality in Years of Schooling 117
4.18: Table D1: Household Expenditure on Primary Education 120
4.19: Table E1: Earning Inequalities 122
4.20: Table E2: Employment for Youth 124
4.21: Table E3: Employment by Sector 126
4.22: Table E4: Earnings by Education Level 128
4.23: Table E5: Economic Independence 130
4.24: Table E6: Returns to Education 131

Tables

2.1: Data Modules and Content of Typical Living Standards
 Measurement Study Survey Questionnaire 19
2.2: Summary of Questionnaire Content in October 2010
 Demographic and Health Survey 20
2.3: Education Indicators Reported in Fourth Round of Multiple
 Indicator Cluster Surveys (2009–11) and Relation to MDGs 23
2.4: Data Available for Estimating Selected Indicators, by
 Type of Survey 25
3.1: ADePT Edu Hardware Requirements 34
3.2: ADePT Edu Software Requirements 34
3.3: Descriptions of Variables Included in the Main Form 46
3.4: Definitions of Variables in the Labor Market Tab 50
3.5: Examples of If-Conditions Available in Stata 58
4.1: Topics Covered by ADePT Indicator Tables 82
4.2: Versions of Tables Available in ADePT 82

Foreword

To support the implementation of its Education Strategy 2020, the World Bank has begun an ambitious multiyear program aimed at assisting countries in improving the performance of their education systems. This program, System Assessment and Benchmarking for Education Results (SABER), is developing an array of technical approaches and tools to examine education systems, diagnose and benchmark their policy and institutional performances, and enhance the amount and quality of information available to society and to decision makers. Expanding access to high-quality educational data is an integral element of this new initiative.

For society—which includes students, parents, and other education sector stakeholders—having more accessible and more reliable information about education opens up a myriad of possibilities for involvement and collaboration, from public-private partnerships in education to the reestablishment of the social contract between parents and teachers. For public officials, better and regularly updated information allows for sharper planning, smarter policy choices, and more productive policy dialogue with providers and the general public.

We began with EdStats, an education statistics portal created by the World Bank to give everyone access to a vast array of education indicators from more than 180 countries. This portal regularly attracts a huge number of visitors, underscoring a wide demand for such data. Now we unveil

Foreword

ADePT Edu, a free software program that makes available education statistics at the household level with a high degree of technical efficiency. The program provides the user with rapid access to microeconomic-level education data for such uses as obtaining the distributional profile of education attainment in a country or estimating the relationship between household wealth or parental education and children's schooling levels. These analyses portray dimensions of education challenges that are also critical for effective policy making.

ADePT Edu marks an important step in opening up worldwide education data to all education stakeholders. This book is a guide to users of the program. I am proud to present this effort from my colleagues in the Development Research Group and in the Human Development Network of the World Bank.

Elizabeth King
Director, Education
Human Development Network
The World Bank

Preface

During our travels to countries engaged in a policy dialogue with the World Bank, we have often found that policy makers needed information to back up their arguments or to reinforce their vision. We have also found situations in which our professional counterparts needed to use statistics and performance indicators to clarify pronouncements made by politicians and opinion makers in popular media outlets. In both cases, quick access to education statistics could have been a determining factor in designing a good education policy or, at least, in generating a consensus around a policy issue.

Although education statistics are now readily available from several international organization websites, there is a clear need for a tool that helps analysts organize education data and lets them use the education portion of household surveys. This type of tool would save time and money for many education ministries and education analysts facing very limited resources, while also improving their ability to analyze education inequality in their countries. This last point is crucial because reducing education inequality is at the heart of public education policy. ADePT Edu is just such a tool for those analysts interested in education inequality and the use of education data and education indicators for policy dialogue.

This book attempts to fill the data access gap that we have observed in our travels, providing free software that facilitates education data analysis and brings inequality to the forefront of the education policy discussion. As

Preface

a result, countries can benchmark their efforts to improve education equity and use ADePT Edu to keep education inequality on the policy agenda of their leaders. Only by addressing education inequality directly can countries meet the Millennium Development Goals and bring access to education to all disadvantaged groups in their societies.

In the process of transforming our idea into practice, several people gave us invaluable professional advice and encouragement. We thank our peer reviewers for taking the time to give the initial manuscript a thorough review. They were Luis Crouch then of RTI International and now at the World Bank's Education for All Fast-Track Initiative; Deon Filmer of the Bank's Development Research Group; Albert Motivans of the UNESCO Institute of Statistics; and Ernesto Schifelbein of the Universidad Autónoma de Chile. Their technical and editorial input was crucial in shaping the tone and scope of this book, and for that, we owe them a great personal and professional debt, although the final responsibility for the book's content remains solely ours. We also thank the co-creators of ADePT, Harry Patrinos and Zurab Sajaia, for their technical leadership and support. We extend thanks to EdStat team members Jennifer Klein and Jian Guo Zhu and consultants Ramón Laguna and Marc-François Smitz for their assistance during the creation of the ADePT database. We are also grateful to Annababette Wils and Ben Sylla of the Education Policy and Data Center and to Mamadou Thiam of the Education for All Fast-Track Initiative for their comments during the development phase of the ADePT software and for their ideas about this book. We thank Ariel Fizbein, chief economist in the Bank's Human Development Network, for his initial idea and intellectual support for ADePT Edu; and we are grateful to our Bank colleagues Juan Diego Alonso, Felipe Barrera, Marguerite Clarke, Juliana Guaqueta, Christine Horansky, Oni Lusk-Stover, Vicente Garcia Moreno, and Vy T. Nguyen for their ideas and comments during the process of creating AdePT Edu. We also thank Elizabeth King, director of education, and Robin Horn, sector manager, in the Human Development Network for their feedback, guidance, and supervision. Finally, we thank Janet Sasser, Stephen McGroarty, and Nora Ridolfi of the Bank's Office of the Publisher for their great editorial and production assistance.

The ADePT Edu software, complete country profiles produced with ADePT Edu for over 80 countries, and the data on the indicators used throughout the book can be downloaded from EdStats (www.worldbank.org/education/edstats).

Abbreviations

ADePT	Automated DEC Poverty Tables
DEC	Development Economics (Vice Presidency at the World Bank)
DHS	Demographic and Health Survey
EMIS	Education Management Information Systems
GER	gross enrollment rates
GPI	gender parity index
IHSN	International Household Survey Network
ISCED	International Standard Classification of Education
LSMS	Living Standards Measurement Study
MDG	Millennium Development Goal
MICS	Multiple Indicator Cluster Survey
NAR	net attendance rate
NAR+	adjusted net attendance rate
NBS	Numerics by Stata
NER	net enrollment rate
NER+	adjusted net enrollment rate
TNER	total net enrollment rate
UIS	UNESCO Institute for Statistics
USAID	U.S. Agency for International Development
UNESCO	United Nations Educational, Scientific and Cultural Organization

Overview

This book gathers in one volume all the information related to ADePT Edu, the software platform created by the World Bank for reporting and analyzing education indicators and education inequality. It includes a primer on the availability of education data, an operating manual for using the ADePT software, a technical explanation of all the education indicators ADePT generates, and an overview of global education inequality using ADePT Edu.

Education policy makers need objective information in order to make good decisions in a difficult political and institutional environment. The analysts providing them with such information need quick and reliable access to educational statistics relevant to their policies and issues. This need compelled the World Bank to invest significant resources in EdStats, a web-based portal that contains administrative source data on education for more than 180 countries.

Although important, administrative source data—including information on enrollment, repetition, and dropouts—still leave gaps in information on education. In particular, information needed for assessing the demand side of education, normally found in household surveys, was missing. Information on education at the household level, especially household expenditures and the characteristics of children out of school, is very important for analyzing the demand side of education. Household surveys are also a good source of information on educational attainment, because they include the last year of education completed by people who are not covered by school administrative data. Household survey data also permit analysts to examine educational access by gender, location, and poverty level, all of which are important for understanding educational inequality.

To correct this omission, the World Bank developed ADePT Edu, which is designed for the analysis of education variables contained in household surveys. ADePT Edu gives users the ability to organize and analyze education data from households. Its software can be used with any household survey, allowing users to process data with the aid of a user-friendly interface that creates education tables and graphics that comply with international standards for performance indicators.

Because this volume is a compendium, readers need a brief road map to its use. Chapter 1 is an introduction to ADePT Edu. It describes its origin and intended use and familiarizes readers with educational statistics under the EDSTAT portal. Chapter 1 also briefly explains why disparities in educational access are a prominent topic, especially as the analysis of inequality is just one of many analyses that can be conducted with the aid of ADePT's 200 educational statistics.

Chapter 2 is intended for users unfamiliar with the different datasets that contain education statistics and household-level data that contain information on education. It includes a short primer on the basic issues associated with data quality, brief descriptions of prominent household surveys, and a list of sample household surveys from different countries.

Chapter 3 is a step-by-step technical guide for potential users. In addition to identifying the hardware and operating system requirements, it provides graphic examples of each of the steps needed to install and operate the software. This chapter also includes detailed explanations for uploading datasets, specifying variables, and generating tables and graphs. It provides a complete how-to guide for processing educational data with ADePT Edu.

Chapter 4 describes the outputs of ADePT and the definitions of all the indicators it generates. ADePT output groups education indicators in five basic groups: school participation, school progression, school attainment, education expenditures, and labor market outcomes. The chapter explains each of the tables produced under these subheadings. Chapter 4 also provides detailed definitions of each of the indicators generated by ADePT Edu. These definitions comply with international standards but are constructed in a way that makes them compatible with any dataset. The indicator tables produced by ADePT Edu can thus be thought of as benchmarks.

Chapter 5 provides a global and regional overview of education inequality, using ADePT Edu outputs obtained from household survey data. It analyzes inequality in school participation, progression, and attainment. This analysis can be considered a primer on education inequality for analysts interested in the association between access to education and socioeconomic variables such as gender, location, and household poverty. Chapter 5 also illustrates how ADePT Edu can be used to readily analyze data from any household survey, a feature that makes this software unique. The analysis of education inequality serves as a backdrop for the potential use of household surveys for analyzing the demand side of education.

Chapter 1

Introduction to ADePT Edu: Broadening Access to School and Household Data in Education

This chapter highlights recent efforts by the World Bank to broaden the availability of education data, especially data used in the analysis of education inequality. It explains the benefits of ADePT Edu, a software program designed to provide common educational indicators from micro-level survey data, and the model behind the structure and organization of the reports users can produce with it.

The Need for Data

As the World Bank's new education sector strategy notes, the production and dissemination of reliable education statistics are essential for effective education sector planning and for monitoring progress toward national and global education targets, such as the Millennium Development Goals (MDGs). Good access to education statistics for all countries is also an important global public good that, by definition, is normally not supplied by the market. In response to the need for greater availability of reliable education statistics, the World Bank, the donor community, and national governments have been working to promote the production, dissemination, and use of education statistics.

Accurate and reliable information on education sector performance is crucial for designing policies and programs. Even in environments in which the political economy of education may suggest that education statistics, education policy analysis, and data on sector performance take second place to political decisions, policy makers often use education data as points of reference for their political decisions (Crouch 1997). In recent years many countries have made substantial reforms to their education systems, moving toward greater decentralization of education and the use of performance indicators and the measurement of learning outcomes to monitor educational performance and reinforce accountability (Bruns, Filmer, and Patrinos 2011). Successful implementation of these reforms requires the intensive use of Education Management Information Systems (EMIS) and, by inference, education statistics and education indicators on school and student performance (Arcia and others 2011; Cassidy 2005).

When evaluating the education sector in any country, analysts often need to use statistical indicators of internal efficiency and other educational statistics that monitor policy impacts. As education systems move toward decentralization and accountability, emphasizing access to and the use of education statistics at the local level becomes a necessary part of policy implementation (Filmer and Rubio-Codina 2011; Kitamura and Hirosato 2009). Analysts also need to know about the context in which internal efficiency operates. Educational expenditures by student and education level and the incidence of private educational expenditures by households are examples of the types of information needed to evaluate the potential winners and losers of changes in education policy. In particular, household-level data can be an important source of information in evaluating the impact of education expenditures on equity, living standards, and social outcomes (Das 2004). After all, education is considered the key element of long-term poverty reduction, because it is a key component of social and economic mobility (Hanushek and Wößmann 2007).

Despite considerable efforts made to improve the availability and quality of data, much work remains to be done to generate reliable and timely education statistics at the global level (Porta and Klein 2010). Some progress has been made. In 1990 publicly available education data allowed for the calculation of only 17.5 percent of 153 key education indicators; by 2000 the figure had risen to 46.7 percent (figure 1.1). Between 2000 and 2008, data availability levels fluctuated slightly over time, reaching 46 percent of nearly 280 education indicators in 2008.[1]

Figure 1.1: Percentage of Countries Reporting Data on Education, 1990–2008

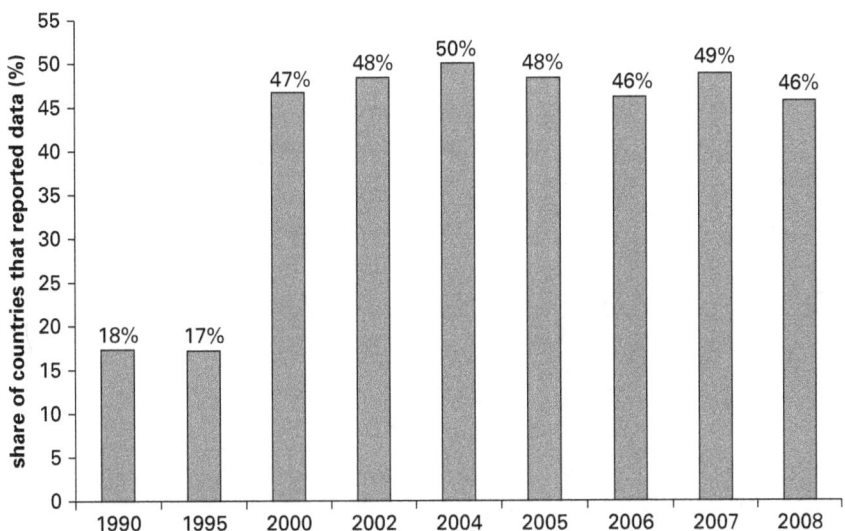

Source: World Bank EdStats calculations based on UIS data 2009.

The number of education indicators on which data are reported has increased. The percentage of countries reporting net enrollment data almost doubled between 1990 (when 32 percent of countries reported data) and 2008 (when 61 percent of countries did so). More data also became available on youth literacy, with 10 percent of countries providing such data in 2007 and 55 percent doing so in 2009. Overall, 62.4 percent of the data needed to estimate the four MDG indicators were available in 2008, an increase of almost 30 percentage points over 1995. Information gaps remain, however: between 2000 and 2008, only about half of all countries collected the data required to estimate the four MDG education indicators (figure 1.2).

Complementing ADePT Edu: Broadening the Availability of Education Projections Modules

In 2007 the World Bank's EdStats website updated its database and menu of education modules to complement UNESCO Institute for Statistics (UIS) data and increase data availability. Its databases are described below.

Figure 1.2: Global Availability of Data Needed to Estimate MDG Indicators for Education, 1990–2008

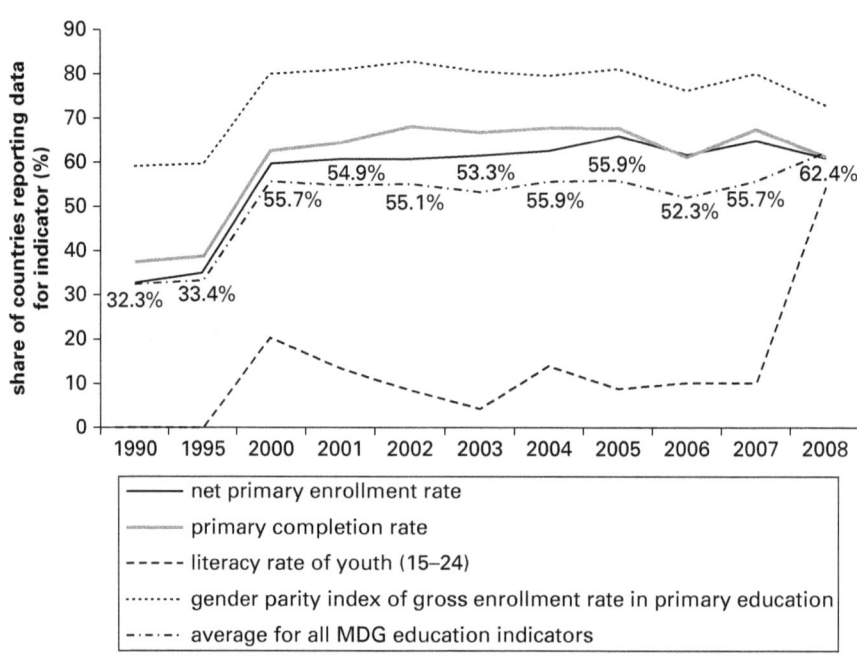

Source: World Bank EdStats calculations based on UIS data 2009.

Education Projections Modules

The Education Projections modules allow users to easily access projections of educational attainment, enrollment rates, and gender parity indexes until 2025 or 2050, depending on the country and data coverage. Three projection models are included in the projections query:

- The International Institute for Applied Systems Analysis/Vienna Institute of Demography (IIASA/VID) Educational Attainment Model includes the reconstruction of educational attainment distributions (primary, secondary, tertiary, and no education) for 120 countries by age for 1970–2000, with projections through 2050.
- The Education Policy and Data Center Educational Attainment Model produces similar projections for 81 countries (as of September 2008) for 2005–25 (the countries covered by these two models do not overlap 100 percent).

- The Education Policy and Data Center Enrollment Rates Model, which projects net enrollment rates (NERs), total net enrollment rates (TNERs), gross enrollment rates (GERs), and gender parity indexes (GPIs) for more than 150 countries until 2025.

Users may choose a model depending on the country and time period covered by each module.

World Bank Education Projects Database

The World Bank Education Projects Database allows users to search Bank education projects approved by the Education Sector Board since 1998. Users can search projects by country to find detailed project information or search by one of more than 100 project components to generate a list of projects that included a specific component. This module includes links to the Project Appraisal Documents, allowing EdStats users to easily access World Bank project descriptions around the world.

Public Expenditure Database

The Public Expenditure Database includes education finance indicators for 79 countries and about 850 education expenditure indicators. Because there is no standard method of calculating most indicators, users are cautioned not to compare data across countries.

ADePT Edu As a Tool for Analyzing Education Inequality

About half of the countries in Sub-Saharan Africa report that 25 percent of their children—about 31 million—do not attend school. Worldwide about 69 million children were out of school in 2008, a figure that is significantly lower than the more than 100 million who were not attending school in 1999 (UN 2010).

Limited access to education does not necessarily reflect inadequate infrastructure—in fact, infrastructure may be the easiest issue to resolve. Poor access may also involve problems in enrollment, attendance, and abandonment, which affect the demand for education. Poverty and education quality are two important factors that help explain access to education and are central to the analysis of educational inequality (Pritchett 2004).

Administrative data collected through school surveys provide information about children attending school. To identify groups that are excluded from the school system and understand the challenges and circumstances that keep them out of school, governments and donors must draw on household survey data. They need better information to design the policies and plan the interventions that will help achieve Education for All.

The World Bank created ADePT Edu to facilitate access to education data and allow education analysts to concentrate on monitoring and analyzing education indicators. ADePT Edu can be used with any household survey to produce tables of all education indicators covered by UIS, as well as indicators associated with educational inequality. ADePT Edu can use Stata (.dta) or SPSS (.sav) datasets as source files; users specify the variables for analysis. Within the Bank, ADePT uses Stata to compute all education indicators, regardless of the type of input file.[2] Users need not have SPSS installed to work with SPSS datasets in ADePT.

Although the analysis of education data—both administrative and survey based—can be done with commercial software available all over the world, many countries cannot afford the cost of producing and publishing a large number of good-quality indicators at the national and subnational levels on an annual basis. ADePT Edu provides these countries with four distinct benefits:

- It is free, alleviating the financial burden on ministries of education and education analysts in poor countries.
- It is already configured to produce a large number of educational indicators, which saves significant amounts of time on country analysis. It eliminates the need to configure commercial software to generate education indicators.
- It ensures the consistency of indicators and their compliance with international standards.
- It allows for the creation of benchmarks at the national level, which can be compared with results in other countries.

The pursuit of equality in access to education has both a moral and an economic basis. Differential access to schooling by children comes through no fault of their own. However, the differential abilities that result have important impacts on individual prosperity and long-term prosperity for society (Bourguignon and Dessus 2007). Unequal opportunities in education reduce the ability of individuals and societies to maximize human potential; the lower levels of human capital created as a result of differential access limit innovation and investment and slow economic growth (OECD 2010; World Bank 2005). The potential impact of increasing education equity is especially important because education is one of the few factors that can break the intergenerational cycle of poverty (World Bank 2003).

In their studies of education inequality in Central America, Porta and Laguna (2007a, 2007b) find that, despite progress in expanding educational services, some groups remain marginalized and are left behind. Among nonindigenous male children of educated parents living in the urban areas of Guatemala, the probability of school attendance is 97 percent. In contrast, among indigenous girls in rural areas whose parents are illiterate and belong to the poorest 20 percent of the income distribution, the probability of school attendance is only 22 percent.

Building on this work and on the conceptual and empirical work of others in education inequality (Bourguignon 2006; Patrinos and Skoufias 2007; Pritchett 2004; World Bank 2005), ADePT Edu was developed to maximize the use of household-level education information and create ready to print reports that allow users to easily visualize inequalities in school participation, school progression, school attainment, education expenditures, and labor market outcomes. These inequalities can also be analyzed for boys and girls, indigenous populations, people living in rural areas, and poor families. The organization of the ready to print reports generated by ADePT Edu follows the logic of the effects of inequality. Those affected by inequality—girls (or sometimes boys), the extreme poor, ethnic groups, and people living in isolated areas—have less access to education because they cannot cover the costs, do not relate to the education content, or are simply discriminated against. Lower access to education may compel them to enter the labor force too early and with a lower level of education than they may desire. The result is a lower level of productivity and innovation for society because people are not given an equal opportunity to control their destinies.

ADePT Edu reports have been generated for more than 80 countries. They are available to the public in EdStat's Household Survey module.[3] More than 40 percent of the surveys come from Sub-Saharan Africa and 23 percent from Latin America and the Caribbean. Forty-two percent of the surveys were carried out in Highly Indebted Poor Countries (HIPC). Many countries in this database have conducted multiple surveys over time; for example, 13 countries conducted four or more surveys between 1985 and 2007.[4]

The inclusion of household survey data in the EdStat portal allows for the analysis of education data at the micro level and the close examination of education inequality. This is an important contribution to education, as school administrative data do not capture information on children outside the school system or information about the private cost of education to households. ADePT Edu allows for the analysis of any type of household survey data, giving analysts a better picture of inequality issues and the need for policy and intervention responses.

Household survey data also allow for more precise interventions. Having information on educational inequality may add significant insight into policy decisions. Household-level data allow for the analysis of educational costs, cost equity, the relationship between educational attainment and levels of household income, and educational inequality from location and gender perspectives. Although the provision of information on educational inequality is not a sufficient condition for policy change, it has the potential to influence policy interventions at the local and national levels. As education systems become more decentralized and accountability begins to take shape at the local level, ADePT Edu can facilitate the analysis of educational inequality, before or after policy implementation.

Notes

1. Because of quality checks and verification procedures, the UNESCO Institute for Statistics publishes data two years after the end of the calendar year.
2. ADePT Edu has an imbedded version of Stata, so there is no need for users to install Stata or to have access to additional statistical software.
3. More reports are regularly added to the database as household data become available. Users should check the website periodically for updated content.
4. Côte d'Ivoire conducted seven household surveys between 1985 and 2007.

References

Arcia, Gustavo, Harry Anthony Patrinos, Emilio Porta, and Kevin Macdonald. 2011. "School Autonomy and Accountability." System

Assessment for Benchmarking Education for Results, Regulatory and Institutional Framework. World Bank, Human Development Network, Washington, DC.

Bourguignon, François. 2006. "Distribution, Equity and Development." In *Equity and Development*, ed. Gudrun Kochendörfer-Lucius and Boris Pleskovic, 29–38. Washington, DC: World Bank.

Bourguignon, François, and Sébastien Dessus. 2007. "Equity and Development: Political Economy Considerations." In *No Growth without Equity? Inequality, Interests and Competition in Mexico*, ed. Santiago Levy and Michael Walton, 45–70. Washington, DC: World Bank.

Bruns, Barbara, Deon Filmer, and Harry Anthony Patrinos. 2011. *Making Schools Work: New Evidence on Accountability Reforms*. Washington, DC: World Bank.

Cassidy, Tom. 2005. *Education Management Information System (EMIS) Development in Latin America and the Caribbean: Lessons and Challenges*. Washington, DC: Inter-American Development Bank.

Crouch, Luis. 1997. "Sustainable EMIS: Who Is Accountable?" In *From Planning to Action: Government Initiatives for Improving School-Level Practices*, ed. David Chapman, Lars Mähéck, and Anna Smulders, 211–39. Paris: UNESCO International Institute for Educational Planning.

Das, Jishnu. 2004. "Equity in Educational Expenditures: Can Government Subsidies Help?" Working Paper 3249, World Bank, Development Research Group, Washington, DC.

Filmer, Deon, and Marta Rubio-Codina. 2011. "Information for Accountability." In *Making Schools Work: New Evidence on Accountability Reforms*, ed. Barbara Bruns, Deon Filmer, and Harry Anthony Patrinos. Washington, DC: World Bank.

Hanushek, Eric, and Ludger Wößmann, 2007. *Education Quality and Economic Growth*. Washington, DC: World Bank.

Kitamura, Yuto, and Yasushi Hirosato. 2009. "An Analytical Framework of Educational Development and Reform in Developing Countries: Interaction among Actors in the Context of Decentralization." In *The Political Economy of Educational Reforms and Capacity Development in Southeast Asia*, ed. Y. Hirosato and Y. Kitamura, 41–54. Berlin: Springer.

OECD (Organisation for Economic Co-operation and Development). 2010. *The High Cost of Low Educational Performance: The Long-Run Economic Impact of Improving PISA Outcomes*. Paris: Program for International Student Assessment.

Patrinos, Harry, and Emmanuel Skoufias. 2007. *Economic Opportunities for Indigenous Peoples in Latin America*. Washington, DC: World Bank.

Porta, Emilio, and Jennifer Klein. 2010. "Increasing Education Data Availability for Knowledge Generation." Background paper for the Education Sector Strategy 2020, World Bank, Washington, DC.

Porta, Emilio, and José R. Laguna. 2007a. "Educational Equity in Central America: A Pending Issue for the Public Agenda." Academy for Educational Development, Washington, DC.

———. 2007b. "Equidad de la educación en Guatemala Centroamérica." Academy for Educational Development, Guatemala City, Guatemala.

Pritchett, Lant. 2004. "Towards a New Consensus for Addressing the Global Challenge of the Lack of Education." Working Paper 43, Center for Global Development, Washington, DC.

United Nations. 2010. *The Millennium Development Goals Report 2010*. New York: United Nations.

World Bank. 2003. *World Development Report 2004: Making Services Work for Poor People*. Washington, DC: World Bank.

———. 2005. *World Development Report 2006: Equity and Development*. Washington, DC: World Bank.

Chapter 2

Using Household Survey Data

The objective of this chapter is to familiarize potential ADePT Edu users with household surveys and their uses. The chapter does not provide complete coverage of statistical issues associated with household surveys; it does provide information on comprehensive studies that do.

There are almost 2,500 questionnaires for household surveys in the world; many of them have enough variations in their design and in the availability of variables to require some familiarization with their structure and potential uses. This chapter underscores the benefits of ADePT Edu as versatile software that can be used to generate comparable education estimators with data from any household survey.

The International Household Survey Network (IHSN 2011) houses a catalog of 4,152 household surveys with economic and social variables from most countries in the world, 266 of which are household surveys on income and expenditures.[1] Achieving consistency in the treatment of education variables requires some degree of harmonization and the use of software that can reduce the problems associated with variation in survey design (EPDC 2009).

The main advantage of using household survey data is that doing so allows the demand for education to be estimated. The decision to enroll and keep children in school is made at the household level, compulsory education notwithstanding, which implicitly involves decisions about the costs and benefits of education perceived by household members (Deaton 1997). Household heads do have a strong influence on enrolling girls in formal schooling, enrolling children at the appropriate age, participating in school governance, and complementing school activities at home, undergoing significant private costs in order to capture the benefits of public education (Strauss and Thomas 1995).

Another advantage of analyzing household data is that it can inform policy makers about the characteristics of children outside the school system—children who are obviously not observed by administrative data from schools. Empirical analyses on children out of school indicate that factors such as extreme poverty, the cost of school uniforms, the lack of relevance of the school curriculum, the distance to school, and personal insecurity on the way to school can be strong barriers to school attendance (Arcia 2003; Ilon and Mock 1991; Pritchett 2004; Sulliman and El-Kogali 2002).

Use of Household Surveys to Analyze Educational Inequality and Education Sector Performance

The measurement of education performance through household surveys is complicated for several reasons:

- Household surveys are very costly or are perceived as costly, particularly if they are underutilized (in which case the benefit-cost ratio is indeed low). To cut costs, countries often reduce their frequency, sample size, and breadth of content (Keogh 2005; Yansaneh 2005). The quality and frequency of household surveys vary significantly between and within countries. Within countries the thematic emphasis may change from one survey to another, depending on the country's policy design needs. Analysts often have to adjust their methods of estimating education indicators, because different waves of surveys generally use different questionnaires and different sample populations (IHSN 2011).
- Household survey methods have evolved over the years. As the cost of computing decreases, the complexity of data processing for analysis has tended to increase. Redundant questions have multiplied in an effort to improve cross-checking and accuracy, and data management has become more complex (Scott, Steele, and Temesgen 2005).
- There is wide variation in the conceptualization and definition of key educational variables. The measurement of school attendance, for example, varies widely in method and scope even across surveys within a country. The differences in variable definition and scope depend on the primary objective of the survey and the institutional dynamics at the time of the survey's implementation (EPDC 2009).

These difficulties notwithstanding, household surveys are very useful for analyzing the education sector. The volume and quality of information on education at the household level tend to be good enough to produce good information on sector performance and to prepare strategies for reducing poverty and achieving the Millennium Development Goals (UN 2010). Household expenditures, ethnicity, gender, and other variables can have a significant impact on educational attainment. Disparities in net intake rates, grade completion, and other indicators of educational performance at the individual level can be analyzed using household surveys. Policy makers can use the results to address education inequality, one of the core issues in education today.

Household surveys include substantial information overlap. International development institutions have mounted efforts to harmonize survey guidelines (IHSN 2011). Since 2004 IHSN has organized periodic high-level meetings to standardize household surveys and increase the coverage and comparability of survey results. To foster harmonization and improve data collection methods, IHSN is supporting technical work in the assessment and improvement of survey methodologies and the documentation of the more than 1,280 questionnaires on file. Harmonization of household data could result in the following benefits:

- Better coordination of internationally sponsored surveys and improved timing, sequencing, frequency, and cost-effectiveness
- Provision of harmonized technical and methodological guidelines for data collection
- Creation of a central survey data catalog
- Provision of tools and guidelines for better documentation, dissemination, and preservation of household survey data compliant with international standards.

Main Household Surveys

Most countries conduct household surveys. Three surveys have invested enormous efforts in solving methodological issues; addressing statistical problems; documenting their preparation, implementation, and analysis; and publicizing results. These surveys are the Living Standards Measurement Study (LSMS), sponsored by the World Bank; the Demographic and Health Survey (DHS), sponsored by the U.S. Agency for International Development (USAID); and the Multiple Indicator Cluster Survey (MICS), sponsored by the United Nations Children's Fund (UNICEF). In many countries, the initial implementation of household surveys in collaboration with one or more of these sponsors has evolved into a national effort, an important goal of the sponsoring institutions.

The Living Standards Measurement Study

The LSMS is a World Bank research project initiated in 1980 in response to the need for policy-relevant data on employment, poverty, and access to social services, such as health care and education. Its main purpose is to better understand the links between the economic and social sectors of an economy and to use those links to make policy decisions (Scott, Steele, and Temesgen 2005).

Institutionally, the LSMS was intended to help countries improve the quality of their household survey data, increase the capacity of their statistical institutes to perform household surveys, improve the ability of statistical institutes to analyze household survey data for policy needs, and provide policy makers with data that can be used to understand the determinants of observed social and economic outcomes (Grosh and Glewwe 1995). An LSMS survey is essentially a dataset containing a variety of topics directly related to household welfare and household behavior. Both the questionnaire and the data share are subject to high levels of quality control, which are transferred to host country institutions.

The LSMS pioneered the use of extensive household surveys in developing countries, collecting information on household expenditures on food, health care, education, nonfood consumer goods, housing, migration, reproductive health, health behavior, nutrition, employment, household production of goods and services, and sources of household income (table 2.1). Collectively, the data approximate household welfare, as measured by food and nonfood consumption, health, and education.

The emphasis in the education section is on educational expenditures by households, along with important information on school attendance by each household member of school age. Information is also collected on school-age household members not attending school, including the reasons for nonattendance. School attainment can be derived from the LSMS, which includes the last grade of education completed by the survey taker.[2] LSMS surveys are divided into modules, each of which contains information for each member of the household as applicable.

Chapter 2: Using Household Survey Data

Table 2.1: Data Modules and Content of Typical Living Standards Measurement Study Survey Questionnaire

Module	Content
Household composition	Household roster, demographic data, information on parents of all household members
Food expenditures	Food expenditures in past two weeks and past year; consumption of home production in past year
Nonfood expenditures	Nonfood expenditures in past two weeks and past year; remittances to other households in past week and past year
Housing	Type of dwelling; housing and utilities expenditures over the week and year of the interview
Durable goods	Inventory of durable goods and their characteristics
Economic and production activities and assets	Nonfarm employment, agro-pastoral production, land, livestock, and equipment owned in past week and past year
Savings	Savings and debts
Education	Completed schooling and schooling expenditures for all household members; attendance and nonattendance information
Health	Health expenditures of all household members and use of health services in past four weeks
Migration	Place of birth, length of stay at current residency
Fertility	Subsample with data on birth history, use of maternity services, and duration of breastfeeding
Anthropometrics	Height and weight measurements of all household members

Source: Adapted from Grosh and Glewwe 1995.

Most LSMS survey findings and their indicators are representative at the regional level (for example, urban and rural regions) and subregional (for example, department, province) levels. Achieving more detailed levels of representation is often too expensive. In addition, because the LSMS produces sample data, the results are affected by sample error. Hence, by definition the indicators derived from cross-sectional data have margins of error delimited by their confidence intervals. The more representative is the sample, the narrower will be the confidence interval and the more reliable and valid will be the indicator. As LSMS data are the property of the country's government, availability tends to be restricted (for the restrictions applicable to each dataset, see www.worldbank.org/lsms).

The Demographic and Health Survey

The DHS is produced by the MEASURE DHS Project, which has been funded by USAID since 1984. Since its inception, the project has conducted more than 240 surveys in 84 countries. With a central focus on reproductive health, the DHS provides data on fertility, family planning, maternal and child health, HIV/AIDS, malaria, and nutrition (Vaasen, Thiam, and Lê 2005). The DHS is part of a larger effort on health that includes more detailed information on HIV/AIDS, the provision of health services, health indicators for small areas, and malaria and its indicators, as well as qualitative research in selected health topics.

Data on education are considered a correlate of health and health behavior. They include information on school achievement of each household member, school attendance by household members of school age, and household educational expenditures (table 2.2).

The MEASURES DHS project coordinated its questionnaire design with the Multiple Indicator Cluster Survey (MICS) to facilitate comparisons across countries. Like the LSMS, the DHS collects a large amount of information on the household's living conditions, including the composition and personal characteristics of household members, housing characteristics, and location.[3]

Data are collected on literacy, school attendance, and educational attainment. These and other data solicited by the survey can be used to derive repetition and dropout rates as well as gross and net attendance rates for different age groups and gender, urban and rural locations, and geographical regions and departments. Many of the health variables are tabulated by

Table 2.2: Summary of Questionnaire Content in October 2010 Demographic and Health Survey

Topic	Information
Household composition	Name, age, sex, marital status
Education	School attendance and attainment, literacy from birth to age 24; literacy test for people older than 7
Characteristics of the dwelling	Water, sanitation, secondhand smoke, construction materials, electricity, mosquito netting, inventory of possessions (durable goods, livestock)
Anthropomorphic measurements	Measurements for each household member; includes hemoglobin and HIV tests
Reproductive health	Contraception, pregnancies, and birth outcomes, pre- and postnatal care
Child immunization, health, and nutrition	Vaccination records for all children; types of food given to infants
Marriage and sexual activity	Data on sexual partners, fertility preference
Work and work decisions	Employment and work decisions by men and women
Human immunodeficiency virus (HIV)	Knowledge, behavior

Source: Authors' compilation based on information from http://www.measuredhs.com/pubs/search/search_results.cfm?Type=35andsrchTp=typeandnewSrch=1.

the level of education of the recipient, allowing for the analysis of the relationship between health access, health outcomes, and educational levels. Many of the costs of health care paid by families are also tabulated by educational level, allowing for a close examination of the link between education and health expenditures. Some countries include a DHS EdData module, in which households report detailed expenditures on education for household members.

The DHS developed the Wealth Index as a substitute for the per capita expenditures approach used in other surveys, such as the LSMS. Using this index, Filmer and Pritchett (2001) were able to predict school attendance in India on the basis of the accumulated assets belonging to the child's family. On a set of health indicators, the Wealth Index explains at least as much of the differences across households as the expenditures approach and requires far less effort from respondents, interviewers, data processors, and analysts. Intuitively, analysts try to use household income as the variable of choice for assessing equity in educational access or educational expenditures. However, income is difficult to measure accurately, even when informants are trying to be truthful. Moreover, in most cases income questions suffer from severe interview biases, because respondents try to hide income, fail to take into account in-kind income, or make errors in reporting average incomes when income fluctuates widely (Rutstein and Johnson 2004).

In the approach taken by the LSMS, families provide detailed information on household consumption, instead of income, on the grounds that household consumption better reflects actual average income. Valuing consumption seems to produce more reliable indicators of household income than measuring income itself, because households make consumption decisions based on their cash flow and home production expectations. However, measuring consumption is a long and complicated process, requiring extensive questionnaires and consumption diaries. Although the information obtained is reliable, collecting it is time-consuming and very costly.

A wealth-based index is a simpler construct for assessing educational inequality. Wealth represents a more permanent status than income or consumption, and it is more easily measured, sometimes by simple observation. Using principal components analysis, the Wealth Index is constructed in the DHS reports using the household's contents, including durable consumer goods, dwelling characteristics, and other underlying indicators of household wealth, such as running water, electricity, indoor toilets, and privacy. Each household in the DHS sample is assigned an index value based on its possessions and underlying wealth. Households are then ranked into population quintiles according to their value on the Wealth Index. The Wealth Index allows the DHS to be used as a data source for assessing educational inequality, significantly increasing the number of countries for which such analysis is possible.

The Multiple Indicator Cluster Survey

Since the mid-1990s, UNICEF has assisted countries in collecting and analyzing data on children and women through its international household survey initiative. The MICS covers a range of indicators in health, education, child protection, and HIV/AIDS. Survey findings have been used extensively to craft policy decisions and program interventions and to influence public opinion.

The MICS was originally developed in response to the World Summit for Children, to measure progress toward an internationally agreed set of mid-decade goals. The first round, with 60 surveys (MICS1), was conducted in 1995; the second round, with 65 surveys (MICS2), was conducted in 2000.[4] In some countries, MICS2 allowed, for the first time, the monitoring of trends in many indicators and the setting of baselines for other indicators. MICS3, conducted in more than 50 countries in 2005–06, has been an important data source for monitoring 21 indicators of the Millennium Development Goals (table 2.3). Starting with MICS4—implemented in 2009–10—survey rounds will be implemented every three years.

UNICEF works closely with other household survey programs, in particular the DHS program, to harmonize survey questions, survey modules, and survey implementation and to increase comparability across surveys and avoid duplication of efforts. Results from the MICS, including national reports and micro-level datasets, can be downloaded from the MICS pages at childinfo.org.

Which Survey Is Best for Analyzing Education Inequality? A Quick Guide

ADePT Edu is a software platform that can be used with any household survey. Because it strives to present consistent data for its indicators, surveys

Table 2.3: Education Indicators Reported in Fourth Round of Multiple Indicator Cluster Surveys (2009–11) and Relation to MDGs

Indicator	Numerator	Denominator	MDG indicator
Literacy rate (for women 15–24)	Number of women 15–24 able to read a short, simple statement about everyday life or who attended secondary or higher education institution	All women 15–24	2.3
School readiness	Number of children in first grade of primary school who attended preschool the previous school year	All children attending first grade of primary school	
Net intake rate in primary education	Number of children of school-entry age currently attending first grade of primary school	All children of school-entry age	
Net primary school attendance ratio	Number of children of primary school age currently attending primary or secondary school	All children of primary school age	2.1
Net secondary school attendance ratio	Number of children of secondary school age currently attending secondary school or higher	All children of secondary school age	
Children reaching last grade of primary school	Children who eventually reach last grade of primary school	Children who entered first grade of primary school	2.2
Primary completion rate	Number of children (of any age) attending last grade of primary school (excluding repeaters)	All children of primary school completion age (age appropriate to final grade of primary school)	
Transition rate to secondary school	Number of children attending first grade of secondary school who were in last grade of primary school during previous school year	All children attending first grade of secondary school	
Gender parity index (primary school)	Net primary school attendance ratio for girls	Net primary school attendance ratio for boys	3.1
Gender parity index (secondary school)	Net secondary school attendance ratio for girls	Net secondary school attendance ratio for boys	3.1

Source: http://www.unicef.org/statistics/index_24302.html.

that are consistently applied in many countries are preferred, especially if the data are readily available. For the estimation of education indicators that use cross-sectional data, the DHS is a good data source because the questionnaire is fairly standard, it has been applied in more than 80 countries, and the data files are readily available. The DHS is the default database used by ADePT Edu; users have immediate access to DHS data for their analysis. The MICS is also a good source of data, but the number of both countries covered and surveys is substantially smaller than it is for the DHS. The LSMS is good for analyzing expenditures in education by households, which allows for analysis of the interaction between poverty and educational access.

Most of the indicators of internal efficiency (enrollment, repetition, dropout, completion, attainment) can be derived from cross-sectional data. For example, attendance rates can be derived by dividing the number of school-age children attending school by the total number of school-age children in the sample. In some cases, cross-sectional indicators can be used to derive cohort-based indicators. This is the case of the indicator for the rate of survival to the sixth grade. Using the repetition and promotion rates obtained from the sample population, one can construct a cohort matrix that can simulate the flow of a cohort of children from the first to the sixth grade. The only important assumption is that the rates of promotion and repetition used in the simulation are the same as the actual rates during the several years it would take for a cohort to flow from first to sixth grade.

A range of indicators can be derived from each type of survey (table 2.4). All three surveys allow for the estimation of the appropriate indicators for school participation, progression, and attainment. (The methods of calculation described in chapters 3 and 4 apply to the DHS only because they follow the order and types of questions asked in the DHS questionnaire.) In the case of primary school survival rates, the method of calculation of the three surveys is indirect, as they are cross-sectional rather than cohort based.

The most complete source of information for assessing student expenditures is the LSMS, but fewer than 50 countries administer it, limiting its usefulness. For assessing education inequality, both the LSMS and the DHS Wealth Index are excellent sources of information. In some countries the DHS also includes a module that collects information on educational expenditures, called the DHS EdData module, but these data are not yet widely available.

Table 2.4: Data Available for Estimating Selected Indicators, by Type of Survey

Survey topic	Demographic and Health Survey (DHS)	Multiple Indicator Cluster Survey (MICS)	Living Standards Measurement Study (LSMS)
School participation			
Gross and net attendance ratios for primary, secondary, and postsecondary education	Yes	Yes	Yes
Proportion of out-of-school children for primary and secondary education	Yes	Yes	Yes
Gross and net intake ratios for first grade of primary education	Yes	Yes	Yes
Survival rate to fifth grade of primary education	Approximated	Approximated	Approximated
Proportion of children on-time, under-age, and over-age by each grade of primary education	Yes	Yes	Yes
Percentage of (sample) population that ever attended school, by year, age 6–17	Yes	Yes	No
School progression			
Promotion, repetition, dropout, and completion rates for each grade of primary and secondary education	Yes	Yes	Yes
Repetition rates for postsecondary education	Yes	Yes	Yes
Primary to secondary education transition rates	Yes	Yes	Yes
School attainment			
School attainment of adult population	Yes	Yes[a]	Yes
Average number of years of schooling by age group (15–19, 20–29, 30–39, 40–49, 50+)	Yes	Yes[a]	Yes
Proportion of population age groups that completed each grade 1–9	Yes	Yes[a]	Yes
Education equity[b]			
Household and per student expenditures on primary, secondary, and postsecondary education	Yes[c]	No	Yes
Household and per student educational expenditure by category (fees, uniforms, books, food, transportation)	Yes[c]	No	Yes
Household and per household member expenditures by poverty level	Yes	Yes	Yes
Household educational expenditures as percentage of household expenditures	Yes[c]	No	Yes
Employment and earnings[b]			
Equality in earnings	No	No	Yes
Employment of youth	Yes	No	Yes
Employment of youth enrolled in school	Yes	No	Yes
Employment of youth not in school	Yes	No	Yes
Employment by sector	Yes	No	Yes
Employment by education level	Yes	No	Yes
Economic independence	Yes	No	Yes
Returns to education	No	No	Yes

Source: Authors' compilation.
a. For household members younger than 24 years old.
b. Data allow estimation of expenditures or wealth indicators.
c. For countries using DHS EdData additional modules.

Advantages and Limitations of Using Household Surveys in Data Analysis

Household surveys contain microeconomic-level data that are crucial for analyzing disparities in access to education by different types of households. These advantages and limitations of these data are described below.

Enrollment versus Attendance

Household surveys such as the DHS usually collect data on household members' school attendance rather than enrollment. Although both enrollment and attendance are used to ascertain school participation, they are two different concepts. A child may be enrolled in school but not attending school at the time of the interview. This is a common problem in administrative data, because schools usually report enrollment but not attendance to their statistics offices. As a result, school enrollment data tend to overstate the effective student population. School attendance at the time of the interview is a more reliable indicator of the proportion of students actually attending school.

Analyzing enrollment and attendance requires careful examination of the language in the questionnaire for subtle but important differences. For example, the terms *enrolled*, *currently attending*, *attended during this school year*, and *attended during last school year* may be misinterpreted and used interchangeably. Users must make sure that clear definitions of enrollment and attendance are specified.

Care must also be taken to ensure that enrollment rates are defined properly. The UNESCO Institute for Statistics (UIS) uses two measures of enrollment, the adjusted net enrollment rate (NER+) and the adjusted net attendance rate (NAR+), both of which include primary school–age children enrolled in primary or secondary school. The NER+ is estimated using only adminstrative data; in the NAR+, both the numerator and the denominator of the indicator come from household survey data (Stukel and Feroz-Zada 2010). These estimates relate to school enrollment and should not be confused with school attendance.

First grade enrollment and attendance can be another source of confusion in countries with limited preschool coverage. Many parents enroll their children in the first grade when the children are five years old because there are no preschools nearby. In most cases, the parents and teachers of these children expect them to repeat the grade the following year. Some education systems may classify this child as a repeater; other systems may classify them as dropouts. Household survey data, which include the age of the child at the time of the interview, can help isolate this problem, revealing the true repetition rate for first grade and providing a better interpretation of what it means to repeat as an analytical category.

The DHS includes questions on both enrollment and attendance. For anyone older than five, the DHS questionnaire asks if the person ever attended school and if so the highest grade completed. It also asks about current attendance. If the question is asked during vacation time, "current attendance" is "the most recent attendance."

Level of Education Reported in Household Surveys

In presenting education indicators based on enrollment, ADePT Edu uses the International Standard Classification of Education (ISCED) developed by UNESCO to define the level of education (primary, secondary, or tertiary). For cross-country comparison purposes, ISCED classifies a level of education based on its content, not its duration. Therefore, the ISCED definition of an education level may differ from a country's definition. For example, primary education in Ethiopia lasts eight years. However, ISCED uses only the first six years, in order to define primary education in a way that is comparable across countries. The level of schooling attended by a household member as recorded in household surveys refers to the national definition. Thus, primary education as used in this query may not necessarily be the same as in the query based on enrollment data.

Age, Timing, and Duration of Household Surveys

Many household surveys, such as the DHS, are not specifically designed to study education. Information on education is collected and used as a background characteristic to explain other behaviors or phenomena, such as fertility levels or contraceptive behavior. Household surveys that do not focus on education may not be timed to coincide with the beginning or end of a school year. As a result, data collection may take place during school vacation or across two school years.

In addition, many household surveys conducted in developing countries do not collect the date of birth of every household member; age at the time of the survey is usually collected in completed years. The lack of a birth date may have implications for age-related indicators, such as gross or net attendance rates, as children's age at the start of the school year is not always known with certainty. For example, in a country in which the official primary school–age range is 6–12, the calculation of the primary net enrollment ratio (NER) will include children who were actually 6–12 years at the time their households were surveyed. If the survey did not coincide with the beginning of the school year, the calculation of NER may include children who were only five years old at the start of the school year but turned six by the time their households were surveyed. Similarly, the calculation may exclude children who were 12 at the start of the school year but who turned 13 by the time their households were surveyed.

The timing and duration of household surveys relative to the school year should be taken into consideration when interpreting education indicators derived from household surveys that are not education surveys. This information is usually available in the household survey report or accessible on the survey website.

Standard Errors

For each indicator produced by ADePT Edu, users are provided with the number of observations used to derive the indicator as well as the corresponding standard error. This information is useful in assessing the reliability of the estimated indicator before using or interpreting it. Education indicators derived from household surveys, like any other survey estimates, have standard errors that are related to the size of the sample. The standard error of the mean is the standard deviation of the sample mean estimate of a population mean. It can be estimated in ADePT using the Taylor linearization method for intracluster correlation robust standard errors.

Poverty Quintiles and Poverty Groups

The LSMS and other surveys that collect consumption expenditures typically analyze equity by defining nonpoor, poor, and extremely poor households according to absolute definitions of poverty lines.[5] Households are allocated to each of these groups according to a mapping of total household consumption expenditures, household size and composition, and the command over essential commodities that these variables entail.

An alternative approach divides households into quintiles, ranging from the richest to the poorest. Surveys such as the DHS and the MICS, which do not contain consumption expenditures, cannot typically be used to define absolute poverty groups, although they may use a proxy for economic status that allows education equity to be analyzed through the lens of relative quintiles based on that proxy.

Missing and Contradictory Values

Data are considered to be missing when the response to a particular question is left blank. Data are considered contradictory when the responses to two questions are incompatible (an example would be a child reported to be attending the ninth grade of primary school in a system in which primary school extends only through sixth grade). As a rule, observations with missing or contradictory values are omitted from the calculation of any indicator to which the problematic values are relevant. When observations are omitted, they are left out of both the numerator and the denominator of a calculation. Consider, for example, the case of a household member who attended primary school during the current year and the previous year, but the grade attended during the previous year is unknown (a blank value). As it is impossible to tell whether this child was promoted or repeated the grade, he or she is omitted from any efficiency calculations (that is, when calculating the primary repetition rate, this child is omitted from both the numerator [the number of repeaters in primary] and the denominator [the number of primary students]). However, the same child is included in both the numerator and the denominator for the primary net attendance rate, because the full set of information needed to perform this calculation is available. In the rare cases in which more than 5 percent of the observations in a dataset include missing or contradictory values for a particular question, the results of any calculations based on that question are discarded, in order to avoid introducing too much bias through omitted observations.

Notes

1. IHSN is an international network of organizations interested in harmonizing household surveys in order to facilitate survey analysis in poor countries (http://www.surveynetwork.org/home/). Its membership includes

the World Bank, the UNESCO Institute for Statistics, the International Labour Office, the World Health Organization, the Food and Agriculture Organization, the World Food Programme, most major international development banks, and other international organizations. A complete listing can be found at http://www.surveynetwork.org/home/index.php?q=about/membership.
2. *School enrollment* refers to the inscription of a student in a given grade at a given school. *School attendance* refers to the presence of the student in a given grade at a given school on a regular basis. *School attainment* refers to the latest grade successfully completed.
3. See www.measuredhs.com.
4. http://www.unicef.org/statistics/index_24302.html.
5. Some countries use relative poverty lines, but their use is rare in developing countries.

References

Arcia, Gustavo. 2003. "The Incidence of Public Education Spending in Nicaragua: The Impact of the Education for All/Fast Track Initiative." Consulting report submitted to the World Bank, Washington, DC.

Deaton, Angus. 1997. *The Analysis of Household Surveys: A Microeconometric Approach.* Washington, DC: World Bank.

EPDC (Education Policy and Data Center). 2009. "How (Well) Is Education Measured in Household Surveys? A Comparative Analysis of the Education Modules in 30 Household Surveys from 1996–2005." IHSN (International Household Survey Network) Working Paper 002, World Bank, Washington, DC.

Filmer, Deon, and Lant Pritchett. 2001. "Estimating Wealth Effects without Expenditure Data—or Tears: An Application to Educational Enrollments in States of India." *Demography* 38 (1): 115–32.

Grosh, Margaret, and Paul Glewwe. 1995. "A Guide to Living Standards Measurement Study Surveys and Their Data Sets." LSMS (Living Standards Measurement Study Surveys) Working Paper 120, World Bank, Washington, DC.

Ilon, Lynn, and Peter Mock. 1991. "School Attributes, Household Characteristics, and the Demand for Schooling: A Case Study of Rural

Peru." *International Review of Education* 37 (4): 429–51. DOI: 10.1007/BF00597620.

IHSN (International Household Survey Network). 2011. "Harmonizing and Improving Survey Methods." January. http://www.surveynetwork.org/home/index.php?q=activities/harmonization/rationale.

Keogh, Erica. 2005. "Developing a Framework for Budgeting for Household Surveys in Developing Countries." In *Household Sample Surveys in Developing and Transition Countries*, 279–300. New York: United Nations.

Pritchett, Lant. 2004. "Towards a New Consensus for Addressing the Global Challenge of the Lack of Education." Working Paper 43, Center for Global Development, Washington, DC.

Rutstein, Shea O., and Kiersten Johnson. 2004. "The DHS Wealth Index. DHS Comparative Reports 6." ORC Macro, Calverton, MD.

Scott, Kinnon, Diane Steele, and Tilahun Temesgen. 2005. "Living Standards Measurement Study Surveys." In *Household Sample Surveys in Developing and Transition Countries*, 523–56. New York: United Nations.

Strauss, John, and Duncan Thomas. 1995. "Human Resources: Empirical Modeling of Household and Family Decisions." In *Handbook of Development Economics* (vol. 3A), ed. J. Behrman and T. N. Srinivasan. Amsterdam: North Holland Press.

Stukel, Diana Maria, and Yassamin Feroz-Zada. 2010. "Measuring Educational Participation: Analysis of Data Quality and Methodology Based on Ten Studies." Technical Paper 04, UNESCO Institute for Statistics, Montreal.

Sulliman, E. D., and S. E. El-Kogali. 2002. "Why Are the Children Out of School? Factors Affecting Children's Education in Egypt." Paper presented at the Ninth Economic Research Forum, Sharjah, United Arab Emirates, October 26–28.

UN (United Nations). 2010. *The Millennium Development Goals Report 2010*. New York: United Nations.

Vaasen, Martin, Mamadou Thiam, and Than Lê. 2005. "The Demographic and Health Surveys." In *Household Sample Surveys in Developing and Transition Countries*, 495–522. New York: United Nations.

Yansaneh, Ibrahim S. 2005. "An Analysis of Cost Issues for Surveys in Developing and Transition Countries." In *Household Sample Surveys in Developing and Transition Countries*, 253–66. New York: United Nations.

Chapter 3

Using ADePT Edu: A Step-by-Step Guide

This technical guide to ADePT Edu illustrates each of the steps required to install and operate the software.[1] The chapter begins by identifying the computer hardware and software needed to run ADePT Edu. It then describes how to install the software. The rest of the chapter provides instructions for operating ADePT Edu. Users who are already familiar with ADePT Edu may want to go directly to chapter 4, which defines all of the indicators estimated by the program, or to chapter 5, which examines the issue of inequality in education and can be used as an example of how to use household survey data.

System Requirements

ADePT Edu can be used with any household survey, broadening the use of educational statistics in sector analysis and planning. The hardware and software requirements are described below.

Hardware Requirements

Table 3.1 describes the hardware needed to operate ADePT Edu.

Software Requirements

Table 3.2 describes the software needed to operate ADePT Edu.

Table 3.1: ADePT Edu Hardware Requirements

Hardware	Requirement
CPU	Any modern computer; faster CPUs reduce time required to process jobs. Multiprocessor computers can be used with Stata MP.
Disk space	40 MB of disk space to install; running ADePT creates temporary copies of datasets 25–50 percent larger than the originals, so disk space required ultimately depends on how large datasets are.
Memory	Minimum of 512 MB of RAM to operate; twice this much physical memory recommended for datasets. Use of dataset larger than 700 MB may require 64-bit Stata and larger memory.
Display	At least 1,024 x 768 screen resolution. Users of netbooks and other computers with small built-in screens may find it necessary to use an external monitor (screen resolution does not affect speed or accuracy of computations).
Internet connection	Internet connection not necessary for generating output results; connection needed for program updates only.

Source: http://siteresources.worldbank.org/EXTADEPT/Resources/ADePT_UserGuide.pdf.

Table 3.2: ADePT Edu Software Requirements

Software	Requirement
Operating system	Microsoft Windows operating system: Windows XP, Vista, Server 2003 and later, and Windows 7, in both 32- and 64-bit Windows environments. Does not work on MAC OS or Linux operating systems.
.Net framework	Microsoft .Net Framework 2.0 or later. Most recent Microsoft operating systems come with .Net Framework or allow for its installation. To check whether computer has .Net Framework installed, navigate Windows Explorer to folder where Windows is installed (typically C:\Windows\), then proceed to folder **Microsoft.Net,** then to **Framework**. There will be several subfolders in this folder with names like 1.0.3705, 1.1.4322, and so on. The largest version shows the newest version of .Net Framework installed. If none of these folders is on disk, computer does not have Microsoft .Net Framework. If system does not have .Net Framework 2.0 or a later version, download and install latest version from Microsoft's website (installation requires administrator rights).
Computations	Stata version 10 or later (all versions except Small Stata) or Numerics by Stata (included in ADePT); both Stata and Numerics by Stata are products of StataCorp LP (http://www.stata.com). If the program will be used on multiple computers, Numerics by Stata is the recommended computational engine (unless all computers have version of Stata).
Output viewer	Microsoft Excel for Windows (version XP or later); free Microsoft Excel Viewer can be used.

Source: http://siteresources.worldbank.org/EXTADEPT/Resources/ADePT_UserGuide.pdf.

Installing ADePT

Administrative privileges are not required for ADePT installation; it can thus be installed by users in usually restricted academic or corporate systems. The ADePT 4.1 installation file (adept_install.exe) is available at www.worldbank.org/adept.

To save the installation file to a disk, right-click it with the mouse, select **Save target as** from the menu, and specify the folder on the disk where the file should be saved. After the file is downloaded, execute it. ADePT installation will display the license agreement (screenshot 3.1). Click **I Agree** and proceed.

Chapter 3: Using ADePT Edu

Screenshot 3.1: Accepting the License Agreement

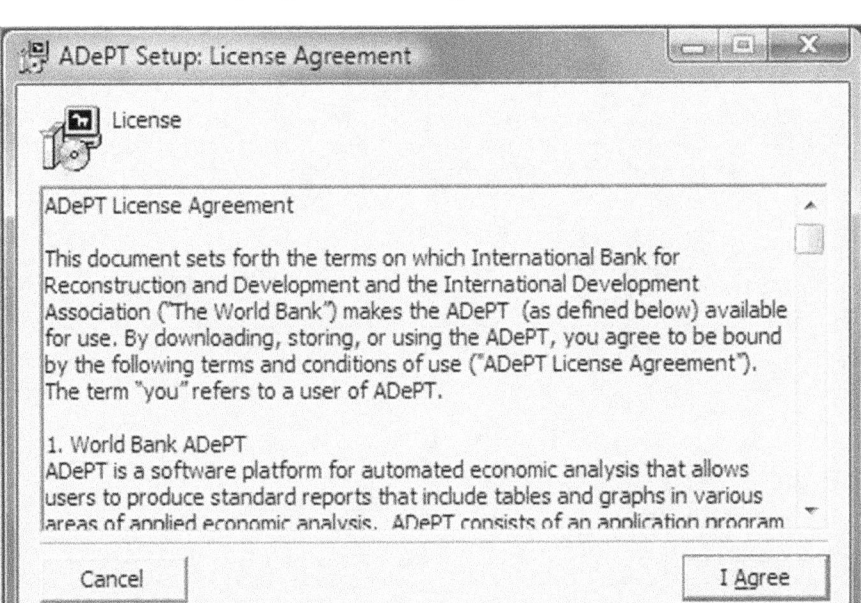

The installation wizard then asks where ADePT should be installed. (You must be authorized to write to the selected directory during installation and when the program is running.) Use the **Browse** button to specify the folder, or type the path in the **Destination Folder** box (screenshot 3.2).

Click **Install** to start copying the files. Once the program has been installed, the screen will look like screenshot 3.3. At this point, close the installation wizard. The ADePT program will start automatically after the installation succeeds.

Users can also install ADePT on an external drive (USB stick), allowing it to be used on more than one computer (administrative privileges are not required to install or run ADePT, meaning it can be run on any computer with suitable hardware and software). Note, however, that the settings will not travel. These settings include options (language, reporting level, path to Excel, and so forth) and the most recent input settings used in every module. In addition, the path to ADePT may change (the drive-letter of the mounted drive depends on the presence of other drives and the configuration of the host computer). If you are using the batch mode of ADePT, you may have to revise your batch files.

Screenshot 3.2: Installing ADePT

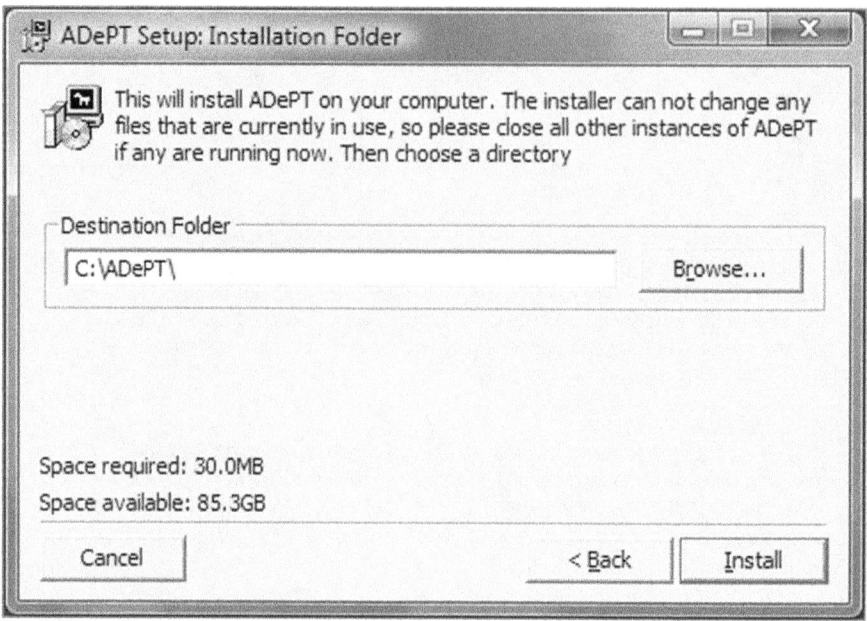

Screenshot 3.3: Completion of Setup

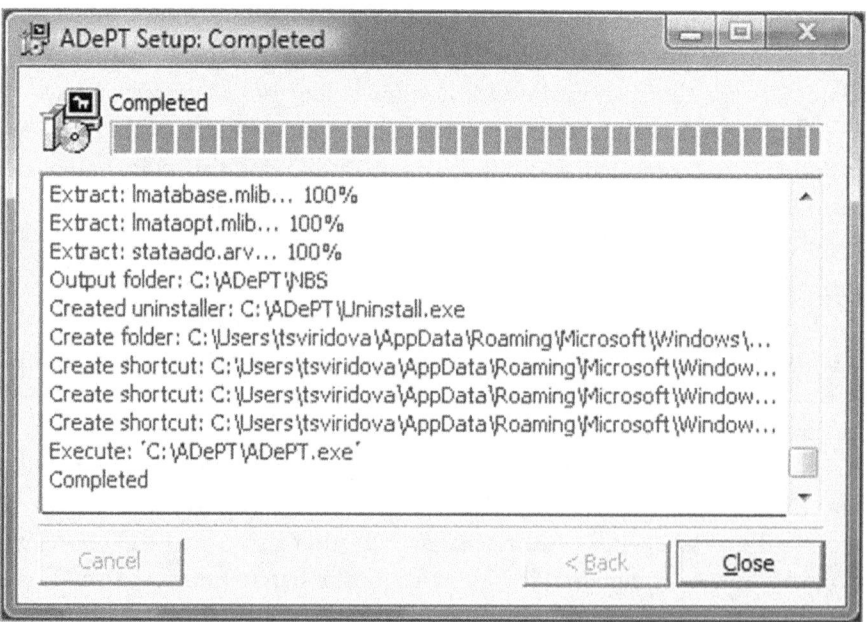

Using ADePT

Once ADePT is installed, users are able to start and close the program.

Starting and Closing ADePT

To start ADePT, go to the **Windows Start** menu and select the ADePT icon from the ADePT software program group (screenshot 3.4). You can also create a shortcut to ADePT on your desktop. To do this, use the mouse to drag the link to ADePT from the **Start** menu and drop it to the desktop.

Upon starting, ADePT indicates all of the modules available. Users who work mostly with one module can suppress this choice by unchecking the corresponding check box labeled "Don't show this window at start up" in screenshot 3.5. If, for example, you chose **Education,** ADePT will automatically load this module when it starts. To switch to a different module, use the **Select module** item in the **Modules** menu of ADePT (on the **Menu bar**).

To close ADePT, select the **Exit** item in the **File** menu or click the red X-button on the Windows navigation bar. Once ADePT is running, it cannot be closed, but the computations can be interrupted by clicking the **Stop** button on the Windows navigation bar.

Upon reopening, ADePT remembers the size of the ADePT window, the last module used, and the settings and content of the input fields. The content of the input fields is saved only if tables were produced during a previous session.

It is recommended that users spend a few minutes examining screenshot 3.6, the guide to the ADePT main screen, which is divided into four quadrants.

ADePT's Computation Process

ADePT consists of modules that generate tables and graphs in a particular area of economic research. To produce the desired set of results, follow these five steps:

1. Start ADePT.
2. Load datasets (one or several) into ADePT.
3. Fill in the **Main form**.

Assessing Sector Performance and Inequality in Education

Screenshot 3.4: Starting ADePT Using the Start Menu

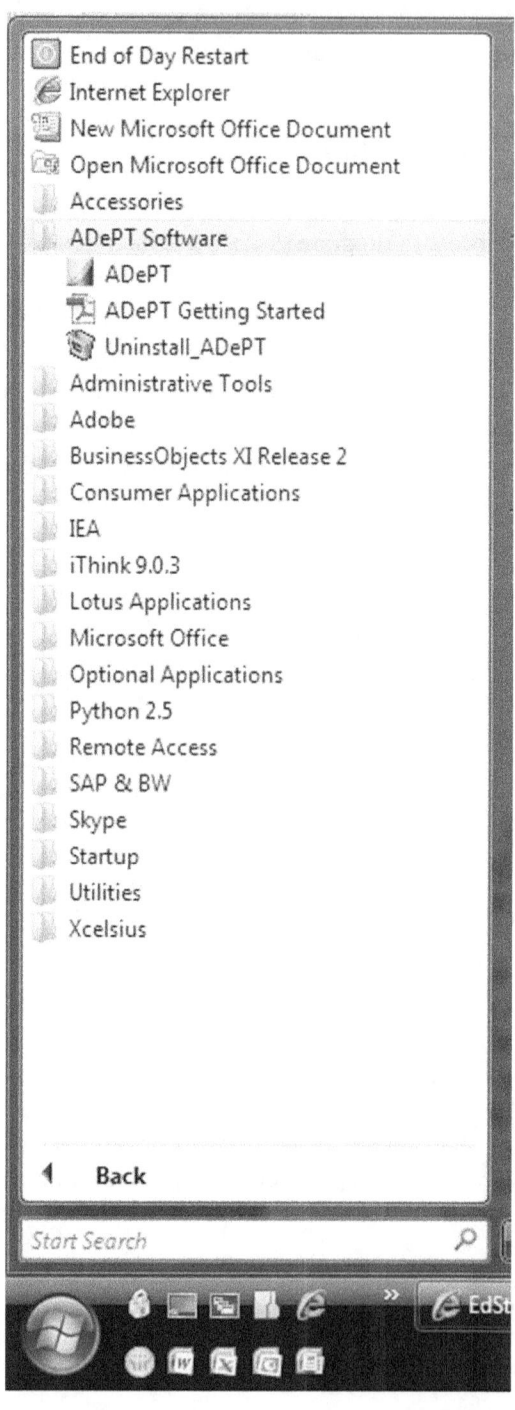

Screenshot 3.5: Selecting a Module

4. Set the weights, survey settings, and missing values.
5. Select tables and graphs to create.

After the required inputs are specified, click **Generate** to produce the output. From this point on, ADePT works automatically, informing users of progress and any problems detected.

There are several stages in this process. First, ADePT prepares the data based on the user's specifications. Two (optional) steps involve recoding missing values and applying a global filter, which restricts the data to a subset of observations satisfying certain conditions. ADePT then checks whether the variables entered correspond to the requirements defined for each variable. While doing so, it checks whether the entered variables are of the correct type (categorical, continuous, dummy, and so forth) and have the proper number of unique values; it also conducts consistency checks on particular variables. This process is repeated for all datasets loaded into ADePT.

Second, ADePT checks the consistency of categories for the variables defined in different files. For example, it checks whether the variable

Screenshot 3.6: Guide to the Main Screen

1. Data/variables quadrant
2. Main form quadrant
3. Table and figure quadrant
4. Table description/system messages quadrant
5. Process indicator
6. Menu bar
7. Datasets tab
8. Variables tab
9. Global filter tab
10. Dataset control buttons
11. Datafile type control
12. List of loaded datasets
13. Show changes window
14. Main variables tab
15. Education tab
16. Labor market tab
17. Missing values tab
18. Survey settings button
19. Status bar
20. Selected table statistics
21. Table and figure tree
22. Frequencies and standard errors check boxes
23. Table description tab
24. System messages tab
25. IF-condition field
26. IF-condition set/clear button
27. Generate/Stop button[2]

entered into the region field in the first year file contains the same number of categories as it does in the second year file. ADePT signals the user with error messages, warnings, and notifications about any problems it finds with the input data. If a problem is found in a particular variable, the program highlights its name in the **Main form**.

Third, ADePT generates temporary variables required for calculations. It tries to use information specified by the user to produce variables that are consistent with one another. For example, ADePT calculates household size and household composition variables from the variables defining household identification (ID), age, and gender of household members. By doing so, it makes sure that all tables in a particular module are internally consistent (that is, numbers in one table do not contradict numbers in other tables).

Finally, ADePT begins producing tables and graphs. Its computational kernel performs calculations and sends the results to the formatting routine, which presents each table and graph on a separate sheet of an output workbook. When all tables and graphs are generated, ADePT instructs the output viewer (MS Excel, MS Excel Viewer, or some other program) to open the file with tables and graphs.

The next sections discuss all of these steps in detail.

Loading Data

ADePT can process data in Stata (.dta) or SPSS (.sav) formats. To load a dataset into ADePT, click **Add** in the **Main form** quadrant and select the dataset you want to load in the **Open dataset** dialog box that pops up (screenshot 3.7).

The full path of the selected dataset and information about the number of variables and observations in the dataset, as well the size of the dataset, are shown in the **Status** bar (screenshot 3.8).

Specify a label for this dataset (screenshot 3.9). The label will be used in tables and graphs to identify the statistics generated. The label could be any word or number, but labeling datasets with the numeric date corresponding to the time of data collection is recommended. Several statistics produced by ADePT use this information to calculate the time span between surveys. For example, you might want to label the dataset from the 2002 survey "2002" and the dataset from the 2005 survey "2005." A separate report will be produced for each dataset you add; specifying multiple

Chapter 3: Using ADePT Edu

Screenshot 3.7: Opening a Dataset

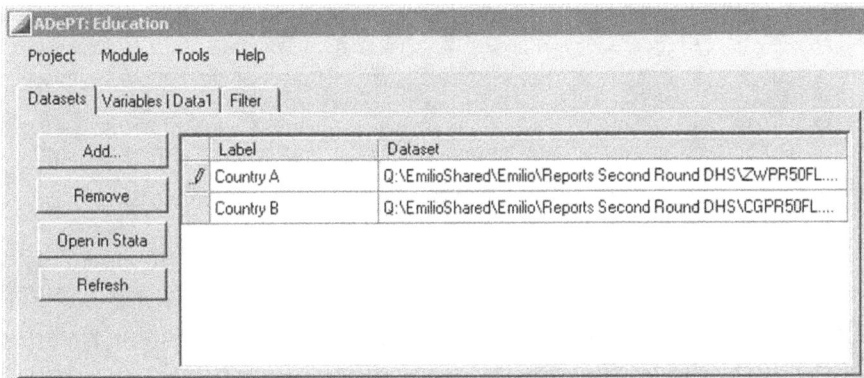

Screenshot 3.8: Full Path of the Selected Dataset

Stata dataset C:\AD_data\Data\Datasets\ADEPT_2002.dta 15 variables 19725 observations ~7243 Kb

Screenshot 3.9: Labeling the Dataset

Label	Dataset
2002	C:\AD_data\Data\Datasets\ADEPT_2002.dta
2005	C:\AD_data\Data\Datasets\ge2005.dta
<Enter label>	C:\AD_data\Data\Datasets\ADEPT_2007.dta

datasets is just a shortcut that works if all variables in the added datasets have the same name.

If Stata is used as the computational engine, the list of **Dataset** control buttons on the left-hand side will change. You can now open the selected dataset in Stata by clicking **Open in Stata** (screenshot 3.10). You can use Stata to browse the observations in the dataset, modify existing data, or create new variables.

To remove a dataset from the list of datasets loaded in ADePT, click **Remove** in the **Datasets** tab (see screenshot 3.10). Removing all datasets from the list will deactivate the ADePT interface; neither variable fields nor tables and graph trees will be accessible.

Screenshot 3.10: Opening a Stata Data File

	Label	Dataset
Add...	2002	C:\AD_data\Data\Datasets\ADEPT_2002.dta
Remove	2005	C:\AD_data\Data\Datasets\ge2005.dta
Open in Stata	2007	C:\AD_data\Data\Datasets\ADEPT_2007.dta
Refresh		

The content of the loaded dataset—the names of the variables and the variables labels—are listed in the **Variables** tab located behind the **Datasets** tab. The **Variables** tab shows the content of the dataset selected (screenshot 3.11). The tab title shows the label of the selected dataset. You can search for a particular text in variables' names and labels by using the search field located at the bottom of the tab.

Specifying Variables

After loading the data, the next step is to tell ADePT what variables in the datasets correspond to the fields required to produce the output. You need to map variables in the data to the fields on the **Main form**. Each module of ADePT has its own set of fields, but the process of defining the fields is similar across modules.

ADePT does not require predefined names to be specified in the input fields: users can enter any variable name from the loaded dataset. The only assumption ADePT makes is that the variables are named consistently if multiple datasets are loaded. In other words, if *S10_Q12* is specified as the urban indicator in one dataset, it should be the urban indicator in all loaded datasets. ADePT checks if this assumption is true and reports to the user if the variable is missing in any of the loaded datasets.

There are four types of input variables on the ADePT forms:

- Continuous variables. A variable is considered continuous if it has more than 50 distinct numeric values. An example of a field that requires a continuous variable is the *Total spending* field.
- Categorical variables. A categorical variable is a numerical or string variable containing less than 50 distinct integer values. If a string value is entered in such a field, ADePT generates a numerical variable

Screenshot 3.11: Variable Names and Labels

Variable name	Variable label
mesto	Enumeration district code
urban	Type of settlement
region	Region
hhweight	Weight

Search ☐ Enable only common variables

with categories corresponding to the distinct values in the string variable. An example of a field that requires a categorical variable is the *Sector of employment* field.
- Dummy variables. A dummy variable is a variable with only two distinct values. The fields requiring dummy variables accept a numerical dummy variable or a logical expression based on an existing variable in the user's dataset. An example of a dummy variable field is the *Gender* field.
- Other parameter inputs used to set scalar parameters.

As in other Windows programs, check boxes are used to specify binary options (for example, whether the missing values should be recoded according to the user-specified rules), and spin-edit controls allow numerical parameters, such as *duration of primary schooling*, to be entered.

Some of the ADePT fields allow multiple variables to be specified that will be treated as a list. Consider, for example, the household ID field. In many datasets, the household ID determines which household an observation belong to, regardless of the values of other variables. This is the type of household ID ADePT expects. In some datasets, however, a household is identified not by household ID alone but also by other variables, such as the regional identifier. This can be the case when household IDs are assigned independently by interviewers in different regions, allowing overlaps in ID values between households in different regions. In this situation, all of the variables that allow a household to be uniquely identified need to be specified in the household ID field, with the individual variables separated by white spaces. For example, if *region* is the variable containing the region codes and the ID is the variable holding the household identifiers within each region, the household ID would be specified as HHID=region id.

ADePT processes this list of variables internally and creates its own household ID variable, which then identifies each household in the loaded datasets. Dragging and dropping variables from the list of variables to ADePT fields that support multiple variables specification will not replace the value, which is already there, but be appended to it.

The **Main form** with variable fields is located below the **Datasets** tab. When the cursor is positioned in a field on the **Main form**, the **Status** bar shows the description and the requirements for the variable to be specified in that field; it indicates which variable is expected to be specified in this field, its type, and whether the variable is required in the current module. The variables included in the **Main form** are shown in table 3.3.

For each household member attending school, ADePT Edu lists educational expenditures by item, such as monthly school fees, transportation to and from school, food purchases while in school, school uniforms (including shoes), special contributions to school projects or for supplementing school expenditures, and other educational expenditures not included elsewhere.

Table 3.3: Descriptions of Variables Included in the Main Form

Variable	Description
Household ID	Continuous variable with unique identification for household. If dataset is composed of separate dataset modules, variable is only element linking one dataset module to another.
Urban	Binary variable with value of 1 if the household is in an urban region and 0 otherwise.
Welfare aggregate	Continuous variable containing value of welfare aggregate used by survey. The most common welfare aggregate is the monetary value of the monthly consumption per capita. Other datasets could use income or an asset-based wealth index instead of consumption as the aggregate of welfare.
Usual resident	Binary variable with value of 1 if household member resides in the house at time of interview. If member did not reside at home at time of interview, variable takes value of 0 or—if dataset specifies so—any value other than 1.
Head of household	Binary variable with a value of 1 if the person is the head of the household and 0 otherwise.
Spouse of household head	Binary variable with a value of 1 if the person is the spouse of the head of the household and 0 otherwise
Age	Continuous variable representing person's age in years.
Gender	Binary variable with value of 1 if person is male and 0 otherwise
Subpopulation	Space reserved for user-specified variable that disaggregates the dataset. For example, the user may want to create separate tables for different regions, levels of income, or ethnic groups. Codes defining the subpopulation go here.
Total spending	Continuous variable showing total annual household expenditures (in currency used by the dataset).

Source: Authors.

Chapter 3: Using ADePT Edu

The weights and survey settings quadrant contains the variable defining household weights in the sample. Household surveys assign a specific household weight to each and every household. The weight is used to give each sample household a level of representation in the total household population. Household weights adjust for differences in the probability of selecting a household in the household population. Household surveys generally have unequal probabilities of selecting households from different regions or from different subpopulations for which statistics are needed. As a result, weights need to be applied when tabulations have to produce a proper representation. Household weights are also necessary when a sample design needs to correct for differential response rates.

The **Survey Settings** button activates a form describing a complex survey design. The characteristics of the survey design are set by the user. For Demographic and Health Survey (DHS) datasets, click **Set default DHS variables' names** in the lower right-hand quadrant of the screen; ADePT will fill in the fields based on the DHS convention. Otherwise the variable names need to be written into the form fields. Each field contains a short hint, which indicates what kind of variable the program expects in each field. By clicking on the **Education** tab, users can fill in the information required to prepare the education tables (screenshot 3.12).

The top left-hand quadrant contains schooling information for the year before the year of the interview (screenshot 3.13). Under the coding conventions of Stata, if the person attended primary school, the code reads Primary = = 1, which means that the number 1 is exclusive to having attended primary school only. Secondary school has a code of 2; postsecondary school has a code of 3. The grade attended the year before the year of the interview is shown at the bottom of this quadrant. If the analyst prefers not to use the Stata variable code, dummy variables, where one school level could be equal to 1 and the others to 0, can be used instead. (The grade variable remains a numeric continuous variable.)

Information on schooling during the year of the interview is shown in the upper right-hand quadrant, labeled **Current school year**. This quadrant contains information on the level of schooling attended during the current year, as well as the grade.

The main reason why previous and current years are included is to permit the calculation of real repetition and dropout rates. The current year information also includes the reasons for not being in school, which can be valuable in explaining the reasons why students drop out of school. The list

Assessing Sector Performance and Inequality in Education

Screenshot 3.12: Variable Names in the Main Form

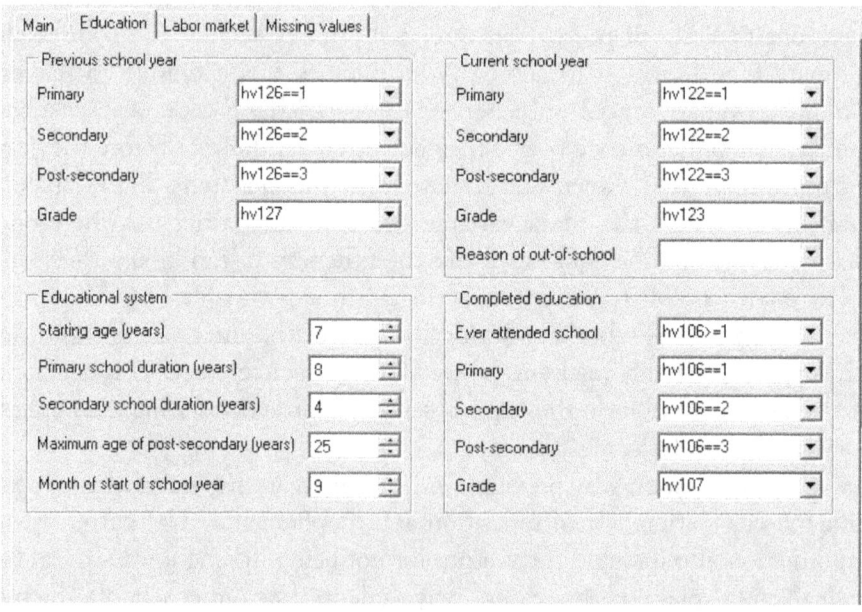

Screenshot 3.13: Specifying Variable Names in the Education Tab

of the reasons for not being in school during the current year is usually different across datasets, as the list is generally country specific.

The bottom left-hand quadrant contains the characteristics of the education system of the country of analysis. This information must be added using the drop-down menu.

The bottom right-hand quadrant shows school attainment (**Completed education** in screenshot 3.13). The first drop-down indicates whether the household member ever attended school. The response can be either 0 (never attended school) or any digit equal to or greater than 1. For a household member who completed the fifth grade of primary school, **Ever attended school** would be equal to 1; **Primary, Secondary,** and **Post-secondary** would be equal to 0; and **Grade** would be equal to 5. This example uses the Stata code convention. Users can instead select binary or dummy codes for each variable.

The next tab, **Labor market**, contains information on employment, the sector of employment, earnings, hours, and work experience (screenshot 3.14). ADePT uses the information in this tab to estimate the returns to education. The variables in this tab are defined in table 3.4.

The list of datasets is shown on the **Datasets** tab in the **Main form**. Once a dataset is selected for analysis, the **Variables** tab displays the variable names and labels in the selected dataset (screenshot 3.15). Users can drag and drop variables from the selected dataset into the corresponding fields on the **Main form**. Once variables are dragged and dropped, the type of variable (numeric or string) and its name and label are shown in the **Status** bar.

Users can search for any part of a variable name or label using the search filter field. For example, typing "ur" selects variables with names or labels that contain the string "ur." To clear the search filter, simply delete all the characters in the search field.

Users can use a drop-down list in the field to specify a variable, type the variable name into the field, or drag and drop the variable. The drag and drop method is recommended, because it is faster and more convenient for datasets that contain a large number of variables and reduces the possibility of errors when entering the variable names. Drop-down lists take a long time to navigate if the loaded datasets contain a large number of variables. Manual entry of variable names can lead to misspelled variable names and thus errors in ADePT execution, but typing into the variable field is the only way to specify expressions in the fields. Variable names are case sensitive and should be specified exactly as they appear in the dataset.

Assessing Sector Performance and Inequality in Education

Screenshot 3.14: Variable Names for the Labor Market Tab

| Main | Education | Labor market | Missing values |

Labor market
- Employed: hv008
- Unemployed: hv002
- Sector: hv004
- Earnings: hv003
- Hours: hv004
- Work experience: hv014

Table 3.4: Definitions of Variables in the Labor Market Tab

Variable	Definition
Employed	Takes value of 1 if household member is working for wages at time of interview and 0 otherwise.[a]
Unemployed	Takes value of 1 if person is not working but is looking for work and 0 otherwise.
Sector	Code provided by each survey.
Earnings	Total amount earned by household member during number of hours reported in next variable.
Hours	Number of hours worked by household member (an average month has 167 hours).
Work experience	For surveys that do not report years of experience, ADePT estimates them using the following formula: experience = (age − years of education − age of entry to the school system). For example, a 35-year-old who completed eighth grade would have 20 years of work experience (35 − 8 − 7).

Source: Authors.
a. Some surveys ask if the person was working during the week before the interview.

If several datasets are loaded, ADePT can disable the drag-and-drop capabilities for variables that are not included in all datasets. Whenever several datasets are loaded, users need to check the **Enable only common variables** checkpoint at the bottom of screenshot 3.15. The enabled common variables appear in black bold lettering; the disabled variables appear in gray. Both types of variables are shown in the **Variables** tab (screenshot 3.16).

Chapter 3: Using ADePT Edu

Screenshot 3.15: Variable Names for a Loaded Dataset

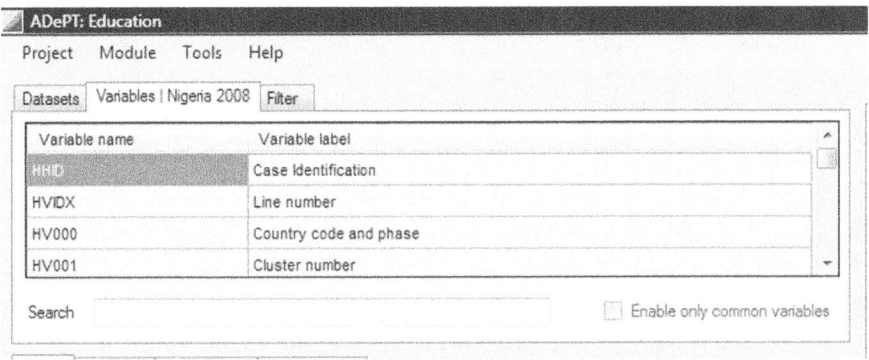

Screenshot 3.16: Disabled Variables in Gray, Active Variables in Bold

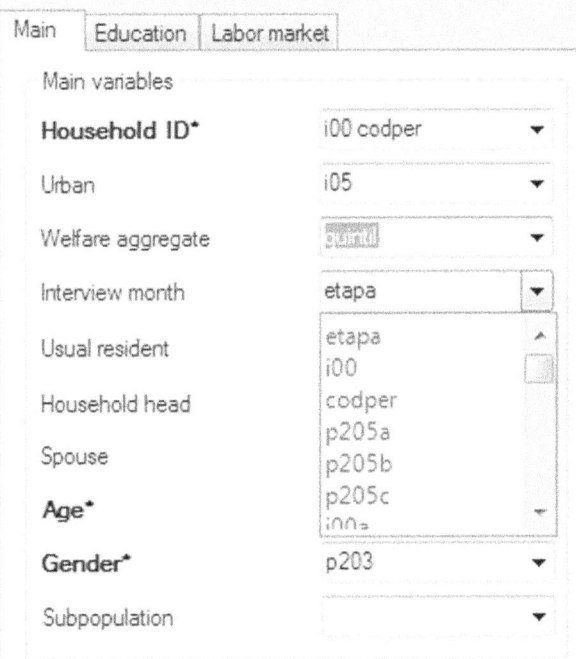

Using Compound Fields

Several modules of ADePT use compound fields. Compound fields allow the management of several input elements as a single unit. For example, in the **Social Protection** module (in the initial ADePT module selection screen), the program type, program name, and benefits amount can be entered as a single element in a list of programs. Although the properties of the compound fields may be different for the different modules, all compound fields have common elements and behavior.

First, compound fields always contain two or more elements, one of which is a field in which the user has to provide a variable name (screenshot 3.17). Variables can be dragged and dropped from the **Variables** tab to fill this field. To add a unit to the list, fill in all required elements of the unit and click **Add**. For example, the **Missing values** tab contains a compound field managing the user-specified list of missing values. Each unit in the list contains two elements: the names of the variables to be recoded (field **Variables**) and the values that should be replaced to missing (field **Missing values**). Both elements are required; users need to specify a variable name and enter a missing value to append the list. Elements already in the list can be removed by clicking **Remove**.

Screenshot 3.17: Compound Field for Missing Values

Second, compound fields can be required for analysis. It is important to distinguish between required elements of a list unit and the compound field that is required. An element is required if a unit cannot be posted in the list without specifying this element. All, some, or none of the elements may be required. The entire compound field is required if ADePT cannot conduct any analysis unless the field is filled in. A compound field is considered filled if it contains at least one unit. For example, the **Missing values** compound field contains two required elements but is not a required field (analysis can be conducted even if the list is empty). For the programs list in the **Social Protection** module, users need not enter all three elements (*Type*, *Variable*, *Label*), but they must enter a program; analysis cannot be performed if no social protection program is specified.

Generating Tables and Figures

After loading data into ADePT and specifying the corresponding variables, users can select the tables and figures (graphs) they want to generate. Tables and figures are chosen from a tree-like structure, in which they are grouped by topic (screenshot 3.18).

Variables need to be specified and options selected to create each table and graph. For example, a table that shows the distribution of poverty rates by geographic regions requires the specification of the welfare aggregate, poverty lines, and regions. If one of these variables is not specified, the table cannot be created.

The title tab in the **Table and figure window** shows the total number of tables and figures in the module (39 tables and graphs in screenshot 3.18); the number of feasible tables that can be generated; and the number of tables selected. The feasible tables are displayed in black; tables that cannot be created for a particular module are displayed in gray. These tables remain inactive if any of the variables required are not specified.

The **Table description** and **if-condition** tab in the lower portion of the **Table and figure window** displays a description of the highlighted table, describing the table layout and its intended use. If it is feasible to generate this table, users can select it by checking the check box next to the table's title in the **Table and figure window**. Multiple tables/figures can be selected by checking the boxes next to the corresponding title. ADePT will select all feasible tables/figures in this group.

Screenshot 3.18: Table and Figure Window: Selecting the Education Tables to Generate

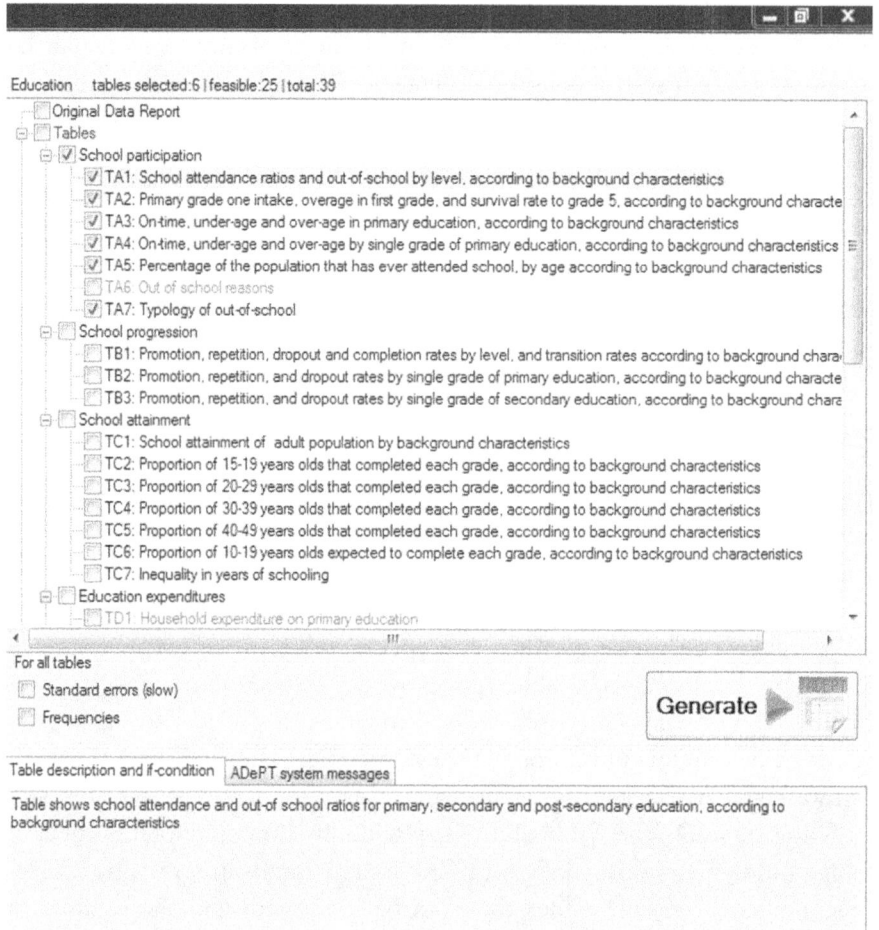

After selecting the tables and figures to produce, click **Generate** to start processing the data. The progress of computations will be displayed in the **ADePT system messages** tab and by the rotation of the **Process** indicator icon in the top left-hand corner of the ADePT window. To interrupt the computations, click the green **Generate** button changes, which turns into a red **Stop** button (screenshot 3.19). No tables or figures are outputted if the **Stop** button is clicked.

Screenshot 3.19: Record and Stop Button for Creating Tables

```
For all tables
  ☐ Standard errors (slow)
  ☐ Frequencies                                Stop

Table description and if-condition | ADePT system messages
Creating Table 4.12...
Creating Table 5.1...
Creating Table 5.2...
Creating Table 5.3...
Creating Figure 5.4...
Creating Figure 5.5...
```

Choosing a Reporting Option

The **System messages** tab located at the bottom of the **Table and figure window** in screenshot 3.18 displays information on data processing, on errors and warnings, and on the progress in the generation of output. To define the level of reporting in the **System messages window**, click **Tools → Options** on the **Menu** bar and select the **Reporting** tab.

Users can select three levels of reporting on the **Reporting** tab (screenshot 3.20). If the default level of reporting (**Main messages and current status**) is selected, ADePT displays only the main messages on the progress of data checking, data preparation, and data analysis and reports warnings and error messages. This level of reporting is recommended. Two other levels of reporting—**Detailed messages and progress indication** and **Service messages (debug mode)**—are designed for troubleshooting ADePT. They are rarely used.

Changing the font can be useful in printing tables and figures for presentations. To change a font or to clear the content of the **System messages window**, right-click the window and select a desired option—**Clear output** and **Select font**—from the menu (screenshot 3.21).

Performing Common Tasks

This section describes several common tasks that can be performed with ADePT. They include generating tables on a subsample of observations,

Screenshot 3.20: Selecting a Level of Reporting

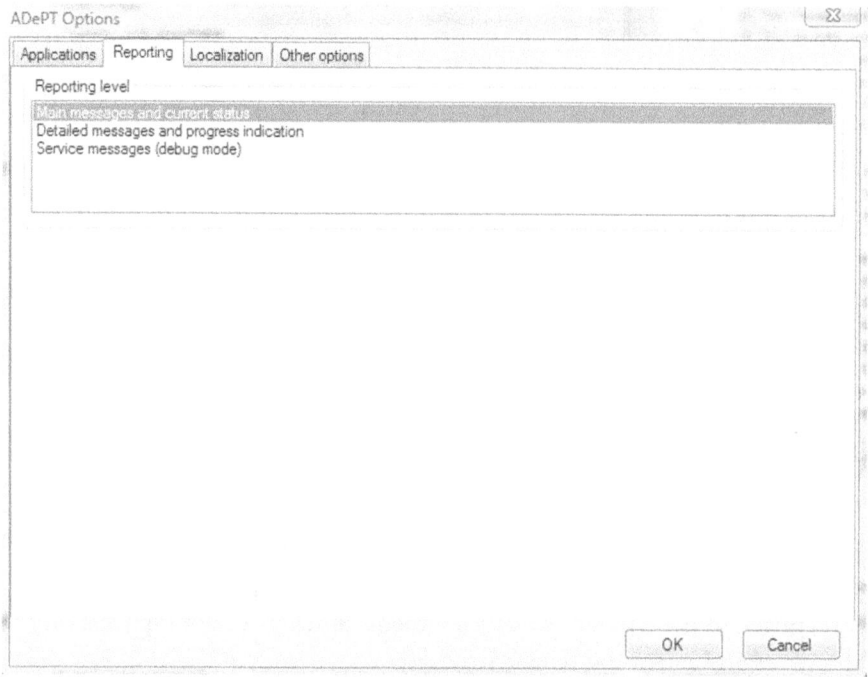

Screenshot 3.21: Clearing Contents or Changing Fonts

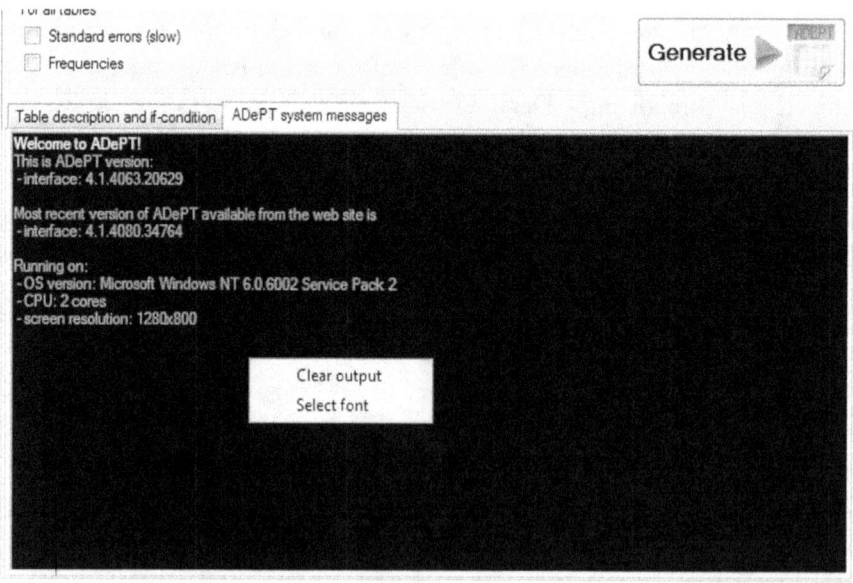

generating tables of frequencies and tables with standard errors, describing complex survey designs, defining missing values, specifying expressions in variables fields, and running simulations.

Generating Tables on a Subsample of Observations

Analysis can focus on a particular subpopulation in all or some tables and figures. A global filter is used to retain in the analysis only those observations that satisfy certain requirements. The variables selected by the global filter apply to all tables and figures in an active module during the computation. The **Global filter** tab is located next to the **Datasets** tab in the **Data/variables window**. It becomes visible when at least one dataset is loaded. The tab contains a check box (**Apply the filter**) and the field for a logical condition to be used in retaining observations for analysis. Any valid Stata logical expression can be specified in this field.

When an expression for the global filter is specified, ADePT retains only the observations that satisfy the conditions specified by the global filter. Because the global filter is applied in the early stage of data processing, using it will result in faster calculations than using it for all tables or figures. For example, to produce tables and figures for respondents under the age of 40 in a particular region of the country, a user enters "age<40 & region=11" in the global filter field (screenshot 3.22). ADePT drops all observations in which region is not equal to 11 and age is greater than 40. It generates tables and figures only for observations that satisfy the specified conditions.

Individual tables and figures may also have restrictions on observations. These tables and figures augment rather than replace the global filter, so that only observations that satisfy both the global filter and the individual if-condition are included in the analysis. Applying an if-condition to a

Screenshot 3.22: Using the Global Filter

Datasets	Filter	Variables	2002
Filter			
☑ Keep observations satisfying the following condition:			
(age<40) & (region=11)			

group of tables or figures (screenshot 3.23) is equivalent to applying the same condition to all tables or figures in that group.

The purpose of an if-condition is to include observations from a particular subgroup of a population. The inclusion condition is formulated as a Boolean expression—a function of the variables existing in the user's dataset. Observations are included in the analysis if they satisfy the inclusion condition (the Boolean expression evaluates to value *true*). In many cases, the conditions are restricting, limiting the observations included in the analysis to a particular region, age group, or other feature. (In Stata, there is no need to write the word *if* before if-conditions, and "= =" can be used interchangeably with "=.") Narrower groups can be selected by restricting several dimensions simultaneously. For example, an if-condition can be rewritten as "(urban=1) and (region!=1)," limiting the observations to all urban locations and excluding the first region (for example, the capital of a country). The symbols "and" and "|" are used to denote logical "AND" and logical "OR" operations. In order for A and B to be *true*, both A and B must be true. In order for A|B to be true, any one of A or B must be true. Any of the functions available in Stata can also be specified as if-conditions (table 3.5).

ADePT follows Stata's convention, where missing values are considered to be infinitely large numbers. Hence, the expression (age > 65) evaluates to *true* not only when the age of the responders is greater than 65 but also when the value of the age variable is missing. Parentheses are used to indicate the order of evaluation for complex expressions.

Screenshot 3.23: Setting an If-Condition

Table 3.5: Examples of If-Conditions Available in Stata

If-condition	Interpretation
inlist(region,1, 3, 5, 6)	Include only observations from regions with codes 1, 3, 5, and 6.
inrange(age, 15, 65)	Include only individuals 15–65.
((male= =1) and inrange(age, 15, 65))|((male= =0) and inrange(age, 15, 60))	Include only individuals of working age, which is defined differently for men and women.
!missing(sector)	Exclude observations with missing values in variable sector.

Source: Authors.

When if-conditions are evaluated, each observation is treated independently. For example, to exclude all households in which the household head was born abroad, users must either be working at the household level (in which case person-specific characteristics refer to household heads) or have a variable for the place of birth of the household head defined for each individual in the dataset (and consistent within each household) instead of the place of birth variable. If the if-condition is based on the place of birth variable, children living in the households with foreign-born household heads will not be excluded.

To specify an if-condition, select a table (or a group of tables), then click on the **IF-condition** field in the bottom of the **Table description** tab. Enter the expression to restrict the sample of observations, and click **Set** (screenshot 3.24).

Tables or figures that have an if-condition applied to them are highlighted in screenshot 3.24. To remove the if-condition, select the object to which the if-condition was applied and click the **Clear** button that appears next to the IF-condition field (screenshot 3.25). The if-condition specified for a table is outputted below the table. The definitions of if-conditions are not saved in the project file.

A combination of the global filter and individual if-conditions for tables may become too restrictive; it is the user's responsibility to make sure the conditions do not contradict one another and do not eliminate all observations from the sample. For example, if the global filter selects only the urban population and an if-condition applied to a particular table selects only the rural population, then no table can be generated, because no observations satisfy both conditions. The contradiction in this example is obvious; it is less apparent in situations in which there are complex dependencies between, say, the sector of employment, education level, and other factors. If the effective condition (the combination of the global filter and the individual IF-condition) is so restrictive that no observations satisfy it, an error message will appear and the table and graph will be marked red in the selection tree.

Setting a global filter and applying an if-condition to all tables and figures may look the same, but the two actions are actually different because the global filter has the higher priority and is applied at the data preparation stage, before the beginning of the analysis. This has two consequences.

First, the global filter can be used to remove observations from the analysis that cause problems with the data checks. Normally, if the problem is

Assessing Sector Performance and Inequality in Education

Screenshot 3.24: Example of an If-Condition

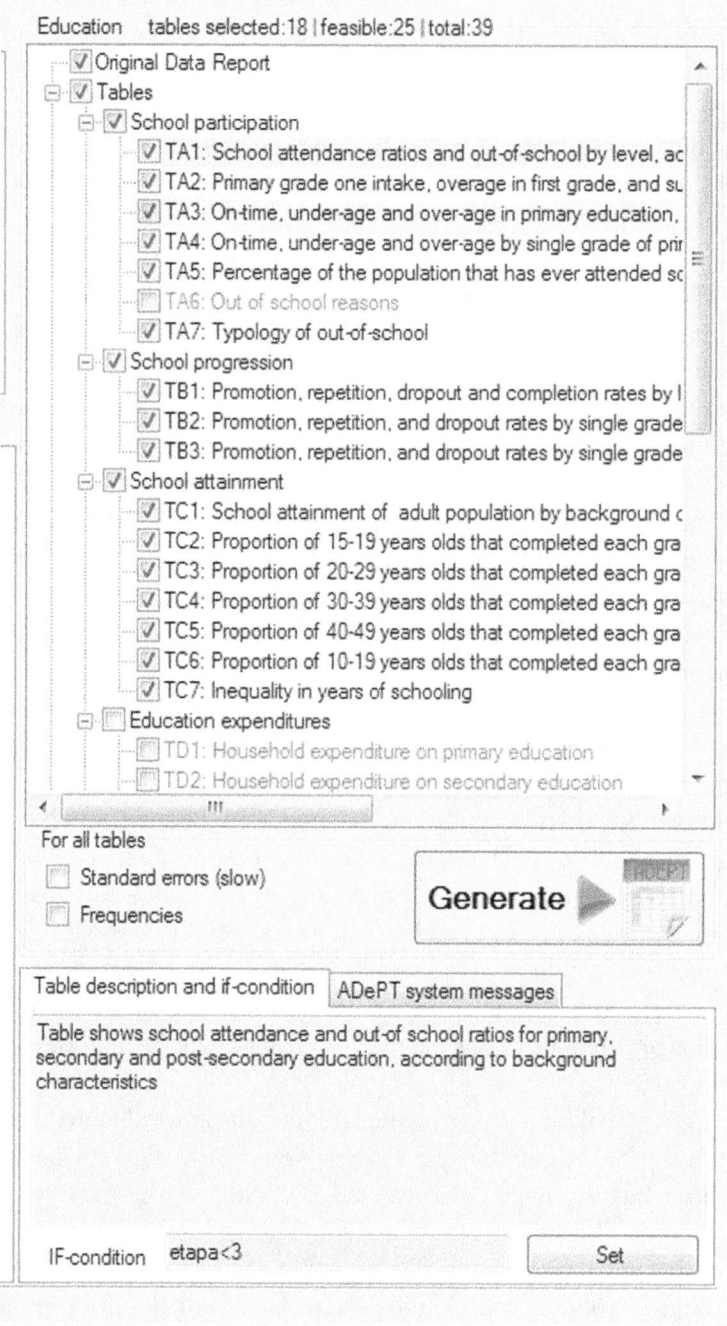

Screenshot 3.25: Clearing an If-Condition

caused by a particular value of a certain variable, that value can be recoded to a missing variable to exclude as an outlier. However, there may be cases in which an observation may have all its individual variables within a normal range but the combination of all the individual variables yields a value that is not possible. For example, a user may want to apply the global filter to remove all respondents under age 5 if they report attending a school. No warning will be issued, as these observations are excluded from the analysis before the checks are conducted. If the same condition were applied to a particular table, a warning that very young children are attending schools would be displayed, even though these observations would later be excluded from that table.

Second, the global filter may affect the values of the variables ADePT derives from the data. Consider household size as an example. In an individual-level dataset, ADePT constructs a variable for household size by counting the number of observations with a unique value of the household ID variable. If a global filter that selects only the working-age population is applied, the variable that ADePT creates for household size will count the number of working-age individuals in a household, which could be different from the number of household members.

Generating Tables with Standard Errors and Tables of Frequencies

In addition to standard tables, ADePT can produce tables with standard errors and tables with frequencies. ADePT uses sophisticated algorithms to calculate the standard errors for estimated statistics. These algorithms often require substantial computational resources. Producing tables with standard errors takes more time than producing standard tables—sometimes substantially more. For this reason, it is advisable to begin by generating standard tables.

Tables with frequencies show the unweighted number of observations used in the calculation of a particular cell in a table. Indicating these frequencies does not take extra time.

To output tables with standard errors and tables with frequencies, check the check boxes **Standard errors (slow)** and **Frequencies,** located to the left of the **Generate** button (screenshot 3.26).

Describing a Complex Survey Design

ADePT can account for a complex survey design when it calculates standard errors for the estimates. It allows users to specify multiple stratification designs, final population corrections, survey weights, and options on how the standard errors of the estimates should be computed.

Most surveys include one or more weighting variables. Users should consult the survey documentation to determine which weighting variable must be used. If the only survey design parameter to specify is the weights, it can be inputted on the **Main form**, with the other variables. Weights entered apply to all household and individual data. If other parameters of the survey design need to be specified, click **Survey Settings** and fill in the form describing a complex survey design (screenshot 3.27).

Defining Missing Values

ADePT does not remove an observation from the sample if any of the used variables has a missing value. Instead, it treats missing values intelligently,

Screenshot 3.26: Generating Tables with Standard Errors, Frequencies, or Both

Screenshot 3.27: Adding Household Weights and Other Parameters

ignoring observations with missing values if the missing values are involved in the analysis for a particular table or graph. Missing values in Stata and SPSS datasets are assigned codes that ADePT recognizes. However, not all data providers use these codes. Some datasets contain values 9, 97, 98, 99, 997, and so forth, which perform the functions of the missing value code (one variable may use multiple codes for "refusal," "don't know," "not applicable," and so forth). If this is the case, it is crucial that ADePT be informed about such codes. The program will ensure that these codes are recoded to missing values before any analysis is performed.

Missing values can be defined in the **Missing values** tab. To activate the tab, on the **Menu** bar click **Tools → Show missing value tab**. The **Missing value** will appear next to the **Variables** tab in the **Main form** window.

ADePT receives information about missing values as a list of pairs of elements: variables and missing value codes. The following combinations are possible:

- One variable and one missing value
- One variable and multiple missing values, separated by spaces
- Multiple variables, separated by spaces, and one missing value
- Multiple variables, separated by spaces, and multiple missing values.

A particular variable can be mentioned in multiple lists of variables and multiple lists of missing values.

The **Missing values** tab contains the (initially empty) list of such pairs and controls to append this list. To define missing values, do the following:

1. Enter one or more variable names into the first field, separating variable names with spaces.
2. Enter one or more values into the second field, separating multiple values with spaces.
3. Click **Add**.
4. Repeat (if necessary) for other variables and values.

Users can add as many definitions of missing values for the variables in the dataset as they wish.

Screenshot 3.28 shows how to recode value 999 in the variable defining education. To do so, drag and drop the **p205a** variable into the **Variable** field, enter 999 into the **Missing values** field, and click **Add**.

Screenshot 3.28: Changing the Code for Missing Values

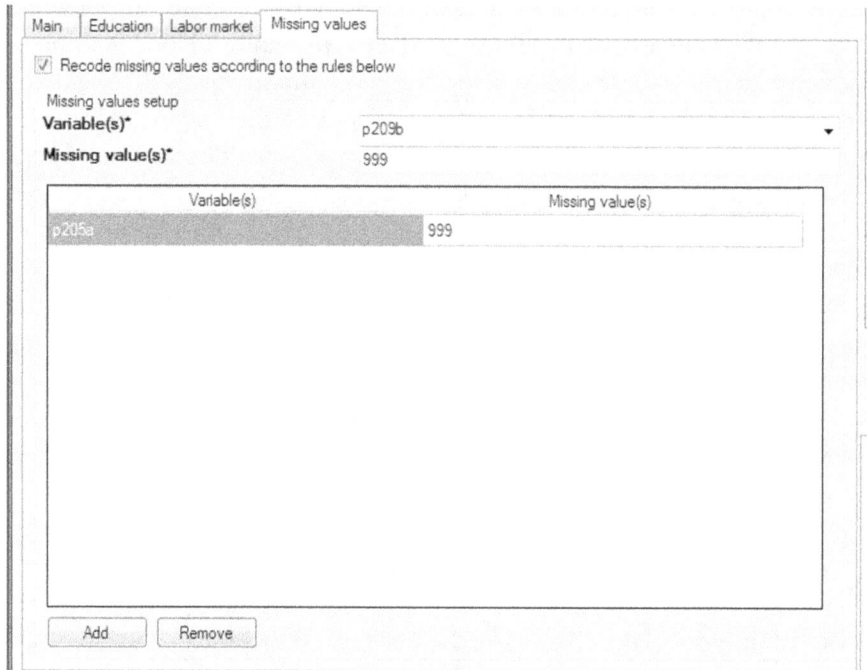

Information about the user-defined missing values is saved in the project file; it is invoked when the project file is opened if **Add to project file** is checked. If the definitions of missing values were stored in a project file, the **Missing values** tab will appear automatically when the project file is loaded.

Specifying Expressions in Variables Fields

Some variables (for example, Urban and Gender) are treated as dummy variables and thus can take on only two values (if a variable is used). ADePT assigns meaning to particular values of these variables (for example, 1 denotes urban population in the Urban variable). The coding of these variables may be different in the user's datasets. If this is the case, do the following:

1. Recode the original data to match ADePT's expectations (for example, set 1 = male, 1 = urban, 1 = household head).
2. Specify an expression instead of a variable name. ADePT will evaluate the expression and take the result as a corresponding indicator.

Expressions come in handy when a variable does not exist in the dataset exactly the way ADePT expects it to be specified but can be derived from the existing variables using a simple transformation. Because the result of expression evaluation is binary, expressions apply only to dummy variables (and to categorical variables to the extent that they are generalizations of dummy variables).

Consider the following example. In the original dataset variable, URBAN takes the value of 1 for rural and 2 for urban populations. Because there are several data files (each corresponding to a different year), it would be cumbersome to recode this variable into the format ADePT expects. It might be easier to specify an expression of the following type:

$$URBAN==2 \ .$$

ADePT generates a new variable in each dataset that takes the value 1 whenever URBAN is equal to 2 (screenshot 3.29). For all other values (that is, values of 1), this new variable take the value of 0. Missing values of URBAN remain missing.

In recoding a variable, the following transformations may be applied:

$$varname == const$$
$$varname != const$$
$$varname > const$$
$$varname >= const$$
$$varname < const$$
$$varname <= const.$$

Screenshot 3.29: Creating an Expression to Recode a Variable

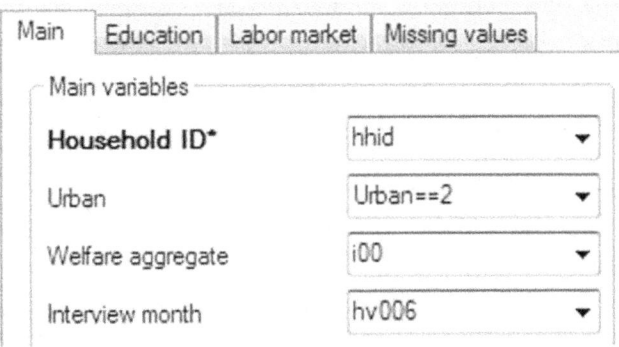

The name of a variable must be the first word of the expression. Whenever an expression evaluates to logical *true*, it takes a value of 1, while a logical *false* takes a value of 0.

Running Simulations

Simulation analysis of a reform or policy intervention involves two steps. The first step involves creating a dataset with simulated data. This dataset is based on the actual data, modified to simulate the effect of a reform or policy.

The second step involves loading the two files (original and simulated) into ADePT and generating tables and graphs comparing the statistics in the original and simulated scenarios. A full version of Stata is needed to run simulations.

To run a simulation, follow these seven steps:

1. Start ADePT and switch to the module most appropriate for the topic of analysis.
2. Add the original file to the list of files. This file will be used to derive the simulated data.
3. Click **Open in Stata**. A new Stata session will start and the dataset will automatically be loaded to Stata. (Refer to the Stata manuals for a description of Stata commands.) Type **Help** in Stata's command line to bring up the electronic documentation for the installed version of Stata.
4. Issue Stata commands that modify the dataset according to the desired assumptions. Rather than create new variables, modify the original variables (recall that when working with multiple datasets, ADePT assumes that the variable names are the same in all datasets). For example, suppose that each individual's consumption is stored in variable v021 and you want to investigate how a 10 percent consumption subsidy to rural households will affect aggregate poverty rates. Type the following command:

    replace v021 = v021 * 1.10 if rural == 1

5. When you finish modifying the data, save them to a new file. To save the simulated data in the file called "simulated," type the command in Stata:

    save simulated, replace

6. Close the Stata session by typing "exit" in the Stata command prompt, and add the simulated dataset to the files list of ADePT.
7. Select **Show Changes** in the files list. If there are only two datasets in the list, ADePT will automatically select them to be compared.

Note that ADePT does not take into account the fact that the second dataset is simulated, so the standard errors reported by ADePT for simulated indicators and differences may be incorrect.

Complex simulations can be run. For example, a user may want to first model the dependency of income and consumption on education, then simulate an increase in education, and then reestimate the income and consumption effects of the reform.

Adjusting Settings

This section presents the setting options available to all modules of ADePT, including the language of interface, the computational engine, and the output viewer.

Changing the Screen and Output Language

ADePT is available in several languages. Changing **Localization** affects the interface of the program (menus, dialogs, error messages, and so forth) (screenshot 3.30). Changing **Reporting** affects the language in tables and graphs produced.

Before changing the language, make sure you have saved your input into an ADePT project file: unless the input is saved, it will be lost when ADePT is restarted. To adjust the language setting, open the **Options Dialog** in the main menu (**Tools → Options**), and switch to the **Localization** tab.

The **Localization** tab contains two selections: one is for the language and one is for the code page. To change the language, select one of the languages from this list and click **OK**. The dialog box will close. To apply the change of language, you must close and reopen ADePT. Once the new language is set, ADePT will display all the menus, dialogs, and error messages in that language. (Because ADePT is a fast-developing project, some new parts of the interface might not yet be translated. In this case, ADePT will display them in English.)

Screenshot 3.30: Changing the Language

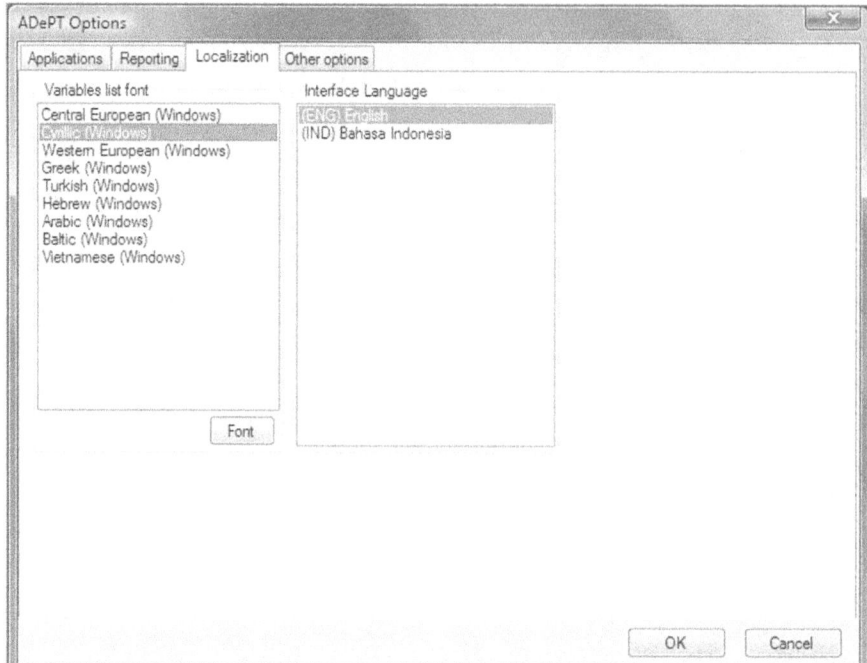

The choice of the coding page allows the variable names and variable labels to be recorded in non-Latin script. You may need to change the coding page if your datasets contain variable names or labels recorded in Cyrillic, Arabic, Greek, or other scripts. This change is necessary because the Stata dataset format allows storage of non-English symbols but does not provide the code page in which they should be represented (this is a setting on the computer on which the data were saved into the file). Thus, users must manually try the different code pages until the localized data labels become readable. ADePT provides a choice of the most common code pages for alphabet-based languages (Cyrillic, Greek, and so forth). Stata datasets cannot store labels in character-based languages; there is thus no code page selection for them. The selection of the coding page is independent of the choice of the language.

To switch to the proper code page, right-click the column header for the value labels and left-click the appropriate encoding name (screenshot 3.31).

Screenshot 3.31: Selecting the Proper Code Page

Datasets	Variables	2004	Filter
Variable name	Variable label		
code_fam	Код домогоспод	Central European (Windows)	
n_member	Код члена домог	✓ Cyrillic (Windows)	
age	Вік	Western European (Windows)	
male	1:male	Greek (Windows)	
edlev		Turkish (Windows)	
reltohed		Hebrew (Windows)	
ecstatus		Arabic (Windows)	
weight	weights for Q3 aft	Baltic (Windows)	
location	1 Kiev, 2 big cities 3 small towns 4 rural	Vietnamese (Windows)	

If the code page is set correctly, the variable labels appear as in screenshot 3.32. If the code page is not set correctly, the variable names appear as in screenshot 3.33.

ADePT will automatically decode labels using the specified code page and show them in the variables list panel. It may take several tries to determine which code page is the correct one. An equivalent but faster way of switching the code page is to right-click the header of the variables column on the **Variables** tab and select a code page in the menu that pops up. ADePT will remember the code page setting and use it in all modules until a new code page is specified.

Selecting the Computational Engine and Output Viewer

ADePT relies on the Stata numerical engine for computations. By default, it uses Numerics by Stata (NBS) to generate tables and graphs. NBS is a library of computational routines developed and distributed by StataCorp. It is included in the ADePT installation package and set up as a numerical engine on installation. Users who have Stata version 10 or later installed on their computers have the option to use ADePT with their own Stata.

NBS has a computational functionality of the Stata SE 32-bit version 11 (the latest version of Stata). Users with 64-bit Stata and users with Stata MP may prefer using their own Stata as a computational engine for ADePT, as these versions allow faster execution (Stata MP) and can load larger

Assessing Sector Performance and Inequality in Education

Screenshot 3.32: Appearance of Variable Names When the Code Page Is Set Correctly

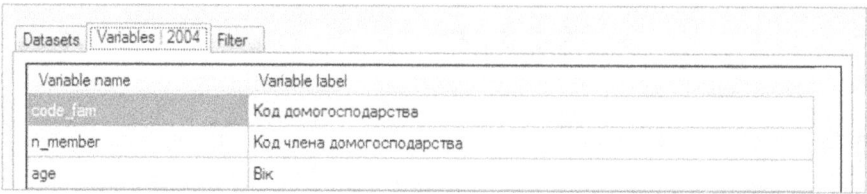

Screenshot 3.33: Appearance of Variable Names When the Code Page Is Not Set Correctly

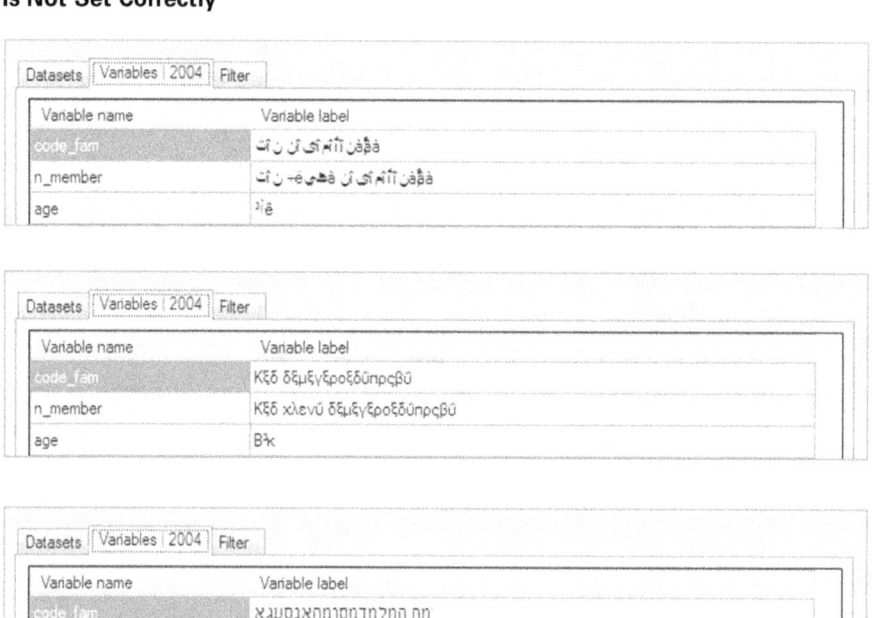

datasets (64-bit Stata SE and MP) than NBS. Using Stata with ADePT also extends ADePT functionality by allowing users to open and modify data files directly from ADePT.

ADePT saves tables and graphs in Microsoft (MS) Excel format. Tables and graphs can be displayed with MS Excel, a free MS Excel Viewer, or OpenOffice Calc.

On installation, ADePT tries to locate the executable file for Excel and use it as a viewer for the generated results. ADePT first tries to read the location MS Excel executables from the Windows registry. If ADePT cannot find this information in the registry, it searches selected folders on the local drives.

Users who do not have Excel installed on their computers can download and install a free Excel Viewer from the Microsoft website (http://www.microsoft.com). This installation requires administrative rights. The functionality of the MS Excel Viewer is restricted to opening, viewing, and printing files generated in MS Excel–supported formats. Users can also copy data from MS Excel Viewer to other programs. MS Excel Viewer does not allow users to modify or save a workbook or to create a new one.

To check the setting of ADePT, on the **Menu** bar click **Tools → Options** and select the **Applications** tab. This tab shows whether during installation ADePT determined the location of the required applications and offers options for installing missing components. The tab contains two selector buttons for switching between Stata and Numeric by Stata, fields with the paths to Stata executables, executables for MS Excel or MS Excel Viewer, and the path to the scripting host executable (this component will be removed in later versions of ADePT).

In screenshot 3.34, ADePT has successfully located all the required components and is ready to run. The fields highlighted in green contain paths to required applications. ADePT will use NBS for computation and MS Excel installed in C:\Program Files\Microsoft Office\Office12 folder as a viewer for output.

In this example, ADePT uses Stata 10 installed on the local (or network) computer as a computational engine. It tries to locate Stata 10 or later executable automatically on installation. If it fails to find the Stata executable, users can point ADePT to a location of this executable by clicking the **Browse** button on the right of the field with the Stata executable path. Users can specify the directory with MS Excel or MS Excel Viewer executables on their computers by pointing ADePT to these locations. If no MS Excel or MS Excel Viewer is found on the local computer, ADePT will still produce the output file with tables and graphs and store it in a user-defined location.

Screenshot 3.34: Final Set, Ready to Run

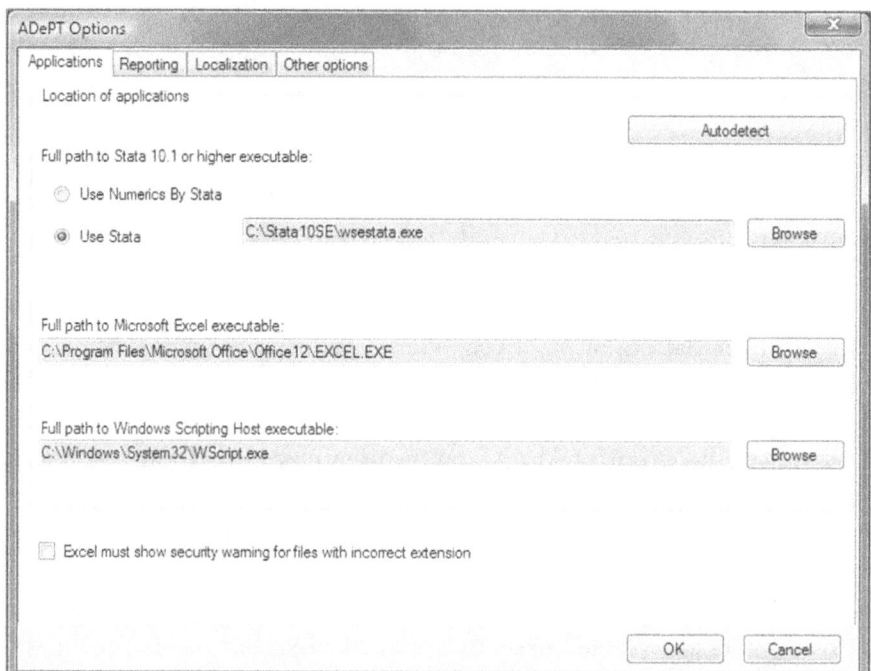

Working with Projects in ADePT

A project is a configuration file that contains paths for the datasets and names of variables specified by the user in a module of ADePT. A project can be useful for saving the information defined in a current session to use again later. The basic commands to work with project files are located in the **Project** menu on the **Menu** bar (screenshot 3.35).

After data files are uploaded and variables specified on the ADePT form, users can save this information for future use by choosing **Project** and then **Save Project** (or **Save Project As** if the files have not been saved previously).

The saved project will store links to datasets, names of specified variables, definitions of the missing values, and the expression used in the global filter. Projects do not retain the list of selected tables and graphs, the corresponding

Screenshot 3.35: Commands for Working with Project Files

Project	Module	Tools	Help
Reset			Ctrl+R
Open Project...			Ctrl+O
Open Last Used Project			Ctrl+L
Save Project			Ctrl+S
Save Project As...			
Exit			

if-conditions and frequencies, or standard errors choices, because these features characterize the output rather than the input.

A previously saved project can be retrieved by selecting **Open Project** on the **Project** menu. In the window that opens, navigate to the folder containing a previously saved project and double-click its name. The datasets are not saved in a project file; instead, the project file contains references to the selected datasets. To start a new project, clear all the fields on the form by choosing **Project** and then the **Reset** command from the drop-down menu.

ADePT saves the settings of the last successfully run configuration (that is, the last creation of a table or graph) on exit and loads them automatically at startup. If you prefer to start working with the blank project instead, you can change the default behavior by going to **Tools → Options → Other Options** and unchecking the corresponding check box. The last successfully run configuration for the current module can be recalled at any time by selecting the corresponding command in the **Project** menu.

You can reuse projects saved in a particular module in other modules. In this case, the project will load the datasets and specify variables that are present in both modules. For example, if the project saved in the **Poverty** module is opened in the **Labor** module, ADePT will automatically fill in the fields for welfare aggregate, poverty lines, urban-rural indicator, and so forth. It will not be able to fill in the fields specific only to the **Labor** module, such as work categories, earnings, and others.

Using ADePT Project Files on a Different Computer

Saved project files can be accessed on a different computer. ADePT projects contain explicit (not relative) paths to the data files. ADePT will try to load data files from the locations stored in the project file. If it fails to find the data files on the paths specified in the project file, it will search for these files in the directory in which the project file is located. Thus, to use a project file in a situation where the locations of the data files are different from those saved in the project file, place the data files in the directory where the project file is located. Saved projects can also be used in batch processing, described later in this chapter.

Replicating Results

To reproduce the results obtained with ADePT, the person replicating the files needs the following:

- ADePT software, which can be downloaded and installed by going to www.worldbank.org/adept
- The project files, with the input specifications used to obtain the original results
- The datasets used to generate the results (note that the datasets are not stored in the project file; only the links to their location on the user's drive are stored).

It may be convenient to pack the project files and datasets into a single archive, such as a zip-archive, to reduce the size of the transfer. When ADePT opens a saved project file, it looks for the datasets in the specified locations. If the people using your files are unable or unwilling to re-create your folder structure on their computers, instruct them to place the datasets in the same folder where they put your project files. If ADePT does not find a dataset in the location specified in the project file, it checks the folder where the project file itself is located; if the dataset is found, it is taken from there.

Note that if-conditions are not saved in project files. If you used any if-conditions to produce the original results, you need to describe which if-conditions were applied to which tables and graphs. The if-conditions for each table and graph are displayed below them on the corresponding sheets of the ADePT output.

Using ADePT in a Batch Mode

ADePT supports a batch mode of operation that can be helpful in producing several reports for many countries or a set of reports for the same country with different parameters (for example, different poverty lines). The batch mode minimizes human involvement in producing the reports; ADePT creates output automatically based on the settings prepared and saved earlier in a project file.

To use the batch mode, start ADePT as usual and provide all inputs. Add the datasets and fill in the variables, then save the input into a project file of your choice (note that you do not need to generate the actual report—that is, click the **Generate** button—to be able to save inputs in the project file). Repeat this procedure for every report you want to produce. After all the project files are prepared, close the ADePT program.

At this step you need to create a new batch file, which will call ADePT to produce the reports. For every report you intend to produce, add the following line to ADePT:

C:\Software\ADePT\ADePT.exe D:\Projects\FirstProject.ini D:\Reports\FirstReport.xml

The line consists of three parameters. The first is the full file name of the ADePT executable. This is the path specified when you installed ADePT, followed by the name of the ADePT executable: ADePT.exe. The second is the full name of the project file saved earlier. The third is the full name of the file in which the report should be saved. If any of these three parameters contains a white space, it should be enclosed in double quotation marks, as follows:

"C:\Program Files\ADePT\ADePT.exe" D:\Projects\FirstProject.ini "D:\Final Reports\FirstReport.xml"

To run the created batch file, double-click it in a Windows Explorer window. If the batch file is written correctly, you will see ADePT running. If you want to schedule an overnight job, use the **Task Scheduler** to schedule this batch file as a new task. On a Windows Vista-based computer, the **Task Scheduler** can usually be found in the **Accessories/System Tools** subfolder of the **Start** menu. Note that not all users may have privileges to schedule tasks (contact your system's administrator for assistance).

The choice of tables and graphs is not specified when ADePT runs in batch mode, because ADePT automatically determines which tables and graphs can be created based on the user-specified inputs and creates all feasible tables and graphs. Because the if-conditions are not stored in the project files, there is no way to specify table-specific inclusion conditions in batch mode. A global filter can be specified.

The following tips can help users create batch files:

- Use a text editor (do not use MS Word). Save the batched files as plain text with the extension ".BAT" so that the Windows operating system recognizes them as batch files.
- If you do not remember where ADePT was installed, right-click its icon in the **Start** menu. The text after the **Target** parameter is the full file name you need for the first parameter.
- Project files can be located in different folders, reports can be saved in different folders, and data can be located in a third place, but it is a good idea to impose some structure on the organization of the files. All prepared projects should be saved in one folder, all data files in its subfolders, and all produced reports in a special output folder. Proper organization of the files will help you navigate and back up your files more easily.
- It is also a good idea to bind the project and the report with a common name. For example, if the project is called "First.ini," name the report "First.xml."
- Some parameters apply to the ADePT program as a whole and cannot be specified in each project individually. These are the language and code page settings and the choice of the Stata executable and other settings specified in the **Options** dialog. If any of them needs adjustment, start ADePT and specify them interactively before running the batch file.

Updating ADePT

The ADePT team is constantly working on improvements in functionality, adding new tables and graphs to existing modules and developing new modules. It is thus important to keep the program up to date by periodically installing the updates.

To check whether a new version of ADePT is available, on the **Menu** bar, click **Help → Check for Updates** (screenshot 3.36). (An Internet connection must be established before opening the updates dialog.) ADePT will try to access the developers' website and check if a newer version is available. In the dialog window that opens, ADePT reports whether an update is necessary. To view detailed information on the components that have changed and their old and new versions, click **Show details**.

It is very important to save the project file before performing an update, as ADePT closes during the update. Click **Update** to perform the update and change the program files. ADePT will download the newest version from the developers' website. Once the newer version is downloaded, ADePT closes and replaces its files with the newer ones. ADePT then restarts automatically. All custom settings and values of the parameters are preserved on updates.

It is also possible to update ADePT by simply installing the most recent version on top of an existing version. A formal uninstallation of ADePT is not required for updates, but it is possible to conduct one. To uninstall ADePT, click the icon in ADePT's program group in the Windows **Start** menu. Uninstalling the program will remove all ADePT program files from your computer.

Screenshot 3.36: Checking for Updates of ADePT

Troubleshooting ADePT

ADePT problems may be encountered during installation or during debugging. Most problems can be resolved by reading the Frequently Asked Questions section.

Resolving Problems Encountered during Installation

The most recent version of ADePT can be downloaded from www.worldbank.org/adept. Carefully study the requirements for hardware and software before installing ADePT. Although ADePT does not require administrative privileges to be installed, its prerequisites do require such special privileges. Contact your system's administrator if you do not have such access rights on your system. If you encounter a problem during installation on a system that satisfies all the requirements for ADePT, check the frequently asked questions (FAQ) section on ADePT's homepage.

If the problem cannot be resolved, contact ADePT through the contact form on the website. To be able to help in the most efficient way, ADePT staff will need the following information about your system:

- Version of the ADePT installation you are trying to install, including the date downloaded from the ADePT site and the size of the installation
- Operating system, bit-version, release version, service packs and updates applied to the operating system, and language of the operating system
- Version of .Net framework installed
- Version of Microsoft Office installed (if applicable)
- Detailed description of the problem, indicating whether it is reproducible
- Any additional information you think may be helpful in resolving the problem.

Using the Debug Mode

If you experience strange behavior during computations, in particular if some tables are not produced or you see indications of possible bugs, activate ADePT's debug mode. In this mode, ADePT will monitor its own behavior during computations, logging the commands issued to transform the data, in order to identify problems with the algorithms on which ADePT is based.

Screenshot 3.37: Debug Mode

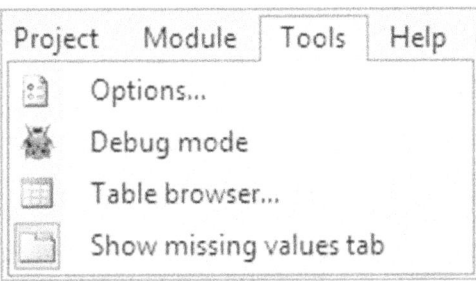

To activate the debug mode, select **Debug mode** in the **Tools** menu before clicking **Generate** (screenshot 3.37). Once the debug mode is activated, it will remain on until switched off (even if ADePT is restarted). An indication that ADePT is currently in debug mode is a check mark next to items in the menu and the words "DEBUG MODE" in the title of the main program window.

After setting all the inputs and clicking **Generate**, wait for the computations to be performed. When they are done, ADePT will suggest saving the error report file. This file (a zip-archive) contains information about the job ADePT was performing that can help the developers identify the problem and fix the program or suggest a work-around. You can save this file to any location on your computer and send it to the developers as an attachment.

The error report file includes the following information:

- The information the user has put into the fields on the form of ADePT.
- The messages ADePT produced while checking the data and performing computations.
- Any output (perhaps incomplete) ADePT managed to produce before the error occurred.
- Traces of the commands ADePT executed to transform the data and compute the indicators.

The error report file does not include any unit-record data or user's datasets. This information would be useful for developers in order to reproduce the problem. All of the information ADePT puts in the error report file can be checked before submission. To do so, open each file in the error report archive in a text editor.

Notes

1. This chapter is an adaptation of the ADePT version 4.1 Technical User Guide.
2. The **Generate** button changes to **Stop** once a computing process is started.

Chapter 4

Generating and Interpreting Output Tables and Graphs

This chapter provides detailed descriptions of the ADePT Edu output. It also presents the formulas for calculating the various indicators and explains how to interpret the indicators.

ADePT Edu produces two types of tables, which appear as formatted Excel spreadsheets.[1] Output information tables include tables of contents, lists of errors and warnings, and variable settings. Indicator tables provide information on school participation, school progression, school attainment, education expenditures, and labor market outcomes (table 4.1).

Indicators are disaggregated by the following characteristics:

- Residence (urban and rural)
- Gender
- Residence and gender
- Household expenditure quintiles
- Household expenditure quintiles and gender
- Gender of household head
- Educational level of household head.

Standard errors or frequencies can be requested for all indicators.[2] All indicator tables can thus be produced in three versions (table 4.2).

The level of geographical representation of the indicators for these subpopulations depends on the sampling framework of the household survey. As long as selection into the survey sample is unrelated to these subpopulations,

Assessing Sector Performance and Inequality in Education

Table 4.1: Topics Covered by ADePT Indicator Tables

Topic	Indicators
School participation	• Gross and net attendance ratios for primary, secondary, and postsecondary education • Proportion of out-of-school children for primary- and secondary-school age • Gross and net intake ratios for the first grade of primary education • Survival rate to the fifth grade of primary education • Proportion of children who are on-time, under-age, and over-age in each grade of primary education • Percentage of the population 6–17 that ever attended school • Reasons why children are out of school • Typology of out-of-school children (late entry, dropout, never in school)
School progression	• Promotion, repetition, dropout, and completion rates for each grade of primary and secondary education • Primary to secondary education transition rates
School attainment	• School attainment of the adult population • Average number of years of schooling by age group (15–19, 20–29, 30–39, 40–49, and 50+) • Proportion of population age groups that completed grades 1–9, by grade • Inequality in years of schooling (Gini coefficients and Theil index)
Education expenditures	• Household expenditures on primary, secondary, and postsecondary education
Labor market outcomes	• Earnings by education level • Returns to education • Employment by sector • Youth employment/unemployment • Earning inequalities (Gini coefficients and Theil index)

Source: Authors.

Table 4.2: Versions of Tables Available in ADePT

Excel spreadsheet contents	Color of tab
Main print-ready tables	Neutral
Main print-ready tables with standard errors	Green
Main print-ready tables with frequencies	Blue

Source: Authors.

the results will generally be unbiased estimators. However, as the sample size gets smaller, there may be an increase in the sampling variation and a decrease in accuracy. Hence, it is important to examine the standard errors reported by ADePT Edu to calculate the confidence interval of the indicator. Users should consult the documentation of the household survey to understand the sampling frame in order to determine how representative the selected subpopulation is.

ADePT Edu allows users to produce eight types of graphs (figures):

- Attainment profiles for young and older cohorts
- Enrollment profiles
- Cohort grade survival profiles
- Enrollment pyramids

Chapter 4: Generating and Interpreting Output Tables and Graphs

- Typology of out-of-school children
- Education attainment Lorenz curves
- Mean hourly earnings by education level
- Mean hourly earnings by years of education.

Output Information Tables

ADePT Edu produces three types of output information tables: the contents table, the notifications table, and the original data report table. Each type of table is described below.

The Contents Table

The first sheet contains the ADePT Edu table of contents (screenshot 4.1). Users select a data table by clicking on its name. Links denoted TABLE_SE (column C) indicate tables with standard errors. Links denoted TABLE_FREQ (column D) indicate tables with frequencies. Not shown in the screenshot is a list of graphs produced by ADePT Edu, which follows the list of tables.

The Notifications Table

The **Notifications** sheet contains error, warning, and notification messages about problems discovered during the preparation of the output file. There are three levels of problem/error reporting in ADePT: notifications, warnings, and errors. To alert users about problems, the color of the **Notification** tab changes from neutral to yellow for warnings and to red for error messages.

During computations, the error, warning, and notification messages appear in the **System Messages** window of the **Main form** (screenshot 4.2). Once the computations are completed, the messages are stored with the report in the **Notifications** sheet.

Notifications convey information about the processing of the data and report names of the loaded data files. They have no impact on the content of the tables or graphs produced. They serve to remind users about parameter values that were used during the analysis that are not in the user's dataset but that still reflect the user's assumptions. For example, if the user specifies that the duration of primary school is five years, this value will appear as a notification.

Screenshot 4.1: ADePT Edu Table of Contents

	A	B	C	D
1		ADePT Education: Table of Contents		
2				
3	Original Data Report	Original Data Report		
4	Table A1	Table A1: School attendance ratios and out-of-school by level, according to background characteristics, [Data1]	TABLE_SE	TABLE_FREQ
5	Table A2	Table A2: Primary grade one intake, overage in first grade, and survival rate to grade 5, according to background characteristics, [Data1]	TABLE_SE	TABLE_FREQ
6	Table A3	Table A3: On-time, under-age and over-age in primary education, according to background characteristics, [Data1]	TABLE_SE	TABLE_FREQ
7	Table A4	Table A4: On-time, under-age and over-age by single grade of primary education, according to background characteristics, [Data1]	TABLE_SE	TABLE_FREQ
8	Table A5	Table A5: Percentage of the population that has ever attended school, by age according to background characteristics, [Data1]	TABLE_SE	TABLE_FREQ
9	Table A7	Table A7: Typology of out-of-school [Data1]	TABLE_SE	TABLE_FREQ
10	Table B1	Table B1: Promotion, repetition, dropout and completion rates by level, and transition rates according to background characteristics, [Data1]	TABLE_SE	TABLE_FREQ
11	Table B2	Table B2: Promotion, repetition, and dropout rates by single grade of primary education, according to background characteristics, [Data1]	TABLE_SE	TABLE_FREQ
12	Table B3	Table B3: Promotion, repetition, and dropout rates by single grade of secondary education, according to background characteristics, [Data1]	TABLE_SE	TABLE_FREQ
13	Table C1	Table C1: School attainment of adult population by background characteristics, [Data1]	TABLE_SE	TABLE_FREQ
14	Table C2	Table C2: Proportion of 15-19 years olds that completed each grade, according to background characteristics, [Data1]	TABLE_SE	TABLE_FREQ
15	Table C3	Table C3: Proportion of 20-29 years olds that completed each grade, according to background characteristics, [Data1]	TABLE_SE	TABLE_FREQ
16	Table C4	Table C4: Proportion of 30-39 years olds that completed each grade, according to background characteristics, [Data1]	TABLE_SE	TABLE_FREQ
17	Table C5	Table C5: Proportion of 40-49 years olds that completed each grade, according to background characteristics, [Data1]	TABLE_SE	TABLE_FREQ
18	Table C6	Table C6: Proportion of 10-19 years olds expected to complete each grade, according to background characteristics, [Data1]	TABLE_FREQ	
19	Table C7	Table C7: Inequality in years of schooling, [Data1]	TABLE_SE	TABLE_FREQ

Chapter 4: Generating and Interpreting Output Tables and Graphs

Screenshot 4.2: Error, Warning, and Notification Messages

	A	B	C
1			Errors, Warnings and Notifications generated by data checking process
2			
3	NOTE		Checking variables in 2002:
4	WARNING	STATUS	Suspected outliers with code(s) 1 3 - in variable aktivnost
5	WARNING	PLINE	poverty line 2 is too low, resulting in HC = 1.1%
6			
7	NOTE		Checking variables in 2007:
8	WARNING	STATUS	Suspected outliers with code(s) 1 3 - in variable aktivnost
9	WARNING	AGE	some respondents might be too young for education level - Primary school
10	WARNING	PLINE	poverty line 2 is too low, resulting in HC = 0.3%

ADePT issues a warning if it detects a suspicious situation in the data but cannot be sure that the finding represents an error. Examples include the following:

- An observation violates assumptions imposed by the parameters of ADePT (for example, students in the sample report that they attend the fifth grade of primary school in a dataset in which the duration of primary schooling is four years).
- A value of a categorical variable seems too far off compared with other values of this variable (an outlier) (ADePT may flag this value as not legitimate).
- Information is inconsistent or implausible (for example, a two-year-old child who is reported as employed).
- Definitions of categories differ across rounds of the same survey (for example, a variable that contains codes for regions contains a different number of unique values in the datasets collected for the same country in two years).

When a warning is issued, no actions are taken; ADePT uses all nonmissing observations in the loaded datasets to produce tables and graphs. Warnings simply inform the user about potential problems with the data. An example of a warning is a message that informs a user that no weight variable is defined and that tables and graphs are produced on unweighted data.

ADePT reports an error when it finds a problem that prevents the use of a variable in the analysis, such as a variable that does not exist in the dataset. After reporting the error, ADePT continues as if the variable were not specified. When ADePT can determine the source of the problem in a particular variable field, this field is highlighted on the form.

Problems may be resolved in one of two ways. First, users can adjust the parameters/input of ADePT—by, for example, checking that parameters of the educational system agree with the actual situation in the country under consideration. Second, users can adjust the input datasets, using Stata or SPSS to correct the problem.

Notifications, warnings, and errors are just as important as the results that ADePT produces. They should be carefully reviewed before any conclusions are drawn from tables and graphs.

Screenshot 4.3 provides an example of ADePT output showing some of the errors and warnings discussed above. In the next to the last line in this screenshot, a warning indicates that 4,105 observations with a grade of secondary are out of the specified range for the country [1, 5]. This discrepancy could reflect an error in the dataset, or it could mean that the variable value specified for the country does not correspond to the variable value used to construct the dataset. Users should review all warnings and decide whether to change the parameters, implement procedures to clean up the data, or use the data as they are.

In the example shown in screenshot 4.3, if the user decides to run the report without changing the parameters or cleaning up the data, the program will not use the 4,105 out-of-range observations in the calculation of any table requiring the out-of-range information; it will treat these values as missing. The 4,105 observations could, however, be included in the estimation of other indicators.

The **Notifications** sheet also includes notes about the definitions of key variables in the dataset. For example, the note for the parameter STAGE

Screenshot 4.3: Examples of Errors and Warnings in ADePT Output

	A	B	C
1			Notifications
2	Type	Tag	Message
3			
4	NOTE		Checking variables in C:\DHS\NICARA~1\2001\NCPR41FL.DTA:
5	WARNING	_GRADE_C	Suspected outliers with code(s): 98 - in variable hv107
6	NOTE	STAGE	Age of start of schooling is set to 7
7	NOTE	PRDUR	Duration of primary schooling is set to 6
8	NOTE	SCDUR	Duration of secondary schooling is set to 5
9	NOTE	MAXAGE	Maximum age of post-secondary schooling is set to 0
10	NOTE	MONST	Beginning of the school year is set to
11	NOTE	AGE	61343 values of age decreased by 1 year to account for the time passed since the beginning of the school year.
12	WARNING	GRADE	4105 observations with grade of secondary out of range [1,5]
13	WARNING	GRADE	91 persons attending grades higher than the next-after-completed.

Chapter 4: Generating and Interpreting Output Tables and Graphs

clarifies that the age at start of schooling is set to seven. The note on the parameter MONST (month to start school) indicates that the beginning of the school year is set to the value 2, meaning the month of February. These parameters are set on the **Education** tab of the form in the **Educational System** group. UNESCO regularly provides updates for the beginning and duration of each educational level in each country.

Original Data Report

The **Original Data Report** table provides basic information on datasets and variables loaded in ADePT (screenshot 4.4). For each variable specified, this table presents information on the number of nonmissing observations; the mean, minimum, maximum, and selected percentiles; and the number of unique values in the variable. It provides useful information about the data loaded into ADePT, in many cases resolving problems related to the discrepancy of the results generated on different datasets. The **Original Data Report** should always be carefully reviewed before starting analysis of the data with ADePT.

The **Original Data Report** lists all the variables required for the tables produced by the report, along with the sample size (denoted N), the average value of each variable (mean), the minimum and maximum values for each variable in the table (min and max), and the variable values for the 1st, 50th, and 99th percentiles (p1, p50, and p99). The column labeled N_unique shows the total number of observations with unique identifiers. In the example shown in screenshot 4.4, there are 6,386 households with unique identifiers.

Screenshot 4.4: Original Data Report

	A	B	C	D	E	F	G	H	I
1			Original Data Report						
2		N	mean	min	max	p1	p50	p99	N_unique
3	2002								
4	id (Household ID)	19,725	3,280.8	1.0	6,386.0	66.0	3,367.0	6,319.0	6,386
5	pline_u (Custom category 1)	19,725	5,234.3	5,234.3	5,234.3	5,234.3	5,234.3	5,234.3	1.0
6	urban (Urban)	19,725	1.5	1.0	2.0	1.0	1.0	2.0	2
7	consump (Welfare aggregate)	19,725	10,544.4	630.1	137,441.6	2,690.4	9,087.7	35,925.7	6,386.0
8	hhweight (Household weights)	19,725	379.2	271.1	4,013.1	271.1	364.8	776.6	62
9	generated (Household size)	19,725	3.9	1.0	10.0	1.0	4.0	8.0	10.0
10									
11	Note: in variable urban value 1 was assumed to mean "Urban"								

Contents / Notifications / Original Data Report / Table 2.1 / Table 7 / Figure 5.5_Total / Figu

School Participation Indicator Tables

ADePT Edu produces seven tables of indicators for measuring school participation:

- Table A1: School attendance ratios and out-of-school children
- Table A2: Primary grade 1 intake, over-age in first grade, and survival rate to grade 5
- Table A3: On-time, under-age, and over-age in primary education
- Table A4: On-time, under-age, and over-age by single grade of primary education
- Table A5: Percentage of the population age that has ever attended school
- Table A6: Reasons for being out of school
- Table A7: Typology of out-of-school children.

In all the formulas below where age of a child is used, the age can be adjusted to take into account the timing of the survey (based on variable interview month) relative to the beginning of the school year (as indicated in the parameters of the educational system).

Table A1: School Attendance Ratios and Out of School, by Level

Tracking the participation of children in school is one of the most basic measures of performance in the education sector. Attendance at primary school is a prerequisite for Education for All. Disaggregating attendance indicators by subpopulation provides a means of capturing inequality in attendance across subpopulations. Measuring the proportion of children out of school is also crucial to policy makers who want to advance Education for All and educational attainment. The disaggregation calculated by ADePT Edu describes who the out-of-school children are (screenshot 4.5).

Indicator A1.1: Gross Attendance Rate for Primary School

The gross attendance rate for primary school[3] is the number of primary school students of any age expressed as a percentage of all children of primary school age:

Screenshot 4.5: Table A1: School Attendance Ratios and Out of School, by Level

	A	B	C	D	E	F	G	H	I	J
1	Table A1: School Attendance Ratios and Out of School, by Level									
2	Table A1: School attendance ratios and out-of-school by level, according to background characteristics, [Data]									
3		Primary				Secondary				Post-secondary
4		Gross Attendance	Net Attendance	Proportion of out-of-school		Gross Attendance	Net Attendance	Proportion of out-of-school		Gross Attendance
5	Total	123.79	79.01	19.64		39.44	27.89	34.10		1.97
6										
7	Gender									
8	Boys	124.05	78.17	20.54		40.22	26.76	32.74		2.00
9	Girls	123.52	79.91	18.68		38.63	29.05	35.48		1.93
10										
11	Area of residence									
12	Urban	131.31	89.56	6.11		89.15	58.41	16.58		7.64
13	Rural	122.86	77.69	21.33		31.62	23.10	36.85		0.77
14										
15	Residence and gender									
16	Urban - Boys	131.97	90.45	5.95		97.59	59.89	11.97		7.93
17	Urban - Girls	130.55	88.56	6.29		81.88	57.14	20.55		7.38
18	Rural - Boys	123.03	76.58	22.42		32.10	22.08	35.68		0.80
19	Rural - Girls	122.68	78.87	20.18		31.12	24.18	38.08		0.75
20										
21	Household wealth									
22	Quintile 1	94.54	60.79	39.16		7.73	5.77	56.76		0.00
23	Quintile 2	124.74	75.63	24.10		14.30	10.79	40.78		0.03
24	Quintile 3	134.60	84.80	15.05		26.28	19.38	34.70		0.04
25	Quintile 4	141.70	90.17	8.55		48.02	35.51	25.04		0.52
26	Quintile 5	128.99	89.31	3.99		93.69	62.94	17.83		7.49
27										
28	Household wealth and gender									
29	Quintile 1 - Boys	94.00	59.03	40.93		8.53	5.61	55.15		0.00
30	Quintile 2 - Boys	124.55	74.47	25.25		14.38	10.22	39.90		0.00

primary gross attendance rate =

$$\frac{\sum_i w_i 1(level_i = primary)}{\sum_i w_i 1(age_i \in [entry\ age, entry\ age + primary\ duration - 1])},$$

where *i* denotes the *i*th individual in the survey, 1( ) is the indicator function (equal to 1 when the condition is true, 0 when false), and w_i is the sample weight for the *i*th individual.

Because children above and below primary school age attend primary school, the gross attendance rate can exceed 100 percent. In the example shown in screenshot 4.5, the gross attendance rate for primary schools is 123.79, indicating that many primary students are likely over-age. There is little difference between girls and boys, with the figure for both rounding to 124 percent.

Indicator A1.2: Net Attendance Rate for Primary School

The net attendance rate for primary school is the proportion of children of the official primary school age who attend primary school:

primary net attendance rate =

$$\frac{\sum_i w_i 1\begin{pmatrix} level_i = primary\ and \\ age_i \in [entry\ age, entry\ age + primary\ duration - 1] \end{pmatrix}}{\sum_i w_i 1(age_i \in [entry\ age, entry\ age + primary\ duration - 1])}.$$

The primary school age is based on the values of the parameters of the educational system—the starting age and the duration of primary school. In the example in screenshot 4.5, 79.01 percent of primary school–age children are attending primary school. Inequality in this measure of attendance is evident: among the top income quintile of households, 89.31 percent of children are attending primary school, while only 60.79 percent of primary children from the poorest quintile of households are attending primary school.

Indicator A1.3: Proportion of Out-of-School Children for Primary School

The proportion of out-of-school children for primary school is the number of children in the official primary school–age range who are not attending

Chapter 4: Generating and Interpreting Output Tables and Graphs

primary or secondary education, expressed as a percentage of children of the official primary school–age range:

proportion out-of-school primary =

$$\frac{\sum_i w_i 1\begin{pmatrix} age_i \in [entry\ age, entry\ age + primary\ duration - 1]\ and \\ level_i \neq primary\ and\ level_i \neq secondary \\ and\ level_i \neq tertiary \end{pmatrix}}{\sum_i w_i 1(age_i \in [entry\ age, entry\ age + primary\ duration - 1])}.$$

By definition, children in the official primary school–age range who are attending preprimary education are considered out of school. The sum of the net primary attendance rate and the proportion out-of-school children does not add to 100 percent because the net primary attendance rate does not count students who are in secondary school.

There may be large differences in household survey data. For example, in many countries, parents can opt to have their student start a year early if they feel the child is prepared. When this child is in the first year of secondary school, he or she is still within the primary school–age group but not in primary school and so would not be counted in the numerator of the net enrollment rate.

Indicator A1.4: Gross Attendance Rate for Secondary School

The gross attendance rate for secondary school is the number of secondary school students of any age, expressed as a percentage of children of secondary school age:

secondary gross attendance rate =

$$\frac{\sum_i w_i 1(level_i = secondary)}{\sum_i w_i 1\left(age_i \in \begin{bmatrix} entry\ age + primary\ duration, \\ entry\ age + primary\ duration \\ + secondary\ duration - 1 \end{bmatrix}\right)}.$$

This rate is typically below 100 percent, because in most countries many children drop out of the education system after finishing primary school. In the example in screenshot 4.5, the secondary gross attendance rate for the poorest quintile is 7.73 percent.

Indicator A1.5: Net Attendance Rate for Secondary School

The net attendance rate for secondary school is the proportion of children of official secondary school age who are attending secondary school:

secondary net attendance rate =

$$\frac{\sum_i w_i 1 \begin{pmatrix} level_i = secondary \text{ and} \\ age_i \in \begin{bmatrix} entry\ age + primary\ duration, \\ entry\ age + primary\ duration \\ + secondary\ duration - 1 \end{bmatrix} \end{pmatrix}}{\sum_i w_i 1 \begin{pmatrix} age_i \in \begin{bmatrix} entry\ age + primary\ duration, \\ entry\ age + primary\ duration \\ + secondary\ duration - 1 \end{bmatrix} \end{pmatrix}}.$$

This percentage is typically well below 100 percent. A large disparity between quintiles is apparent in the example shown in screenshot 4.5: the top quintile has a rate of 62.94 percent, whereas the bottom quintile has a rate of 5.77 percent.

Indicator A1.6: Proportion Out of School for Secondary School

The proportion out of school for secondary school is the number of children in the official secondary school–age range who are not attending primary, secondary, or postsecondary school, expressed as a percentage of the number of children of the official secondary school–age range.[4]

proportion out of secondary school =

$$\frac{\sum_i w_i 1 \begin{pmatrix} age_i \in \begin{bmatrix} entry\ age + primary\ duration, \\ entry\ age + primary\ duration \\ + secondary\ duration - 1 \end{bmatrix} \text{ and} \\ level_i \neq primary \text{ and } level_i \neq secondary \text{ and } level_i \neq tertiary \end{pmatrix}}{\sum_i w_i 1 \begin{pmatrix} age_i \in \begin{bmatrix} entry\ age + primary\ duration, \\ entry\ age + primary\ duration \\ + secondary\ duration - 1 \end{bmatrix} \end{pmatrix}}.$$

In the example in screenshot 4.5, 34.10 percent of secondary school–age children are out of school.

Indicator A1.7: Gross Attendance Rate for Postsecondary Education

The gross attendance rate for postsecondary education is the number of postsecondary school students of any age, expressed as a percentage of children of postsecondary school age:

tertiary gross attendance rate =

$$\frac{\sum_i w_i 1(level_i = tertiary)}{\sum_i w_i 1\left(age_i \in \begin{bmatrix} entry\ age + primary\ duration \\ + secondary\ duration, \\ maximum\ age\ of\ tertiary \end{bmatrix}\right)}.$$

Postsecondary school age is defined as the age range from graduation from secondary school to the maximum age set as a parameter of the educational system. This age, which the user of the program selects, is usually the age by which it is expected that a person must complete studies. In the example in screenshot 4.5, the postsecondary gross attendance rate is 1.97 percent.

Table A2: Primary Grade 1 Intake, Over-Age in First Grade, and Survival Rate to Grade 5

Table A2 (screenshot 4.6) shows the gross and net intake rates for the first grade of primary school, the percentage of students who are over the age of entry into first grade, and the survival rate to grade 5. These indicators provide evidence on access problems and the internal efficiency of the educational system. Their disaggregation indicates whether the education system serves some subpopulations differently from others and identifies which groups of individuals are struggling most within the school system.

Indicator A2.1: Gross Intake Rate to Grade 1

The gross intake rate to grade 1 is the number of new students attending the first grade of primary education, regardless of age, expressed as a percentage of the children of official entrance age to primary education:

$$\text{gross intake rate to grade 1} = \frac{\sum_i w_i 1(grade_i = 1)}{\sum_i w_i 1(age_i = entry\ age)}.$$

Assessing Sector Performance and Inequality in Education

Screenshot 4.6: Table A2: Primary Grade 1 Intake, Over-Age in First Grade, and Survival Rate to Grade 5

	A	B	D	F	H
1	Table A2: Primary grade one intake, overage in first grade, and survival rate to grade 5, according to background characteristics, [Data1]				
2		Gross Intake Rate	Net Intake Rate	Grade 1 students older than official grade 1 age, (%)	Survival rate to grade 5
3					
4	Total	150.92	46.37	44.86	35.88
5					
6	Gender				
7	Boys	148.85	44.80	47.49	36.12
8	Girls	153.19	48.09	42.05	35.58
9					
10	Area of residence				
11	Urban	140.45	44.35	29.15	37.15
12	Rural	152.05	46.59	46.44	35.79
13					
14	Residence and gender				
15	Urban - Boys	143.33	42.09	29.49	40.06
16	Urban - Girls	137.26	46.86	28.75	34.28
17	Rural - Boys	149.45	45.10	49.37	35.52
18	Rural - Girls	154.91	48.23	43.32	36.01
19					
20	Household wealth				
21	Quintile 1	152.59	36.64	58.01	28.94
22	Quintile 2	152.18	48.40	48.96	33.45
23	Quintile 3	167.07	55.48	44.37	37.30
24	Quintile 4	151.65	53.97	36.94	37.28
25	Quintile 5	121.22	37.88	18.96	38.65

In the example in screenshot 4.6, there are 150.92 students in grade 1 for every 100 children of entry age for primary.

Indicator A2.2: Net Intake Rate to Grade 1

The net intake rate to grade 1 is the number of new students attending the first grade of primary education who are of the official primary school entrance age, expressed as a percentage of the children of official entrance age to primary education:

Chapter 4: Generating and Interpreting Output Tables and Graphs

$$\text{net intake rate to grade } 1 = \frac{\sum_i w_i \mathbf{1}(grade_i = 1 \text{ and } age_i = entry\ age)}{\sum_i w_i \mathbf{1}(age_i = entry\ age)}.$$

In the example shown in screenshot 4.6, 44.80 percent of entry-age boys are in grade 1.

Indicator A2.3: Percentage of Grade 1 Students Older Than Official Grade 1 Age

The percentage of grade 1 students older than official grade 1 age is the number of children in the first grade of primary school who are one or more years older than the target entry age for the grade, expressed as a percentage of the total number of students attending grade 1:

percentage of grade 1 students older than official grade 1 age =
$$\frac{\sum_i w_i \mathbf{1}(grade_i = 1 \text{ and } age_i > entry\ age)}{\sum_i w_i \mathbf{1}(grade_i = 1)}.$$

In the example in screenshot 4.6, the proportion of average students in grade 1 is 46.44 percent in rural areas and 29.15 percent in urban areas.

Indicator A2.4: Survival Rate to Grade 5

The survival rate to grade 5 is the percentage of a cohort of students (total, male, female) attending the first grade of a primary cycle in a given school year who are expected to reach grade 5, regardless of repetition. It is calculated on the basis of the reconstructed cohort method of UNESCO (UNESCO 2010). In the example in screenshot 4.6, 38.65 percent of students in the top quintile reach grade 5 and 28.94 percent of students in the bottom quintile reach grade 5.

Table A3: On-Time, Under-Age, and Over-Age in Primary Education

Table A3 (screenshot 4.7) presents indicators on the extent to which children are in the correct grade for their age. Like the indicator on over-age in grade 1, these indicators measure how efficient the education system is at enrolling children of primary age range in primary school.

Assessing Sector Performance and Inequality in Education

Screenshot 4.7: Table A3: On-Time, Under-Age, and Over-Age in Primary Education

Table A3: On-time, under-age and over-age in primary education, according to background characteristics, [Data1]

	Children on time for Primary, (%)	Under-age children in Primary, (%)	Over-age children in Primary, (%)
Total	21.85	15.21	62.95
Gender			
Boys	20.62	13.96	65.42
Girls	23.16	16.55	60.29
Area of residence			
Urban	27.46	26.97	45.57
Rural	21.10	13.64	65.26
Residence and gender			
Urban - Boys	26.87	26.89	46.25
Urban - Girls	28.14	27.06	44.80
Rural - Boys	19.76	12.17	68.07
Rural - Girls	22.52	15.20	62.28
Household wealth			
Quintile 1	17.38	10.74	71.88
Quintile 2	18.79	9.75	71.45
Quintile 3	20.85	11.26	67.90
Quintile 4	24.33	15.77	59.91
Quintile 5	29.08	32.88	38.04

Indicator A3.1: Percentage On-Time for Primary School

The on-time for primary school rate is the sum of the number of students in each grade of primary school who are of the official age for that grade, expressed as a percentage of the number of students attending primary school:

on-time for primary school =

$$\frac{\sum_i w_i 1(age_i = \text{entry age} + grade_i - 1 \text{ and } grade_i \in (1; p))}{\sum_i w_i 1(level_i = \text{primary and } grade_i \in (1; p))},$$

where p is the highest grade of primary school.

In the example in screenshot 4.7, 21.85 percent of primary school students are in the grade they should be in for their age, ranging from 17.38 percent in the poorest wealth quintile to 29.08 percent in the richest quintile.

Indicator A3.2: Percentage Under-Age in Primary School

Under-age in primary school is the sum of the number of students in each grade of primary school who are one or more years younger than the official age for that grade, expressed as a percentage of the number of students attending primary school:

$$\text{under-age in primary school} = \frac{\sum_i w_i 1(age_i < \text{entry age} + grade_i - 1)}{\sum_i w_i 1(level_i = \text{primary})}.$$

In the example in screenshot 4.7, 13.96 percent of boys and 16.55 percent of girls are under-age.

Indicator A3.3: Percentage Over-Age in Primary School

Over-age in primary school is the sum of the number of students in each grade of primary school who are one or more years older than the official age for that grade, expressed as a percentage of the number of students attending primary school:

$$\text{over-age in primary school} = \frac{\sum_i w_i 1(age_i > \text{entry age} + grade_i - 1)}{\sum_i w_i 1(level_i = \text{primary})}.$$

The sum of this indicator and the preceding two indicators is 100 percent. In low-income countries, resource constraints by the household, distance to the school, and other factors often prevent children from starting school or force them to stop going. In the example in screenshot 4.7, 45.57 percent of students in urban areas and 65.26 percent of students in rural areas are over-age.

Table A4: On-Time, Under-Age, and Over-Age by Single Grade of Primary Education, according to Background Characteristics

Table A4 is similar to table A3 except it calculates on-time, over-age, and under-age by grade level, giving a more detailed picture of how efficient the education system is at enrolling children and youth at the targeted schooling level.

Indicator A4.1: Percentage On-Time for Grade X

The percentage on-time for grade X is the number of students who are of the official primary school age for grade X, expressed as a percentage of the number of students attending grade X:

$$\text{on-time for grade } X = \frac{\sum_i w_i 1(age_i = \text{entry age} + X - 1 \text{ and } grade_i = X)}{\sum_i w_i 1(grade_i = X)}.$$

Indicator A4.2: Percentage Under-Age for Grade X

The percentage under-age for grade X is the number of students who are one or more years younger than the official primary school age for grade X expressed as a percentage of the number of students attending grade X:

$$\text{under-age for grade } X = \frac{\sum_i w_i 1(age_i < \text{entry age} + X - 1 \text{ and } grade_i = X)}{\sum_i w_i 1(grade_i = X)}.$$

Indicator A4.3: Percentage Over-Age for Grade X

The percentage over-age for grade X is the number of students who are one or more years older than the official primary school age for grade X expressed as a percentage of the number of students attending grade X:

$$\text{over-age for grade } X = \frac{\sum_i w_i 1(age_i > \text{entry age} + X - 1 \text{ and } grade_i = X)}{\sum_i w_i 1(grade_i = X)}.$$

Chapter 4: Generating and Interpreting Output Tables and Graphs

Table A5: Percentage of the Population That Has Ever Attended School, by Age

Table A5 presents the percentage of the student-age population that has ever attended school, by age (screenshot 4.8). This figure is the number of people of a given age who have ever attended school, expressed as a percentage of the population of that age:

ever attended school at age $X =$

$$\frac{\sum_i w_i 1(\text{ever attended school} = 1 \text{ and } age_i = X)}{\sum_i w_i 1(age_i = X)}.$$

Table A5 yields insights into who is being excluded by the education system. In the example in screenshot 4.8, 67.66 percent of 6-year-olds and 86.73 percent of 17-year-olds have attended school. Among 8-year-olds, 97.26 percent in urban areas and 86.03 percent in rural areas have attended school.

Table A6: Out-of-School Reasons

Table A6 shows why children are out of school (screenshot 4.9). For household survey datasets that contain a question about why a student is out of school, ADePT provides a breakdown of these reasons. This information is important to policy makers wishing to reduce the incidence of out-of-school children.

Screenshot 4.8: Table A5: Percentage of the Population That Has Ever Attended School, by Age

	Age 6	Age 7	Age 8	Age 9	Age 10	Age 11	Age 12	Age 13	Age 14	Age 15	Age 16	Age 17
Total	67.66	82.51	87.25	90.66	88.99	91.70	90.20	90.85	89.64	88.80	87.88	86.73
Gender												
Boys	65.55	81.66	86.49	90.06	89.59	91.90	88.87	89.28	88.27	88.97	87.79	86.92
Girls	69.98	83.36	88.06	91.34	88.37	91.48	91.64	92.43	91.03	88.63	87.97	86.52
Area of residence												
Urban	85.46	95.94	97.26	97.93	99.40	99.28	97.85	98.17	98.69	97.85	98.53	98.11
Rural	65.73	80.64	86.03	89.65	87.74	90.56	89.17	89.78	87.99	87.32	85.96	84.53

Screenshot 4.9: Table A6: Reasons Why Children Are Out of School

Table A6: Out of school reasons. [Nicaragua LSMS 2005]

	because of age	Not interested	Finished studies	Need to do house work	Work/field work	School full	Grade was not offered	School too far	No teacher	Personal Safety	Pregnancy
Primary											
Total	0.00	10.78	0.00	0.94	2.67	2.52	0.83	11.35	2.19	3.25	0.21
Gender											
Boys	0.00	14.25	0.00	0.04	4.21	3.22	0.45	8.94	2.87	3.49	0.00
Girls	0.00	4.91	0.00	2.48	0.06	1.34	1.47	15.43	1.03	2.83	0.56
Area of residence											
Urban	0.00	15.44	0.00	0.00	0.76	2.16	0.00	0.00	0.00	0.00	0.00
Rural	0.00	8.72	0.00	1.36	3.52	2.68	1.20	16.38	3.16	4.68	0.30

Indicator A6.1: Percentage Out of School by Reason, Primary School–Age Children

ADePT calculates the number of primary school–age children out of school for a particular reason per 100 primary age children out of school:

percentage out of primary school for reason X =

$$\frac{\sum_i w_i \mathbf{1}\begin{pmatrix} \text{reason out of school}_i = X \text{ and} \\ \text{age}_i \in [\text{entry age}, \text{entry age} + \text{primary duration} - 1] \end{pmatrix}}{\sum_i w_i \mathbf{1}\begin{pmatrix} \text{age}_i \in [\text{entry age}, \text{entry age} + \text{primary duration} - 1] \\ \text{and level}_i = \text{none} \end{pmatrix}}.$$

Note that ADePT allows only one variable for each reason for being out of school. If the survey contains multiple variables with this information, users enter the main reason for being out of school in the form. In the example shown in screenshot 4.9, the main reason (40.90 percent) why primary school–age children are out of school is lack of money. The second most important reason is different for girls and boys: 14.25 percent of out-of-school boys but just 4.91 percent of girls report that school does not interest them.

Table A7: Typology of Out of School

Table A7 classifies out-of-school children into three categories: late entry, dropout, and never in school (screenshot 4.10). It uses UNESCO's methodology for estimating these percentages (box 4.1).

Chapter 4: Generating and Interpreting Output Tables and Graphs

Screenshot 4.10: Table A7: Typology of Reasons for Being Out of School (UNESCO Method)

	A	B	C	D	E	F	G	H
1		Table A7: Typology of out-of-school, [Data1]						
2		Primary				Secondary		
3		Never in school	Late entry	Drop out		Never in school	Late entry	Drop out
4								
5	Total	62.24	34.56	3.19		88.13	11.40	0.47
6								
7	Gender							
8	Boys	62.11	36.34	1.55		86.67	13.24	0.09
9	Girls	62.22	32.61	5.17		86.95	11.41	1.64
10								
11	Area of residence							
12	Urban	48.95	51.05	0.00		81.26	18.04	0.69
13	Rural	63.24	33.59	3.17		89.16	10.35	0.48
14								

Box 4.1: UNESCO's Method for Estimating the Percentage of Children Out of School

UNESCO estimates the percentage of out-of-school children in the following manner:

Let R_{age} = rate of out-of-school children for each age; R_{min} = minimum of all R_{age}; AGE_{min} = age for which R_{age} is the minimum; and POP_{age} = population by single year of age. The number of out-of-school children expected to never enter school is estimated as follows:

$$OOSC_{never} = Sum(R_{min} \cdot POP_{age}) \text{ for all ages.}$$

The number of out-of-school children expected to enter school in future years is estimated as follows:

$$OOSC_{late\ entry} = Sum(\ (R_{age} - R_{min}) \cdot POP_{age}) \text{ for ages} < AGE_{min}$$

The number of out-of-school children who drop out is estimated as follows:

$$OOSC_{dropout} = Sum(\ (R_{age} - R_{min}) \cdot POP_{age}) \text{ for ages} > AGE_{min}.$$

AGE_{min} is the youngest age for which R_{age} is zero.

Source: UNESCO 2005.

Late entry refers to the proportion of out-of-school children who are currently out of school but are expected to enter the education system later than they should. *Dropout* refers to children who were in school but are no longer attending school. *Never in school* refers to children who are very likely to never go to school and are not classified in either of the first two categories.

Assessing Sector Performance and Inequality in Education

Understanding this typology is important for policy makers trying to reduce the number of out-of-school children. If the majority of out-of-school children are late entrants, mitigating the out-of-school problem requires different policy choices than if a majority are dropouts.

Indicator A7.1: Percentage of Out-of-School Children Classified as Never in School

This indicator is probabilistic, as no survey can tell if a student-age person will never attend school. UNESCO's methodology (2005) estimates the proportion of children who will never attend school as the proportion out of school for the age group with the highest rate of attendance. This methodology assumes no dropout before the age at which enrollment rates peak and no late entry after the age with peak enrollment. In figure 4.1, the age-nine group has the highest attendance rate, so the proportion of out-of-school children from this age group is assumed to equal the highest proportion of children who will never attend school. In screenshot 4.10,

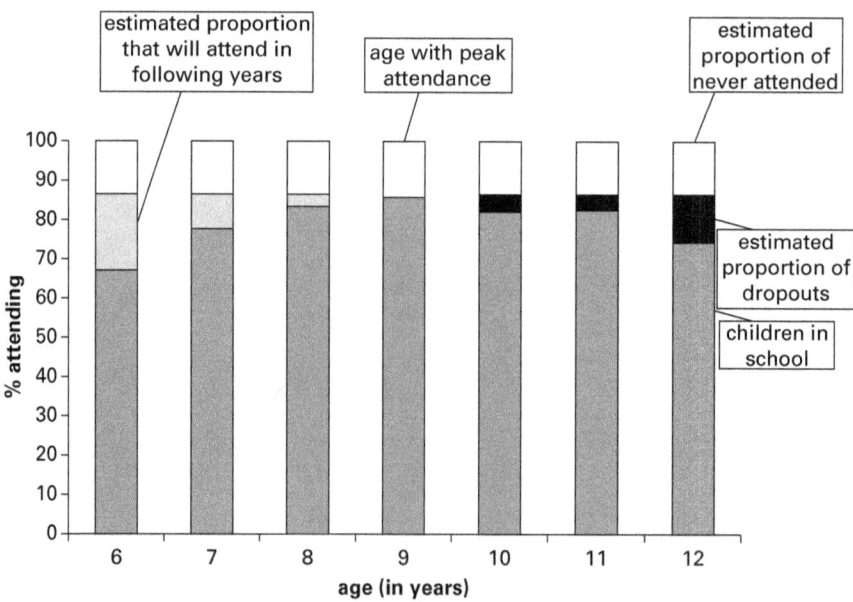

Figure 4.1: Estimates of Percentage of Out-of-School Children, by Type

Source: UNESCO 2005.

Chapter 4: Generating and Interpreting Output Tables and Graphs

62.24 percent of out-of-school primary school–age children are classified this way.

Indicator A7.2: Percentage of Out-of-School Children Classified as Late Entry, by Level

The proportion of out-of-school children classified as late entrants at each level is the proportion left over after the percentages of children never in school and in school are summed, expressed as a percentage of the proportion out of school for children younger than the age with the highest attendance rate (the black area in figure 4.1). In the example in screenshot 4.10, the percentage of primary school–age children who are out of school because they are late entrants is 51.05 in urban areas and 33.59 in rural areas.

Indicator A7.3: Percentage of Out-of-School Children Classified as Dropouts, by Level

The proportion of out-of-school children classified as dropouts at each level is the proportion of children not classified as never in school, expressed as a percent of the proportion of out-of-school children older than the age with the highest attendance rate (the gray portion of the bar in figure 4.1). In the example in screenshot 4.10, dropouts account for 1.55 percent of out-of-school boys and 5.17 percent of out-of-school girls.

School Progression Tables

School progression tables display information on promotion, repetition, dropout, and completion rates for primary and secondary school and by grade level. These indicators provide a measure of internal efficiency, because they describe the extent to which children progress toward completion once they enter the school system.

Table B1: Promotion, Repetition, Dropout, and Completion Rates by Level, and Transition Rates

Table B1 presents the promotion, repetition, dropout, and completion rates for primary, secondary, and postsecondary school (screenshot 4.11).

Screenshot 4.11: Table B1: Rates of Promotion, Repetition, Dropout, and Completion

Table B1: Promotion, repetition, dropout and completion rates by level, and transition rates according to background characteristics, [Zimbabwe 2005-06]

	Primary				Secondary				Primary to Secondary transition rate, (%)	Post-secondary Repetition rate, (%)
	Promotion rate, (%)	Repetition rate, (%)	Drop out rate, (%)	Completion rate, (%)	Promotion rate, (%)	Repetition rate, (%)	Drop out rate, (%)	Completion rate, (%)		
Total	92.18	3.15	4.58	90.72	75.23	3.14	21.16	12.31	79.80	4.86
Gender										
Boys	91.74	3.63	4.54	92.39	76.47	2.98	19.91	16.57	76.80	4.12
Girls	92.62	2.66	4.62	89.20	73.95	3.31	22.47	8.39	82.52	6.19
Area of residence										
Urban	94.77	1.66	3.52	89.23	73.51	3.91	21.80	22.76	82.89	1.87
Rural	91.34	3.63	4.92	91.19	76.45	2.60	20.70	5.38	78.36	21.74

Note: The results for table B1 are specific to Zimbabwe and are used only for illustrating ADePT Edu's Output. The remaining tables use data from Nicaragua.

Indicator B1.1: Primary Promotion Rate

The primary promotion rate is the proportion of students in any grade of primary school promoted to the next grade the following school year. Sometimes this rate includes a small number of students who move forward more than one grade (that is, skip a grade).

$$\text{primary promotion rate} = \frac{\sum_i w_i \begin{pmatrix} 1(\text{last year level}_i = \text{primary}) \\ -1\begin{pmatrix} \text{level}_i = \text{none and highest level attained}_i < \text{primary} \\ \text{and last year level}_i = \text{primary} \end{pmatrix} \\ -1(\text{grade}_i = \text{last year grade}_i \text{ and last year level}_i = \text{primary}) \end{pmatrix}}{\sum_i w_i 1(\text{last year level}_i = \text{primary})}.$$

Indicator B1.2: Primary Repetition Rate

The primary repetition rate is the proportion of students in any grade of primary school in a given school year that attend the same grade the following school year:

$$\text{primary repetition rate} = \frac{\sum_i w_i 1\begin{pmatrix} \text{grade}_i = \text{last year grade}_i \text{ and} \\ \text{last year level}_i = \text{primary} \end{pmatrix}}{\sum_i w_i 1(\text{last year level}_i = \text{primary})}.$$

Students who remain in the same grade are counted as repeaters. In the Zimbabwe example in screenshot 4.11, 3.63 percent of boys and 2.66 percent of girls in primary school the previous year were in the same grade in the current year.

Indicator B1.3: Primary Dropout Rate

The primary dropout rate is the proportion of students in any grade of primary in a given school year that no longer attends school the following school year:

$$\text{dropout rate} = \frac{\sum_i w_i 1\begin{pmatrix} \text{level}_i = \text{none and highest level attained}_i < \text{primary} \\ \text{and last year level}_i = \text{primary} \end{pmatrix}}{\sum_i w_i 1(\text{last year level}_i = \text{primary})}.$$

In screenshot 4.11, 1.66 percent of urban students in primary school the previous year were not in school in the current year.

Indicator B1.4: Primary Completion Rate

The primary completion rate is the total number of students of any age in the last grade of primary school minus the number of repeaters in that grade, divided by the number of children of official graduating age:

primary completion rate =

$$\frac{\sum_i w_i 1\begin{pmatrix} level_i = primary\ and\ grade_i = primary\ duration \\ and\ last\ grade_i \neq primary\ duration \end{pmatrix}}{\sum_i w_i 1(age_i = entry\ age + primary\ duration - 1)}.$$

The completion rate can exceed 100 percent if many over-age students in the system graduate. This is not the case in screenshot 4.11, where the primary completion rate in urban areas is 89.23.

Indicator B1.5: Secondary Promotion Rate

The secondary promotion rate is the proportion of students in any grade of secondary school who are promoted to the next grade the following school year (screenshot 4.11):

secondary promotion rate =

$$\frac{\sum_i w_i \begin{pmatrix} 1(last\ year\ level_i = secondary) \\ -1\begin{pmatrix} level_i = none\ and\ highest\ level\ attained_i < secondary \\ and\ last\ year\ level_i = secondary \end{pmatrix} \\ -1(grade_i = last\ year\ grade_i\ and\ last\ year\ level_i = secondary) \end{pmatrix}}{\sum_i w_i 1(last\ year\ level_i = secondary)}.$$

As with the primary promotion rate, this rate may include a small number of students who move forward more than one grade the following school year. In screenshot 4.11, 73.95 percent of girls who were in secondary school the previous year were promoted to the next grade.

Chapter 4: Generating and Interpreting Output Tables and Graphs

Indicator B1.6: Secondary Repetition Rate

The secondary repetition rate is the proportion of students in any grade of secondary in a given school year who attend the same grade the following school year. Students who stay in the same grade are counted as repeaters.

$$\text{secondary repetition rate} = \frac{\sum_i w_i 1\begin{pmatrix} grade_i = last\ year\ grade_i\ and \\ last\ year\ level_i = secondary \end{pmatrix}}{\sum_i w_i 1(last\ year\ level_i = secondary)}.$$

In screenshot 4.11, 3.14 percent of secondary students repeated a grade.

Indicator B1.7: Secondary Dropout Rate

The secondary dropout rate is the percentage of students in any grade of secondary in a given school year and who no longer attend school the following school year and did not graduate:

secondary dropout rate =

$$\frac{\sum_i w_i 1\begin{pmatrix} level_i = none\ and\ highest\ level\ attained_i < secondary \\ and\ last\ year\ level_i = secondary \end{pmatrix}}{\sum_i w_i 1(last\ year\ level_i = secondary)}.$$

In the example in screenshot 4.11, the secondary dropout rate for urban areas is 21.80 percent.

Indicator B1.8: Secondary Completion Rate

The secondary completion rate is the total number of students of any age in the last grade of secondary school, minus the number of repeaters in that grade, divided by the number of children of official graduation age:

$$\text{secondary completion rate} = \frac{\sum_i w_i 1 \begin{pmatrix} grade_i > last\ year\ grade_i\ and \\ grade_i = primary\ duration \\ + secondary\ duration \end{pmatrix}}{\sum_i w_i 1 \begin{pmatrix} age_i = entry\ age + primary\ duration \\ + secondary\ duration - 1 \end{pmatrix}}.$$

In the example in screenshot 4.11, the secondary completion rate among urban areas is 22.76, while for rural areas, it is much lower at 5.38 percent.

Indicator B1.9: Primary to Secondary Transition Rate

The primary to secondary transition rate is the proportion of students in the last grade of primary who are promoted to the first grade of secondary the following school year:

$$\text{primary to secondary transition rate} = \frac{\sum_i w_i 1 \begin{pmatrix} level_i = secondary \text{ and} \\ last\ year\ level_i = primary \end{pmatrix}}{\sum_i w_i 1 \begin{pmatrix} last\ year\ level_i = primary \text{ and} \\ last\ year\ grade_i = duration\ of\ primary \end{pmatrix}}.$$

In the example in screenshot 4.11, boys have a lower primary to secondary transition rate (76.80 percent) than do girls (82.52 percent).

Indicator B1.10: Postsecondary Repetition Rate

The repetition rate postsecondary is the proportion of students in any grade of postsecondary in a given school year who also attend that same grade in the following school year:

$$\text{postsecondary repetition rate} = \frac{\sum_i w_i 1 \begin{pmatrix} grade_i \leq last\ year\ grade_i \text{ and} \\ last\ year\ level_i = postsecondary \end{pmatrix}}{\sum_i w_i 1 (last\ year\ level_i = postsecondary)}.$$

Students who stay in the same grade one school year after another are counted as repeaters. In the above example, the postsecondary repetition rate is 4.86 percent.

Table B2: Promotion, Repetition, and Dropout Rates by Single Grade of Primary Education

Table B2 contains the same information as table B1 (promotion, repetition, dropout, and completion rates) broken down by grade level (screenshot 4.12).

Screenshot 4.12: Table B2: Promotion, Repetition, and Dropout Rates by Single Grade of Primary Education

	A	B	C	D	E	F	G	H	I	J	K	L	M	N	O	P	Q	R
1		Table B2: Promotion, repetition, and dropout rates by single grade of primary education, according to background characteristics, [Data]																
2				Promotion						Repetition						Dropout		
3		Grade 1	Grade 2	Grade 3	Grade 4	Grade 5		Grade 1	Grade 2	Grade 3	Grade 4	Grade 5		Grade 1	Grade 2	Grade 3	Grade 4	Grade 5
4																		
5	Total	80.41	84.89	82.68	87.36	32.34		17.92	13.31	14.55	8.50	17.97		1.68	1.80	2.78	4.13	47.84
6																		
7	Gender																	
8	Boys	79.95	82.96	81.60	86.20	33.40		18.24	15.11	15.50	9.22	16.98		1.81	1.92	2.90	4.57	48.19
9	Girls	80.89	87.13	83.84	88.52	31.19		17.57	11.21	13.51	7.78	19.04		1.54	1.66	2.65	3.70	47.47
10																		
11	Area of residence																	
12	Urban	86.66	89.45	87.09	91.05	32.61		12.45	9.97	10.92	7.69	14.78		0.89	0.59	1.99	1.25	51.69
13	Rural	79.69	84.29	82.02	86.69	32.28		18.54	13.75	15.08	8.65	18.77		1.77	1.96	2.89	4.66	46.89
14																		

Indicator B2.1: Promotion Rate by Grade in Primary School

The promotion rate by grade in primary school is the proportion of students in a given grade of primary school who are promoted to the next grade the following school year:

promotion rate in grade $X =$

$$\frac{\sum_i w_i \left[1\begin{pmatrix} \text{last year grade}_i = X \text{ and last year} \\ \text{level} = \text{primary} \end{pmatrix} -1\begin{pmatrix} \text{level}_i = \text{none and highest level attained}_i \\ < \text{primary and last year grade}_i = X \text{ and last year} \\ \text{level}_i = \text{primary} \end{pmatrix} -1\begin{pmatrix} \text{grade}_i = X \text{ and last year grade}_i = X \\ \text{and last year level}_i = \text{primary} \end{pmatrix} \right]}{\sum_i w_i 1(\text{last year grade}_i = X \text{ and last year level}_i = \text{primary})}.$$

In the example in screenshot 4.12, the promotion rate drops dramatically as the grade level increases, falling from 80.41 percent in grade 1 to 32.34 percent by grade 5.

Indicator B2.2: Repetition Rate by Grade in Primary School

The repetition rate by grade in primary school is the proportion of students in a given grade of primary school who were enrolled in the same grade the previous school year:

repetition rate in grade $X =$

$$\frac{\sum_i w_i 1\begin{pmatrix} \text{grade}_i = X \text{ and last year grade}_i = X \text{ and} \\ \text{last year level}_i = \text{primary} \end{pmatrix}}{\sum_i w_i 1\begin{pmatrix} \text{last year grade}_i = X \text{ and} \\ \text{last year level}_i = \text{primary} \end{pmatrix}}.$$

Indicator B2.3: Dropout Rate by Grade in Primary School

The dropout rate by grade in primary school is the proportion of students in a given grade of primary school who no longer attend school the following school year:

dropout rate in grade $X =$

$$\frac{\sum_i w_i 1\begin{pmatrix} level_i = none\ and\ highest\ level\ attained_i < primary \\ and\ last\ year\ grade_i = X \\ and\ last\ year\ level_i = primary \end{pmatrix}}{\sum_i w_i 1(last\ year\ grade_i = X\ and\ last\ year\ level_i = primary)}.$$

Table B3: Promotion, Repetition, and Dropout Rates by Single Grade of Secondary Education

Table B3 contains the same information as table B2 (promotion, repetition, dropout, and completion rates by grade) for secondary school (screenshot 4.13).

School Attainment Tables

The next set of tables describes school attainment by various segments of the population. In addition to providing measures of how effective the education system has been, these tables provide a picture of the structure of human capital within a country, which has implications for economic performance.

Table C1: School Attainment of Adult Population

Table C1 presents two types of indicators: attainment by age group and average years of schooling by age group (screenshot 4.14).

Screenshot 4.13: Table B3: Promotion, Repetition, and Dropout Rates by Single Grade of Secondary Education

Table B3: Promotion, repetition, and dropout rates by single grade of secondary education, according to background characteristics, [Data1]

	Promotion						Repetition						Dropout					
	Grade 1	Grade 2	Grade 3	Grade 4	Grade 5	Grade 6	Grade 1	Grade 2	Grade 3	Grade 4	Grade 5	Grade 6	Grade 1	Grade 2	Grade 3	Grade 4	Grade 5	Grade 6
Total	87.34	88.17	89.69	65.53	94.04	94.33	6.98	7.53	5.40	21.50	3.21	4.45	5.68	4.29	4.91	12.97	2.74	1.19
Gender																		
Boys	87.10	88.80	90.31	64.62	93.71	96.59	8.25	7.69	5.17	22.86	4.89	3.41	4.65	3.51	4.51	12.52	1.40	0.00
Girls	87.59	87.60	89.08	66.48	94.47	91.41	5.69	7.39	5.62	20.07	1.07	5.79	6.72	5.01	5.30	13.45	4.47	2.71

Chapter 4: Generating and Interpreting Output Tables and Graphs

Screenshot 4.14: Table C1: School Attainment

	A	B	C	D	E	F	G
1	Table C1: School attainment of adult population by background characteristics, [Nicaragua LSMS 2005]						
2		School attainment for 15-19 Year-olds					
3		No education	Incomplete primary	Primary	Incomplete secondary	Secondary	Some higher
4							
5	Total	10.01	20.44	16.70	41.94	8.27	2.63
6							
7	Gender						
8	Boys	12.54	22.73	17.86	38.21	6.61	2.06
9	Girls	7.30	17.98	15.46	45.96	10.06	3.24
10							
11	Area of residence						
12	Urban	4.94	10.95	14.49	52.88	12.69	4.05
13	Rural	16.12	31.86	19.37	28.78	2.95	0.92
14							

Indicator C1.1: Percentage of Age Group by Attainment Level

The percentage of the specified age range that has attained a specified level of education is calculated as follows:

percentage of people age X–Y with education =

$$\frac{\sum_{i} w_i 1 \left(\begin{array}{l} \text{highest level attained}_i = Z \\ \text{and age}_i \geq X \text{ and age}_i \leq Y \end{array} \right)}{\sum_{i} w_i 1 (\text{age}_i \geq X \text{ and age}_i \leq Y)}.$$

Age ranges are broken into five categories: 15–19, 20–29, 30–39, 40–49, and 50 and over (screenshot 4.16 shows the screenshot for the 10–19 age group). Attainment levels are broken into six categories: no education, incomplete primary, primary, incomplete secondary, secondary, and some higher.

Indicator C1.2: Average Years of Schooling by Age Group

The average years of schooling of an age group population is calculated as follows:

average years of school of people age X–Y =

$$\frac{\sum_i w_i \text{ highest grade attained}_i \mathbf{1}(age_i \geq X \text{ and } age_i \leq Y)}{\sum_i w_i \mathbf{1}(age_i \geq X \text{ and } age_i \leq Y)}.$$

Tables C2–C5: Proportion of Adult Population That Completed Each Grade

Tables C2–C5 present the percentage of an age group that completed each of the grades in a series, calculated as follows:

percentage of population age X–Y that attained grade Z =

$$\frac{\sum_i w_i \mathbf{1}\begin{pmatrix} age_i \geq X \text{ and } age_i \leq Y \text{ and highest} \\ \text{grade attained}_i \geq Z \end{pmatrix}}{\sum_i w_i \mathbf{1}(age_i \geq X \text{ and } age_i \leq Y)}.$$

Screenshot 4.15 displays these data for 15- to 19-year-olds.

Table C6: Proportion of 10- to 19-Year-Olds Expected to Complete Each Grade

Table C6 presents estimates of grade completion based on survival analysis of the sample data. It shows the percentage of each subgroup of a given age range that is expected to complete each grade (screenshot 4.16).

In the example shown in screenshot 4.16, 48.84 percent of boys 10–19 and 44.88 percent of girls are expected to complete eight grades of education.

Table C7: Inequality in Years of Schooling

Table C7 presents the application of the Gini and Theil measures of income and wealth equality to years of schooling (screenshot 4.17). This information helps policy makers understand how equally human capital within a country is distributed. (Chapter 5 provides full explanations of the Gini coefficient and the Theil index.)

Screenshot 4.15: Table C2: Proportion of 15- to 19-Year-Olds That Completed Each Grade

	A	B	C	D	E	F	G	H	I	J	K	L	M	N	O	P	Q	R
1	Table C2: Proportion of 15-19 years olds that completed each grade, according to background characteristics, [Data]																	
2		1 year		2 years		3 years		4 years		5 years		6 years		7 years		8 years		9 years
3																		
4	Total	84.31		79.20		69.57		59.10		45.02		34.42		27.18		20.22		10.73
5																		
6	Gender																	
7	Boys	84.05		78.69		68.62		57.90		44.24		33.52		26.10		19.46		10.27
8	Girls	84.57		79.71		70.51		60.28		45.80		35.31		28.25		20.97		11.18
9																		
10	Area of residence																	
11	Urban	96.31		95.27		92.51		87.65		78.66		70.04		62.02		51.43		34.68
12	Rural	81.99		76.09		65.12		53.56		38.50		27.51		20.42		14.17		6.08

Screenshot 4.16: Table C6: Proportion of Population 10–19 Expected to Complete Each Grade

	A	B	C	D	E	F	G	H	I	J
1	Table C6: Proportion of 10-19 years olds expected to complete each grade, according to background characteristics, [Data]									
2		1	2	3	4	5	6	7	8	9
3										
4	Total	87.01	83.46	77.43	70.84	61.70	53.84	50.16	46.71	41.38
5										
6	Gender									
7	Boys	86.54	82.96	76.94	70.37	61.88	54.65	51.56	48.84	44.31
8	Girls	87.50	83.97	77.93	71.31	61.57	53.12	48.94	44.88	38.87
9										
10	Area of residence									
11	Urban	97.19	96.20	94.20	91.02	85.51	80.72	77.33	73.27	67.25
12	Rural	85.34	81.36	74.61	67.31	57.24	48.35	44.42	40.94	35.37
13										

Screenshot 4.17: Table C7: Inequality in Years of Schooling

Table C7: Inequality in years of schooling, [Data]

	Gini coefficient				Theil index			
	15-19	20-24	25-29	15+	15-19	20-24	25-29	15+
Total	41.73	50.39	54.57	53.60	17.98	28.72	33.68	34.65
Gender								
Boys	41.71	49.38	56.81	53.05	16.80	29.30	41.77	37.29
Girls	41.72	51.39	52.11	54.03	19.05	28.07	24.63	31.59
Area of residence								
Urban	25.76	30.42	36.03	37.11	11.87	12.93	22.06	24.31
Rural	43.15	52.85	55.74	55.22	17.69	32.37	34.23	35.68

Indicator C7.1: Gini Coefficient for Years of Schooling, by Age Group

The Gini coefficient[5] for years of schooling is calculated like the Gini coefficient for income or wealth. It measures the degree of inequality in years of schooling. The Gini coefficient ranges from 0 to 100, with 0 indicating perfect equality and 100 indicating perfect inequality. The ADePT Edu software estimates this indicator for three age groups (15–19, 20–24, 25–29) as well as for the 15+ age group.

Gini coefficient for years of schooling =

$$\frac{n}{n-1} \cdot \frac{\sum_{i=1}^{n}\sum_{j=1}^{n}|\text{highest grade attained}_i - \text{highest grade attained}_j|}{2n\sum_{i}^{n}\text{highest grade attained}_i}.$$

Knowing the inequality of human capital among youth, for example, is important because it is a measure of equality of opportunity. (This topic is covered in detail in chapter 5.)

Indicator C7.2: Theil Index for Years of Schooling, by Age Group

The Theil index is an alternative indicator of inequality. Although it is less intuitive than the Gini coefficient, it has a distinct advantage in that it can provide information on the contribution of different subgroups to total inequality.

Theil index for years of schooling =

$$\frac{\sum_{i=1}^{n}\ln\left(\frac{\sum_{j=1}^{n}\text{highest grade attained}_j}{n\times\text{highest grade attained}_i}\right)}{n}.$$

Education Expenditure Tables

Many countries have adopted a policy of free primary education in order to eliminate barriers to access. Even when schools are free, however, households still have to pay for transportation, school uniforms, school supplies, and other expenditures, depending on the country, and contribute to parent-teacher associations. For children from extremely poor families, such expenditures can be an effective barrier to entry. Policies targeting those facing financial barriers to education can be implemented rapidly. Household education expenditures are shown for primary (table D1), secondary (table D2), and postsecondary (table D3) levels.

Table D1: Primary Level

Indicator D1: Average Share of Household Expenditure on Education, per Student, by Level of Education

The education share of household expenditure by level of education is the proportion of annual educational expenditures divided by the total annual household expenditures:

average share of household expenditure on education for level X =

$$\sum_i w_i 1(level_i = X) \frac{household\ expenditure\ on\ education_i}{total\ household\ expenditure_i}.$$

This indicator is based on how much the household spends per child in school. In screenshot 4.18, the average share of household expenditure per primary school student is 3.99 percent—4.04 percent for girls and 3.93 percent for boys.

Table D2: Secondary Level

Indicator D2: Average Education Spending per Student, by Level of Education

The annual average education spending per student by level of education is the total educational expenditures divided by the total enrollment in each level:

average per pupil spending at level X =

$$\frac{\sum_i w_i 1(level_i = X)\ household\ expenditure\ on\ education_i}{\sum_i w_i 1(level_i = X)}.$$

In the example in screenshot 4.18, average spending per student in primary school was 1,702.44 Nicaraguan córdobas.

Screenshot 4.18: Table D1: Household Expenditure on Primary Education

Table D1: Household expenditure on primary education, [Nicaragua LSMS 2005]

	Education share of household expenditure, (%)	Annual average education spending per child attending	Proportion of household education spending, (%)						
			School registration fees	Books and school supplies	Transportation to/from school	Foods, board and lodging at school	School uniforms	Contribution to parent-teacher association	Other educational expenditures
Total	3.99	1,702.44	3.41	0.68	17.84	51.09	19.61	2.84	4.54
Gender									
Boys	3.93	1,724.40	3.26	0.76	18.01	50.09	20.00	3.04	4.84
Girls	4.04	1,679.57	3.56	0.59	17.66	52.13	19.20	2.63	4.24
Area of residence									
Urban	3.57	1,974.68	6.70	1.14	27.45	32.12	21.16	4.14	7.28
Rural	4.37	1,455.38	0.32	0.24	8.81	68.90	18.14	1.61	1.98

Chapter 4: Generating and Interpreting Output Tables and Graphs

Table D3: Postsecondary Level

Indicator D3: Percentage of Household Education Expenditure by Category, by Level

The proportion of household education spending by category is the amount of annual per student spending on a selected category divided by the annual educational expenditures of the household:

average proportion of household education expenditure spent on Z =

$$\sum_i w_i \mathbf{1}(level_i = X) \frac{expenditure\ on\ Z_i}{household\ education\ expenditure_i}.$$

The categories include school registration fees; books and school supplies; transportation to and from school; food, board, and lodging at school (where applicable); school uniforms; contributions to parent-teacher associations; and other educational expenditure. In the example in screenshot 4.18, 51.09 percent of education expenditure goes to food and lodging at school, 19.61 percent is spent on school uniforms, and 17.84 percent goes to transportation.

Labor Market Outcome Tables

Labor market outcomes are an important measure of the success of a country's education system in terms of both quality and equality. Earnings of youth are often considered a measure of the quality and relevance of their education. Highly unequal earnings have important implications for the country's overall welfare. Tables E1–E6 present several indicators of earnings, earnings inequality, and returns to education.

Table E1: Earning Inequalities

Table E1 (screenshot 4.19) presents the Gini coefficients and Theil index values for earnings for various age groups.

Indicator E1.1: Gini Coefficient for Earnings, by Age Group

In general, there is a positive correlation between educational attainment and earnings. If access to education is unequal, earnings are also likely to be

Screenshot 4.19: Table E1: Earning Inequalities

	A	B	C	D	E	F	G	H	I	J
1			Table E1: Earning Inequalities, [Nicaragua LSMS 2005]							
2			Gini coefficient for earnings					Theil index for earnings		
3			15-19	20-24	25-29	15+	15-19	20-24	25-29	15+
4										
5	Total		49.34	51.45	53.89	58.94	42.31	48.12	54.80	77.99
6										
7	Gender									
8	Boys		45.97	49.96	52.16	59.68	36.84	45.69	49.77	82.91
9	Girls		55.78	50.34	54.09	55.90	59.90	45.24	61.37	61.48
10										
11	Area of residence									
12	Urban		49.11	50.28	52.52	57.50	41.54	44.81	52.11	76.52
13	Rural		48.80	51.15	55.37	58.50	41.84	51.07	57.74	69.28
14										

Chapter 4: Generating and Interpreting Output Tables and Graphs

unequal. As a rule of thumb, a Gini coefficient above 40 is considered unequal and one above 50 as highly unequal. A high degree of inequality suggests that access to education needs to be improved, along with education quality. In the example shown in screenshot 4.19, the Gini coefficient among 15- to 19-year-olds is higher for girls (55.78) than for boys (45.97). For all individuals 15 and older, however, women have lower earnings inequality than males.

Indicator E1.2: Theil Index for Earnings, by Age Group

The same pattern for gender inequality is found using the Theil index: initially women have more inequality in earnings than men, but for all people 15 and older, the Theil index is much higher for men (82.91) than women (61.48).

Tables E2, E2a, and E2b: Employment for Youth

Table E2 presents three key employment indicators by age group and subpopulation (screenshot 4.20). These data provide a general picture of how youth are faring in the labor market, as well as a picture of how different subpopulations are faring.

The employment of youth who have finished their education is an indirect indicator of the success of the education system. Table E2 provides information on the employment status of youth and young adults by age groups.

Indicator E2.1: Percentage Employed, by Age Group

The percentage of an age cohort that is employed is calculated as follows:

percentage of people age X–Y who are employed =

$$\frac{\sum_i w_i 1\left(\begin{array}{l} status_i = employed \\ and\ age_i \geq X\ and\ age_i \leq Y \end{array}\right)}{\sum_i w_i 1(age_i \geq X\ and\ age_i \leq Y)}.$$

In the example shown in screenshot 4.20, 39.69 percent of 15- to 19-year-olds in Nicaragua are employed. This percentage increases with age. At all ages, the inequalities in employment between men and women are large. For the 20–24 cohort, 80.92 percent of men but only 38.82 percent of women are employed.

Screenshot 4.20: Table E2: Employment for Youth

	A	B	C	D	E	F	G	H	I	J	K	L
1						Table E2: Employment for youth, [Nicaragua LSMS 2005]						
2			Population 15-19				Population 20-24				Population 25-30	
3		Employed	Unemployed	Inactive		Employed	Unemployed	Inactive		Employed	Unemployed	Inactive
4												
5	Total	39.69	0.66	59.66		60.85	1.25	37.90		65.94	0.71	33.36
6												
7	Gender											
8	Boys	59.59	0.84	39.58		80.92	1.51	17.56		88.12	0.56	11.32
9	Girls	18.31	0.46	81.23		38.82	0.97	60.21		46.52	0.83	52.65
10												
11	Area of residence											
12	Urban	29.23	1.11	69.66		59.32	1.81	38.87		68.50	0.93	30.57
13	Rural	52.27	0.11	47.62		63.24	0.38	36.38		62.09	0.37	37.53
14												

Chapter 4: Generating and Interpreting Output Tables and Graphs

Indicator E2.2: Percentage Unemployed, by Age Group

The percentage of an age cohort that is unemployed is calculated as follows:

percentage of people age X–Y who are unemployed =

$$\frac{\sum_i w_i 1\left(\begin{array}{l} status_i = unemployed \\ and\ age_i \geq X\ and\ age_i \leq Y \end{array}\right)}{\sum_i w_i 1(age_i \geq X\ and\ age_i \leq Y)}.$$

In the example shown in screenshot 4.20, unemployment rates for youth are relatively low, with only 0.71 percent in the 25–30 cohort unemployed (the figure may be low because job seekers stop looking for work). Unemployment is higher among women (0.83 percent) than men (0.56 percent).

Indicator E2.3: Percentage Inactive, by Age Group

The percentage of an age cohort that is inactive is calculated as follows:

percentage of people age X–Y who are inactive =

$$\frac{\sum_i w_i 1\left(\begin{array}{l} status_i = inactive \\ and\ age_i \geq X\ and\ age_i \leq Y \end{array}\right)}{\sum_i w_i 1(age_i \geq X\ and\ age_i \leq Y)}.$$

$$inactive = \begin{cases} 1, if\ status_i \neq employed\ and\ status_i \neq unemployed \\ 0, if\ status_i = employed\ or\ status_i = unemployed. \end{cases}$$

Data on inactivity need not be inputted into ADePT. The variable is calculated based on data on employment and unemployment.

In the example shown in screenshot 4.20, large gender differences are evident, with 11.32 percent of men 25–30 and 52.65 percent of women inactive.

Table E3: Employment by Sector

Table E3 presents the percentage of employment of each sector by age group (screenshot 4.21). This information reveals the types of work youth engage in. Because this information confounds the skills demanded with the skills

125

Screenshot 4.21: Table E3: Employment by Sector

Table E3: Employment by sector, [Laos 2007-08]

	Agriculture, hunting and related service activities	Forestry, logging and related service activities	Fishing, aquaculture and service activities incidental to fishing	Mining of coal and lignite; extraction of peat	Extraction of crude petroleum and natural gas; service activities incidental to oil and gas extraction, excluding survey	Mining of metal ores	Other mining and quarrying	Manufacture of food products and beverages	Manufacture of tobacco products	Manufacture of textiles
Total	72.28	2.46	2.69	0.00	0.06	0.06	0.14	0.85	0.13	2.12
Gender										
Boys	73.41	1.75	4.14	0.00	0.13	0.06	0.29	0.92	0.00	0.20
Girls	71.30	3.07	1.41	0.00	0.00	0.06	0.00	0.79	0.24	3.80
Area of residence										
Urban	43.38	1.51	3.61	0.00	0.00	0.17	0.42	1.49	0.48	3.17
Rural	82.82	2.80	2.35	0.00	0.08	0.02	0.03	0.61	0.00	1.73

Chapter 4: Generating and Interpreting Output Tables and Graphs

supplied, however, it cannot be used as a measure of the types of skills the economy needs or the types of skills students were prepared for.

The percentage of people of a certain age employed in a particular sector is calculated as follows:

percentage of people age X–Y employed in sector Z =

$$\frac{\sum_{i} w_i 1\begin{pmatrix} status_i = employed\ and\ sector_i = Z \\ and\ age_i \geq X\ and\ age_i \leq Y \end{pmatrix}}{\sum_{i} w_i 1(age_i \geq X\ and\ age_i \leq Y\ and\ status_i = employed)}.$$

Table E4: Earnings by Education Level

Table E4 reveals the relationships between earnings and education among youth (screenshot 4.22 displays the data for the 15–19 and 20–24 cohorts; the table also includes data on people 25–30 and 15–30). The education levels are no education, incomplete primary, primary, incomplete secondary, secondary, and some higher education. These categories are mutually exclusive. This information highlights the opportunity cost of attending school in terms of forgone income and the impact of inequality in education access across subgroups in the population.

The earnings of a cohort with a given level of education are calculated as follows:

earnings of people age X–Y with level Z education =

$$\frac{\sum_{i} w_i 1\begin{pmatrix} age_i \geq X\ and\ age_i \leq Y\ and \\ highest\ level\ attained_i = Z \end{pmatrix} earnings_i}{\sum_{i} w_i 1\begin{pmatrix} age_i \geq X\ and\ age_i \leq Y\ and \\ highest\ level\ attained_i = Z \end{pmatrix}}.$$

The data shown in screenshot 4.22 suggest that education has no impact—or even a negative impact—on earnings: people in Nicaragua with no education earn more than those with some education. There are many reasons why educational attainment may be negatively correlated with earnings. The main reason is that people with less education may have more work experience.

Screenshot 4.22: Table E4: Earnings by Education Level

	A	B	C	D	E	F	G	H	I	J	K	L	M	N
1														
2					Population 15-19							Table E4: Earnings by education level, [Nicaragua		
3												Population 20-24		
4		No education	Incomplete primary	Primary	Incomplete secondary	Secondary	Some higher		No education	Incomplete primary	Primary	Incomplete secondary	Secondary	Some higher
5	Total	2,152.53	4,272.26	1,293.22	3,439.07	3,657.53	0.00		3,208.87	1,616.12	1,555.41	3,334.20	2,496.39	3,357.32
6														
7	Gender													
8	Boys	2,152.53	4,418.65	1,324.96	4,116.08	5,266.93			3,105.77	1,659.35	1,826.46	3,690.21	3,388.60	5,231.14
9	Girls		1,673.62	251.67	281.14	1,011.36	0.00		4,185.21	1,241.04	814.33	2,211.78	815.59	1,150.88
10														
11	Area of residence													
12	Urban	3,832.70	1,394.45	2,998.35	1,637.57	4,624.70	0.00		2,846.11	1,847.82	1,810.05	3,905.67	2,726.77	3,357.32
13	Rural	1,873.42	4,607.87	839.32	4,701.00	2,085.20			3,378.62	1,586.60	1,326.48	574.77	1,758.27	

Table E5: Economic Independence

The status of the household head or spouse of the household head is used as a proxy for economic independence. Based on this proxy, table E5 shows the percentages of people in a cohort that can be considered economically independent:

percentage of people age X–Y that are household heads =

$$\frac{\sum_i w_i 1 \begin{pmatrix} age_i \geq X \text{ and } age_i \leq Y \\ and \begin{pmatrix} household\ head_i = yes\ or \\ spouse\ of\ household\ head_i = yes \end{pmatrix} \end{pmatrix}}{\sum_i w_i 1(age_i \geq X \text{ and } age_i \leq Y)}.$$

The relationship between education and economic independence is strongly mediated by the economic situation of the country, the quality and market relevance of formal education, and the returns to education in a given economic context. The results from table E5 indicate that in the 25- to 29-year-old age group, the percentage of people who are economically independent is higher among people with lower levels of education (screenshot 4.23).

Table E6: Returns to Education

A measure of the success of an education system is the productivity of various levels of educational attainment or years of schooling. One common way to measure this productivity is to look at the economic returns to education—that is, the net financial return of additional schooling. Intuitively, an individual's decision to continue studying will depend on the difference between the cost of pursuing additional studies and the added earnings received as a result. Information on returns to additional education provides an idea of the incentives students face when deciding to continue their formal education. High rates of return may induce students to spend more time in school; low rates may discourage them from staying in school longer.

Indicator E6.1: Rate of Return for Years of Schooling

The rate of return for years of schooling is calculated using the Mincer earnings function, where the natural log of earnings is a function of the years of

Screenshot 4.23: Table E5: Economic Independence

	Table E5: Economic independence, [Nicaragua LSMS 2005]			
	Group share of people that are household heads or spouses			
	15-19	20-24	25-30	15-30
Total	3.00	15.64	36.01	15.66
Gender				
Boys	1.50	11.16	30.98	11.75
Girls	4.61	20.56	40.42	19.67
Level of education				
No education	5.32	23.11	46.15	25.62
Incomplete primary	5.60	21.11	44.56	20.77
Primary	1.76	17.96	38.32	15.14
Incomplete secondary	2.17	13.56	36.25	10.89
Secondary	0.55	13.20	22.98	12.40
Some higher	2.75	5.03	21.60	11.40

schooling, experience, and the square of experience (to capture the diminishing marginal effect of experience).[6]

$$\ln(earnings_i) = \beta_0 + \beta_1 \text{ years of schooling}_i = \beta_2 \text{ experience}_i = \beta_3 \text{ experience}_i^2 + u_i.$$

This equation is estimated using linear regression. This approach assumes that each additional year of schooling has an equal impact on earnings.

Indicator E6.2: Returns by Level of Schooling

An alternative specification of the Mincer earnings function uses binary variables for the level of schooling. In the above example, the return to primary school compared with less than primary is 12.75 percent, the return to secondary is 3.99 percent, and the return to more than four years of higher education is 20.89 percent (see screenshot 4.24).

$$\text{earnings}_i = \beta_0 + \beta_1 1\begin{pmatrix} \text{highest level attained}_i \geq \text{primary} \\ \text{and highest level attained}_i < \text{secondary} \end{pmatrix}$$

$$= \beta_2 1\begin{pmatrix} \text{highest level attained}_i \geq \text{secondary} \\ \text{and highest level attained}_i < 4 \text{ years of tertiary} \end{pmatrix}$$

$$+ \beta_3 1(\text{highest level attained}_i \geq 4 \text{ years of tertiary})$$

$$+ \beta_4 \text{ experience}_i + \beta_5 \text{ experience}_i^2 + u_i.$$

Table E6 indicates that the annual economic return to university education in Nicaragua is high (20.89 percent) (screenshot 4.24). For individuals who just finished secondary education, this information is very valuable. It indicates that they could expect to increase their annual earnings by about 21 percent by completing a university education. In contrast, the decision to continue from primary to secondary education is less clear: the annual economic returns of adding secondary education are low (3.99 percent). The results suggest that some education policy intervention may be needed to increase the relevance of secondary education to the labor market.

Screenshot 4.24: Table E6: Returns to Education

	Years of schooling	Primary	Secondary	More then 4 years of higher
Table E6: Returns to education, [Nicaragua LSMS 2005]				
Total	9.26	12.75	3.99	20.89
Gender				
Boys	10.84	16.40	5.71	18.33
Girls	6.99	-1.20	5.70	23.03
Area of residence				
Urban	7.14	4.88	2.35	21.59
Rural	7.73	8.71	1.43	12.44

Assessing Sector Performance and Inequality in Education

ADePT Education Graphs

In addition to tables, ADePT Edu creates related graphs (figures). These graphs are based on the table results and an algorithm that produces enrollment pyramids and grade survival profiles by age and other characteristics. The ADePT Edu software produces more than 30 graphs, classified into 10 groups. The graphs in this section are taken from the 2005 Living Standards Measurement Survey results for Nicaragua.

Graph 4.1 shows the percentage of 15- to 19-year-olds that completed each grade from 1 to 9. Graphs are available by income level for the following age groups: 15–19, 20–29, and 30–39. The graph shows the percentage differences between the income groups and the large gap between the highest and lowest income quintiles. For example, nearly 90 percent of people in the highest income quintile but only about 10 percent of those in the lowest income quintile completed seven years of education.

Graph 4.2 presents attendance rates for the 6–14 age group, for boys and girls in urban and rural areas. It shows that urban girls have the highest and most stable rates of enrollment; their enrollment rates are about

Graph 4.1: Educational Attainment of 15- to 19-Year-Olds in Nicaragua, by Income Quintile

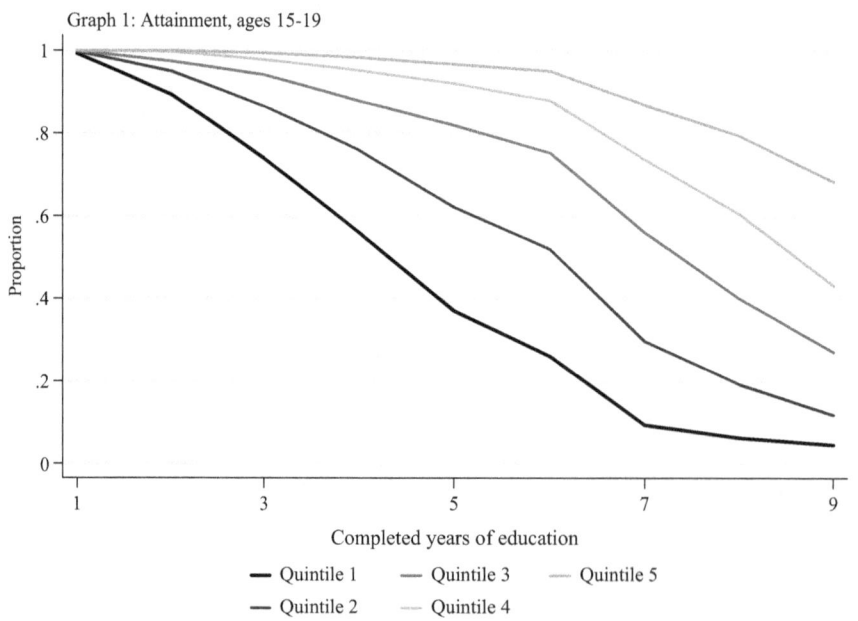

Graph 4.2: Enrollment Rates for Boys and Girls 6–14 Years Old in Rural and Urban Areas of Nicaragua

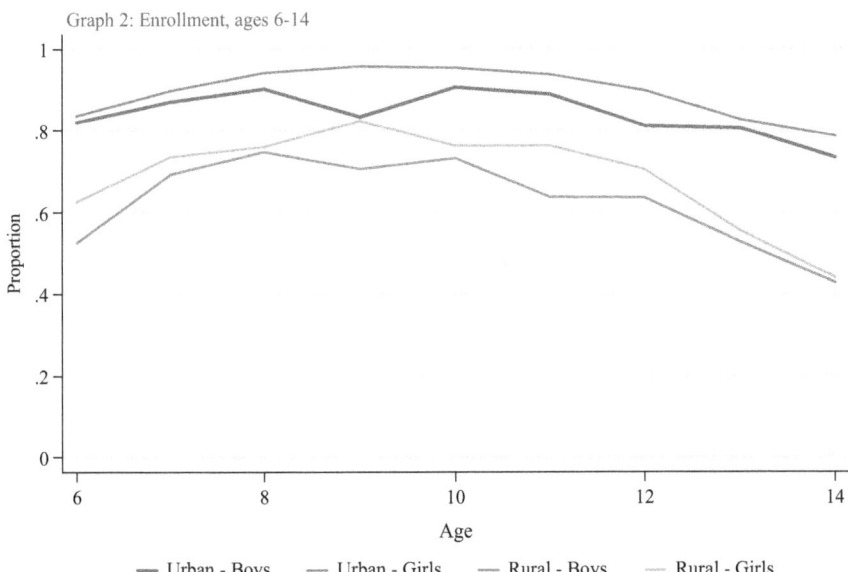

20 percentage points higher than the rates of rural boys. The graph also shows that enrollment peaks between the ages of 8 and 12.

Graph 4.3 shows the grade survival profile of children 10–19 by income quintile. It indicates that children from poorer households are less likely than children from less poor households to reach grade 7. Grade survival rates of children from the bottom two income quintiles are substantially lower than the rates of children from the top three quintiles.

Enrollment pyramids depict attendance rates by age group. In graph 4.4 the percentage of 6- to 24-year-olds currently enrolled in school is shown for the highest and lowest income quintiles. The results indicate that by age 10, there is a considerable difference in the rates of primary school enrollment by income level. By age 11, a significant proportion of children from households in the top quintile have moved on to secondary school, perhaps a year earlier than the official age of entry. By age 13, most children from households in the top quintile are enrolled in secondary school; for children from the bottom quintile, the proportion of children enrolled in primary or secondary school has decreased substantially. By age 15, more than 75 percent of children from the top quintile and only about 25 percent of children from the bottom quintile are still in school. These results

Assessing Sector Performance and Inequality in Education

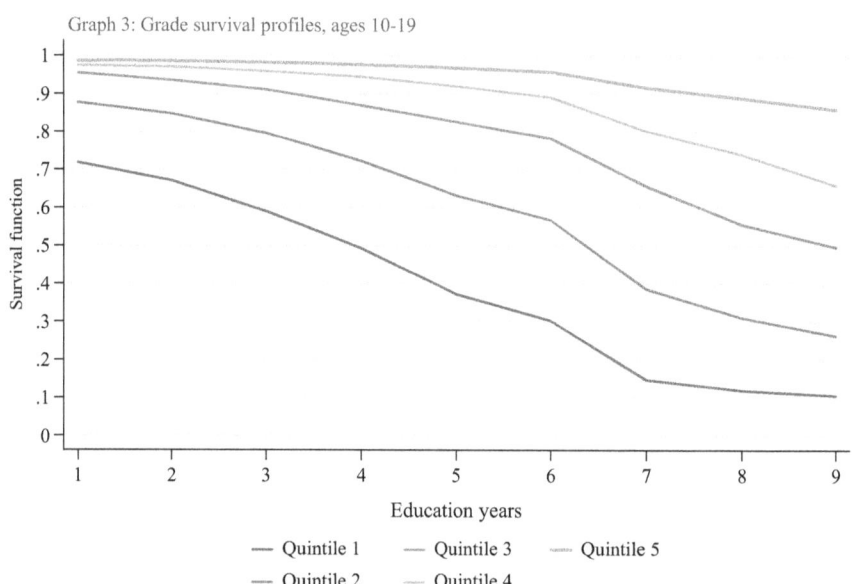

Graph 4.3: Grade Survival Profiles for 10- to 19-Year-Olds in Nicaragua, by Income Quintile

point to the need to increase school attainment of the poor if poverty is to be reduced in the long run.

Graph 4.5 presents educational attainment rates for men and women 30–39 in urban and rural areas. It shows that attainment rates are lower in rural areas, where only about 30 percent of the population has seven years of schooling. In contrast, 75 percent of people in urban areas attained this level of schooling. In both areas, women have more years of schooling than men.

Graph 4.6 shows the typology of out-of-school children (never in school, late entry, and dropout). It shows that 75 percent of rural children classified as out of school were never in school, a percentage that is slightly higher than that of urban children. Dropouts account for only a small proportion of out-of-school children overall but the highest proportion of out-of-school children in urban areas.

Graph 4.7 presents a breakdown of the reasons given by out-of-school children for not attending school (following the classification given by the household survey). The main reason why primary school–age children are out of school is because they have to work in the fields (33.4 percent); the second most important reason is lack of money (26.3 percent).

Chapter 4: Generating and Interpreting Output Tables and Graphs

Graph 4.4: Enrollment Pyramid for 6- to 24-Year-Olds in Nicaragua, by Income Quintile

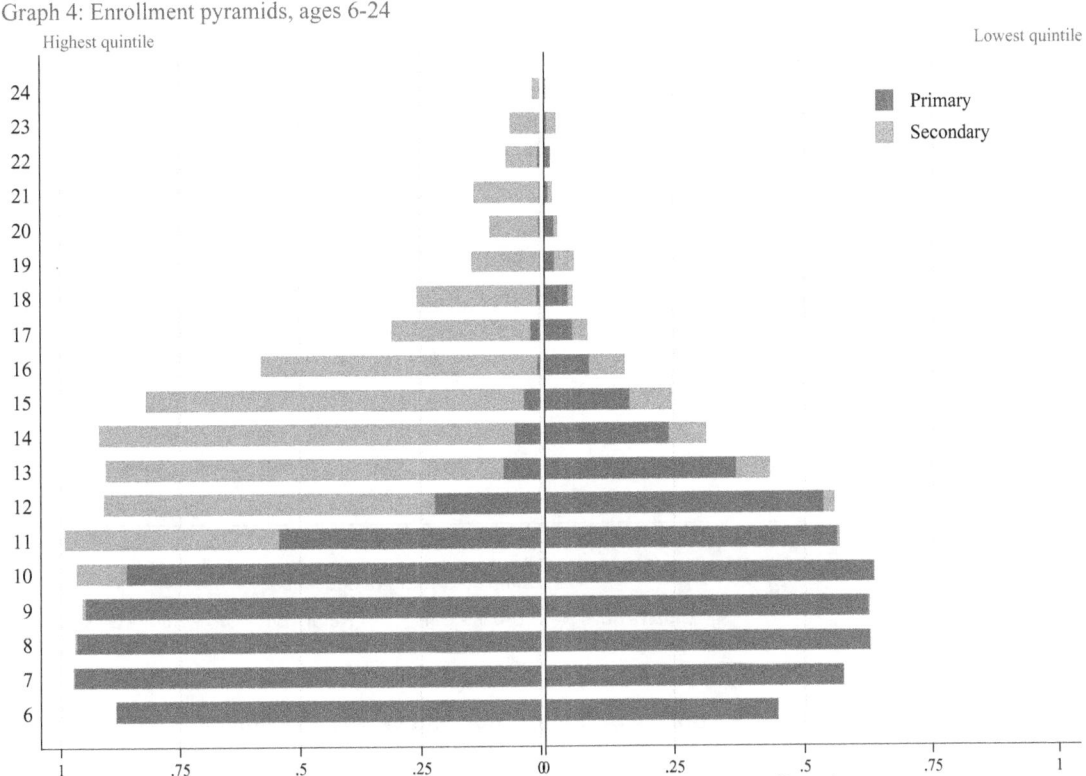

Graph 4.8 presents the Gini index and Lorenz curve for years of schooling. Briefly, the Lorenz curve is a measure of the cumulative distribution of schooling attainment (see chapter 5 for a full explanation of the Lorenz curve and other indicators of education inequality). If the Lorenz curve followed the 45-degree line, the distribution of schooling attainment would be perfectly equal: every fraction of the population would have the same fraction of total years of schooling. In graph 4.8, the Lorenz curve for years of schooling diverges significantly from the line of equality: about 60 percent of the population has about 25 percent of the total years of schooling, meaning that the remaining 75 percent of the total years of schooling is held by 40 percent of the population. These data indicate that human capital (represented by the years of schooling) is unequally distributed across the population.

Assessing Sector Performance and Inequality in Education

Graph 4.5: Educational Attainment Profiles for Men and Women 30–39 Years Old in Rural and Urban Areas in Nicaragua

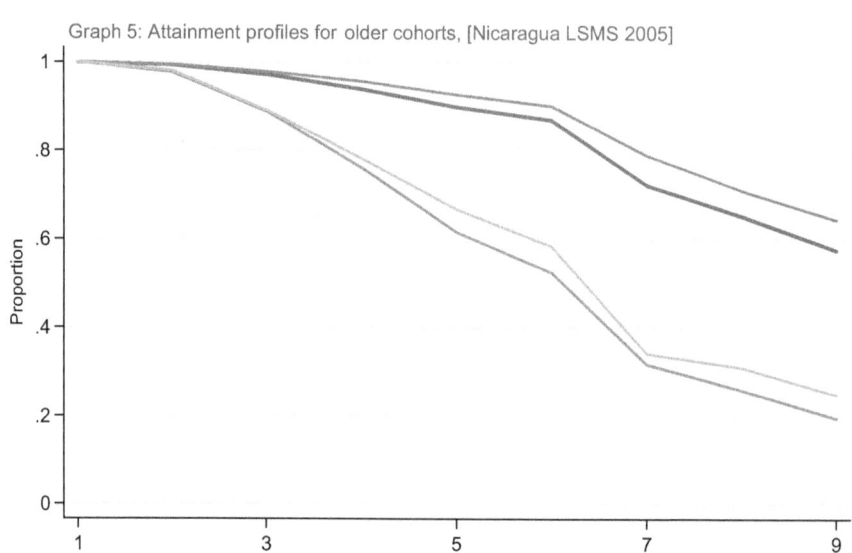

Graph 4.6: Typology of Out of School, by Subpopulation and Level in Nicaragua

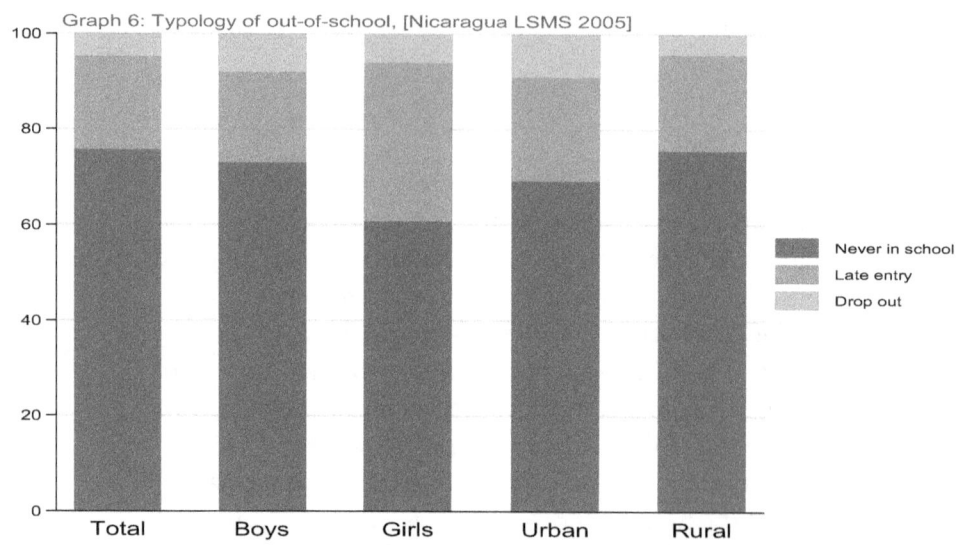

Graph 4.7: Reasons Why Primary School–Age Children Are Out of School in Nicaragua

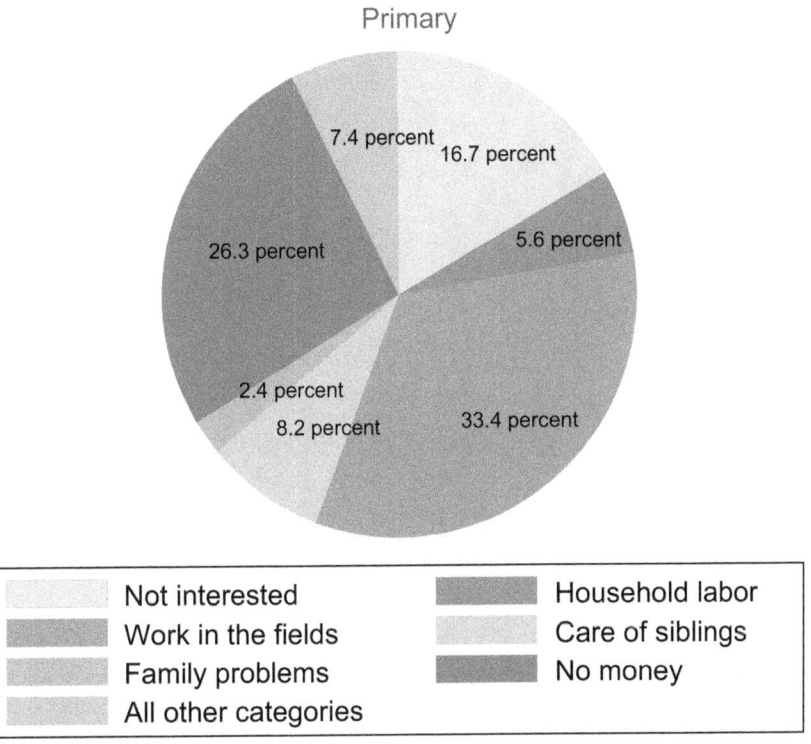

Graph 4.9 is an age-earnings profile by education level. It shows average hourly earnings for various age groups and educational levels. People with some higher education earn more than people with less education for most age groups (although the variance of the sample is high). There is no clear pattern for other levels of education.

Graph 4.10 plots average hourly earnings by years of schooling for three different levels of labor market experience (1, 5, and 10 years). It shows that hourly earnings increase as the number of years of schooling increase for all years of experience. An individual with 10 years of experience and 5 years of schooling earns less per hour than one with 12 years or more of schooling and 1–5 years of experience.

Assessing Sector Performance and Inequality in Education

Graph 4.8: Lorenz Curve for Years of Schooling in Nicaragua

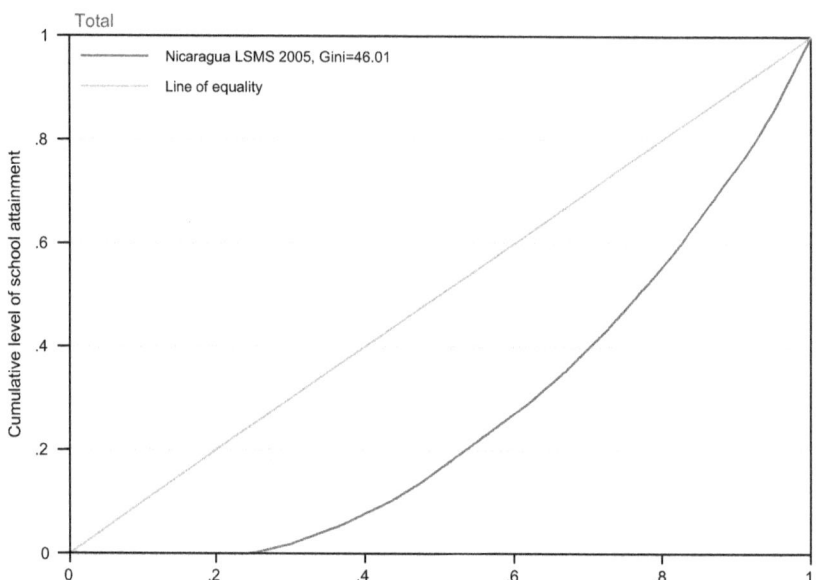

Graph 4.9: Age-Earnings Profile by Education Level

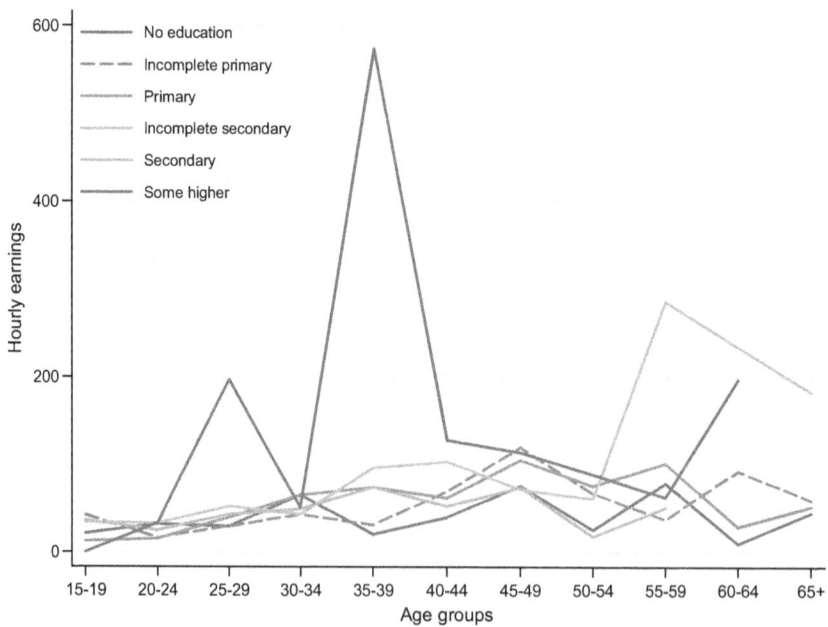

Graph 4.10: Earnings by Years of Schooling and Labor Market Experience in Nicaragua

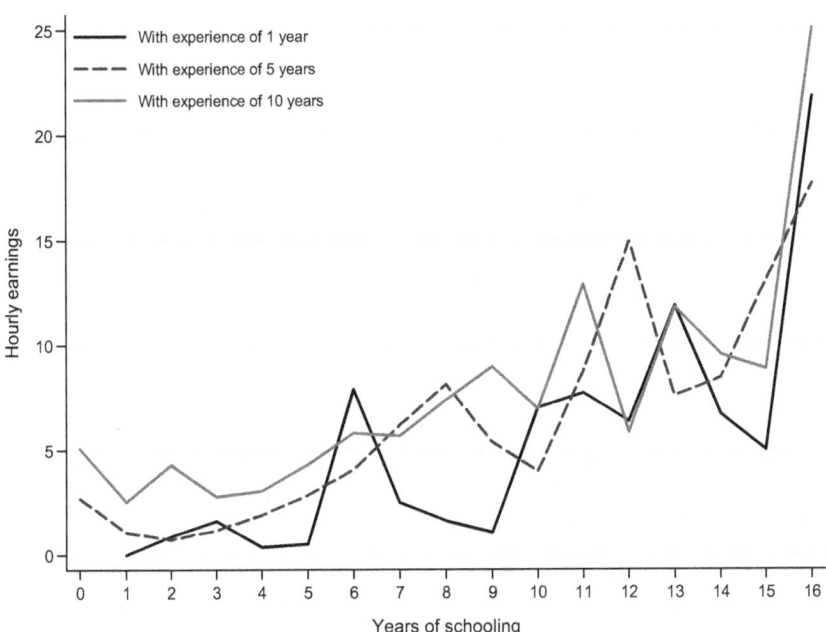

Notes

1. ADePT formats the output, but all data are stored with full precision, facilitating further analysis.
2. Standard errors in the indicator tables are calculated using Stata's implementation of the linearized standard errors to account for intracluster correlation. BRR (balanced repeated replication) and Jackknife methods are also available. See the Stata documentation for details on these calculations.
3. For simplicity, all formulas for proportions, percentages, and rates do not show the multiplication of the result by 100. It is assumed that users will do the multiplication themselves.
4. Some estimates count secondary school–age children who are enrolled in primary or postsecondary education as being out of school. This approach results in overestimation, especially in countries with high gross attendance rates for primary school. Considering youth attending primary

school as out of school can lead to erroneous conclusions about the number of out-of-school children and adolescents, potentially misguiding policy.
5. The formula for the Gini coefficient is conceptually accurate, but it is not intended for computation. The computational algorithm involves a large amount of source code that is too cumbersome to be included here.
6. The Mincer function is named after Jacob Mincer, who established the relationship between earnings and schooling in the United States in 1958. For a recent estimation of the returns to education in other countries in the world, see Psacharopoulos and Patrinos (2002).

References

Psacharopoulos, George, and Harry Anthony Patrinos. 2002. "Returns to Investment in Education: A Further Update." Policy Research Working Paper 2881, World Bank, Washington, DC.

UNESCO (United Nations Education, Scientific and Cultural Organization), and UNICEF (United Nations Children's Fund). 2005. *Children Out of School: Measuring Exclusion from Primary Education.* Montreal: UNESCO Institute for Statistics.

———. 2010. "Use of Cohort Analysis Models for Assessing Educational Internal Efficiency." Technical Note, Paris. http://www.uis.unesco.org/i_pages/indspec/cohorte.htm.

Chapter 5

Analyzing Education Inequality with ADePT Edu

This chapter describes the state of global education inequality, based on household survey data analyzed with the aid of ADePT Edu. It provides a primer on education inequality for analysts interested in the association between access to education and socioeconomic variables such as gender, location, and household poverty.

The concept of equity—as the opposite of inequality—is based on a simple norm: all people should have equal opportunities "to pursue a life of their choosing" (World Bank 2005, p. 2). Aside from moral reasons—after all, equity is a merit good in most societies—there are economic reasons to pursue increased equity or reduce inequality. In its *World Development Report 2006: Equity and Development*, the World Bank sets forth two broad sets of reasons for reducing inequality: to reduce the concentration of economic benefits on elite groups (which can impose high economic and social costs on society) and to allow all people to use their talents and exercise their creativity for the benefit of their families and society.

Education has been identified as a key factor in economic and social development, and the equitable access to education of good quality has become a crucial objective of development policy. Countries with high levels of educational inequality consistently show lower levels of innovation, lower levels of production efficiency, and a tendency to transmit poverty across generations (World Bank 2005). Broader access to education, irrespective of gender, location, ethnicity, or level of income, is most likely to increase innovation and economic growth (Mankiw, Romer, and Weil 1992). Although there is a moral argument for reducing educational inequality, there is an economic argument as well: increased access to education by all helps middle- and lower-income groups realize the full potential of their talent, increasing the level of productivity, innovation, and investment in society and, by inference, increasing the level of welfare of its population (Bourguignon 2006; Bourguignon and Dessus 2007). Although there can be economic growth in the presence of educational inequality, there is compelling evidence showing a close connection between education and productivity and between productivity and income growth (Hanushek and Wößmann 2007; Ravallion 2006; Stevens and Weale 2004).

The reduction of education inequality alone has the potential to produce quick gains in economic and social welfare—if by "equal access to education" one means equal access to the opportunities for learning and not simple equality of access to schooling (Pritchett 2004). Equal access to schooling must be complemented with increases in the quality of education and changes in school governance to address the sustainability of reforms through increased accountability (Arcia and others 2011).

Given this conceptual framework, what is the role of ADePT Edu in fostering educational equity? In a seminal paper on education inequality, Pritchett (2004) argues that many of the international goals in education refer to increases in enrollment and completion, which are merely approximations of competencies and learning achievement. Keeping children in school requires the explicit recognition that there is a demand for education, which does not equate with a demand for schooling. The demand for schooling is based on the information received by households, especially poor households, about the benefits of education, the innate abilities of their children, and the quality of schools. If education providers recognize this demand for education, the pursuit of educational equity requires the constant monitoring of educational indicators and any sources of information that promote accountability for increased learning. Hence, there is an implicit need for information about education inequality in school access and school completion, as well as information about learning outcomes. The information on education inequality presented in this chapter is just the first step in this direction.

Chapter 5: Analyzing Education Inequality with ADePT Edu

Reporting Education Inequality with ADePT Edu

This chapter analyzes education inequality in the following three areas:

- School participation, which is a clear indicator of educational access
- School progression, which tracks a student's timely progress from primary to secondary education
- School attainment, which reports the number of years of formal education attained by youth 15–19.

ADePT Edu addresses the first two issues and is expanding its coverage of the third. ADePT Edu developers are updating the software to allow users to analyze learning outcomes data as well.

ADePT Edu was used to process nearly 200 household surveys from more than 80 countries.[1] The results produced global and regional snapshots of educational inequality, particularly in relation to gender, urban/rural location, and household income. These snapshots identified several broad findings about primary school–age children:

- Almost 20.0 percent of children from the bottom expenditure quintile and just 7.0 percent of children from the top expenditure quintile are out of school.[2] Geography is also an important barrier to educational access: 15.0 percent of rural children are out of school, compared with just 8.5 percent of urban children.
- Net primary attendance rates are 8.7 percentage points higher among children from the top expenditure quintile than they are among children from the bottom quintile. Net rates of attendance are almost 5 percentage points higher in urban than in rural areas. Gender differences are relatively small.
- In general, girls are more likely to drop out than boys, rural children are more likely to drop out than urban students, and children from poorer households are more likely to drop out than children from households that are not as poor.
- Completion rates are higher for boys than for girls, and they are higher for urban than for rural children. However, the largest difference is based on expenditure quintile, with the primary completion rate of students from the bottom quintile 34 percentage points lower than the completion rate of students from the top quintile.[3]

- Average years of schooling follows a similar pattern, with the largest difference caused by income: children from households in the top expenditure quintile have 4.2 years more of schooling, on average, than children from the bottom income quintile.

Global Educational Inequality

The pursuit of educational inequality requires an assessment of its global magnitude and scope to identify the regions of the world where it is most problematic. This is a necessary first step, because resources are limited and some regions will undoubtedly be in greater need of intervention than others.

This section analyzes educational inequality with the aid of the Gini coefficient for educational attainment. Using educational attainment as the main metric for assessing educational inequality is very useful, because the number of years of formal education received is a simple objective metric that can be compared across countries and regions. Relating key socioeconomic variables with the Gini coefficient for educational attainment provides a good assessment of educational inequality on a global scale.

The Gini Coefficient in Education

The Lorenz curve tracks income inequality in a population. It plots the proportion of total income earned by each percentile of the population. Figure 5.1 shows a triangle containing the Lorenz curve, where the triangle's hypotenuse is a 45-degree line representing total equality in the income distribution. At every point along the hypotenuse, the cumulative percentage of total income equals the cumulative percentage of the total population.[4]

The Gini coefficient summarizes the Lorenz curve by estimating the ratio of the area between the Lorenz curve and the 45-degree line (area A in figure 5.1) over the total area of the triangle $A + B$:

$$\text{Gini coefficient} = A/(A + B).$$

The Gini coefficient ranges from 0 (complete equality) to 1 (complete inequality).[5] A low Gini coefficient indicates a more equal distribution than a higher Gini coefficient; a rising Gini coefficient indicates increasing inequality.

Figure 5.1: The Education Lorenz Curve

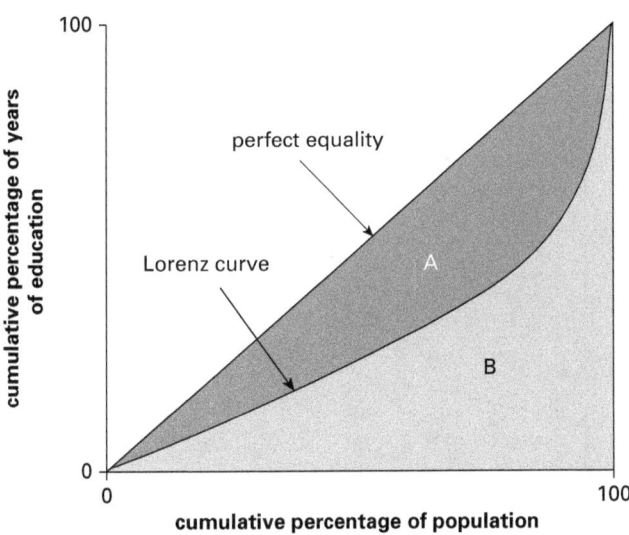

Source: Thomas, Wang, and Fan 2001.

Correlation between Inequality in Income and Inequality in School Attainment

Estimating and plotting the Gini coefficient for income for each of the world's regions in relation to the Gini coefficient for education reveals the relationship between income inequality and educational inequality. The results, shown in figure 5.2, show some consistency across regions: regions—and countries within regions—that have high degrees of income inequality also tend to have higher degrees of educational inequality (these results should be taken with caution because of the low R^2). For example, countries in the Europe and Central Asia region have lower income inequality than other regions; they also have low Gini coefficients of school attainment, indicating low levels of education inequality. In contrast, countries in Sub-Saharan Africa are clustered about Gini values of 0.40–0.50, indicating a high degree of education inequality; these countries also show a high degree of income inequality. Inequality in grade attainment means that children from poorer households tend to have fewer years of formal schooling than children from households that are not as poor. It can be argued that such inequality strongly favors the perpetuation of intergenerational

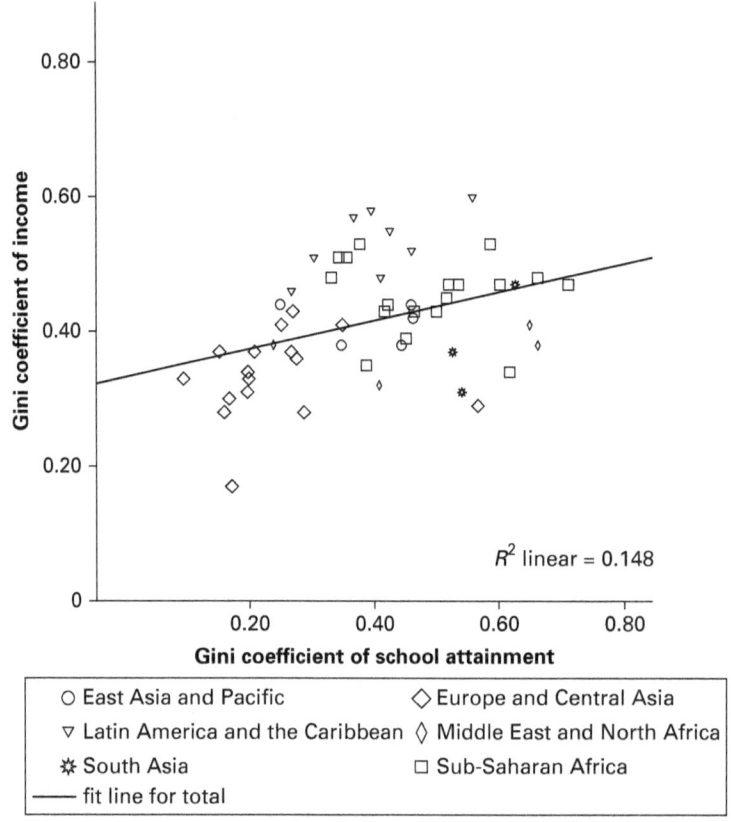

Figure 5.2: Relationship between Gini Coefficient of School Attainment and Gini Coefficient of Income

Source: Estimated by Porta (2011) using data from the Demographic and Health Surveys, Multiple Indicator Cluster Surveys, and Living Standards Measurement Studies for 1985–2007.
Note: Figures are for individuals 15 and older.

poverty in Sub-Saharan Africa, suggesting the need for targeted programs that increase educational attainment among the poor.

Correlation between Inequality in School Attendance and Inequality in School Attainment

Another way to examine educational inequality is to examine the impact of differences in school attendance on educational attainment. Countries with high net attendance ratios also tend to be highly equitable in school

Chapter 5: Analyzing Education Inequality with ADePT Edu

attainment (figure 5.3). Most countries in Sub-Saharan Africa tend to have low net attendance ratios and high degrees of inequality in educational attainment. This correlation suggests that policies aimed at increasing attendance among the poor should be a first step for increasing educational attainment and—more important—reducing school attainment inequality.

Figure 5.3: Relationship between Gini Coefficient of School Attainment and Net Primary School Attendance Ratios

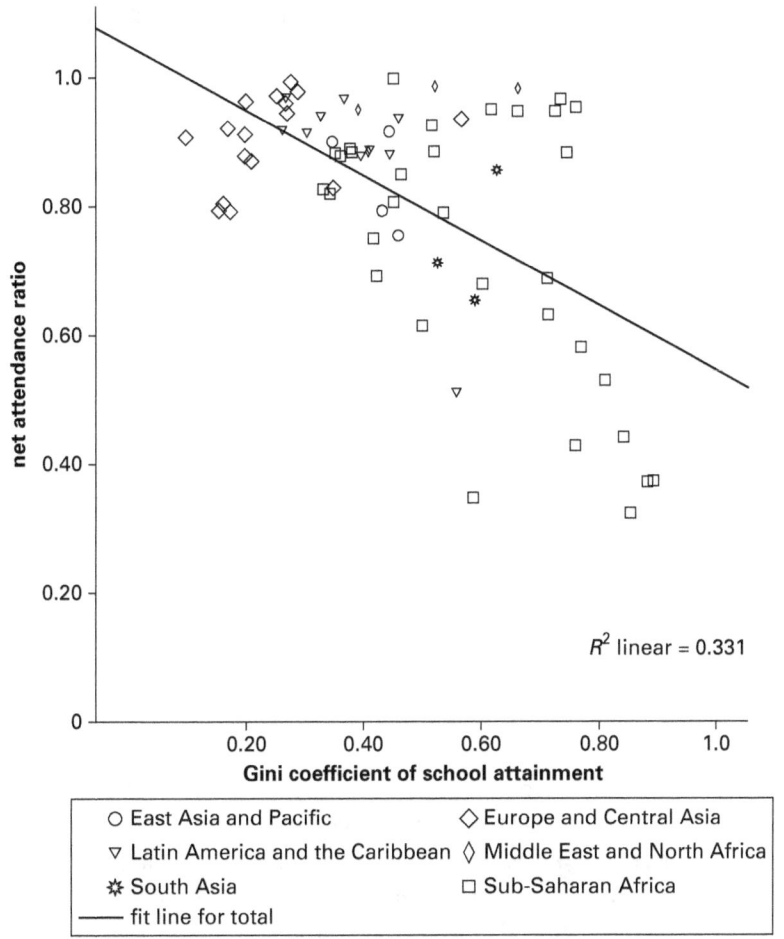

Source: Estimated by Porta (2011) using data from the Demographic and Health Surveys, Multiple Indicator Cluster Surveys, and Living Standards Measurement Studies for 1985–2007.
Note: Figures are for individuals 15 and older.

Correlation between School Completion and Inequality in School Attainment

Inequality in school attainment is also correlated with low rates of primary school completion. Countries with a high degree of inequality in school attainment—as evidenced by the low Gini coefficients of school attainment—also have low rates of primary school completion. Moreover, the trend in figure 5.4 shows that as inequality in school attainment increases, the primary completion rate decreases. The pattern of correlation

Figure 5.4: Relationship between Gini Coefficient of School Attainment and Primary Completion Rate

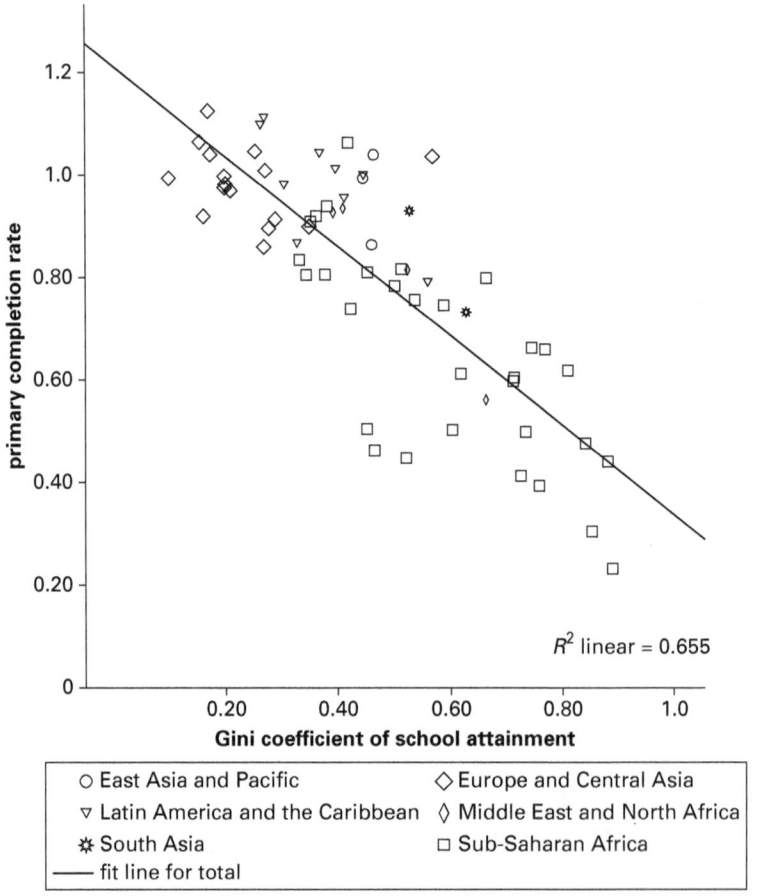

Source: Estimated by Porta (2011) using data from the Demographic and Health Surveys, Multiple Indicator Cluster Surveys, and Living Standards Measurement Studies for 1985–2007.
Note: Figures are for individuals 15 and older.

Chapter 5: Analyzing Education Inequality with ADePT Edu

between these two variables—inequality in school attainment and primary completion rates—is very strong for countries in Sub-Saharan Africa.

Correlation between Extreme Poverty and Inequality in School Attainment

Extreme poverty—represented by people who survive on $1.25 a day—is somewhat associated with inequality in school attainment (figure 5.5), but

Figure 5.5: Relationship between Gini Coefficient of School Attainment and Extreme Poverty

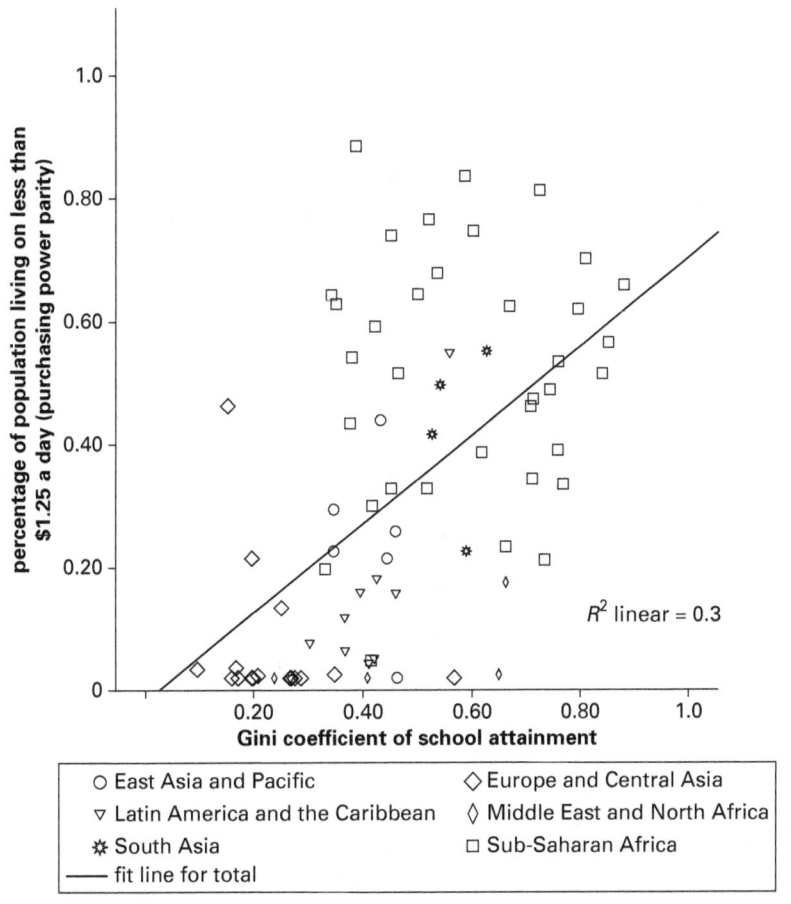

Source: Estimated by Porta (2011) using data from the Demographic and Health Surveys, Multiple Indicator Cluster Surveys, and Living Standards Measurement Studies.
Note: Figures are for individuals 15 and older. Data for poverty headcount are for the most recent year for which data were available between 2000 and 2008.

the variation around the trend line is wide, suggesting that the relationship between extreme poverty and educational inequality should be treated with some caution. Still, the trend suggests that poor countries tend to have greater inequality in school attainment. This finding is important if one has to make the case to policy makers about the design and implementation of targeted educational programs. Most countries showing a relationship between extreme poverty and educational inequality are in Sub-Saharan Africa and South Asia.

Several trends are apparent from the evidence on global education inequality:

- Regions and countries with high degrees of income inequality tend to have high degrees of educational inequality.
- Regions and countries with low net attendance ratios in primary school tend to have high degrees of educational inequality.
- Regions and countries with low rates of primary school completion tend to have high degrees of educational inequality.
- Extreme poverty and educational inequality are positively correlated in Sub-Saharan Africa and South Asia.

How Has Inequality in Educational Attainment Changed over Time?

ADePT Edu provides access to household surveys conducted since 1985. It thus allows trends over more than 30 years to be analyzed.

Education inequality can be analyzed by examining disparities in the incidence of key educational indicators between males and females, rural and urban residents, and people from the highest and lowest income quintiles. The figures in this section calculate the disparities in the incidence of indicators as follows:

- Value for males and value for females
- Value for urban residents and value for rural residents
- Value in top quintile of household expenditures per capita and value in lowest quintile of household expenditures per capita.

A negative result for gender in a figure indicates that the value for females is larger than the value for males. A negative result for location

Chapter 5: Analyzing Education Inequality with ADePT Edu

indicates that the value for rural residents is larger than the value for urban residents; a negative value for income means that the value for households from the bottom quintile of per capita expenditures is larger than the value for families in the top quintile of capital expenditures.

Examination of household survey data on people 26–29 years old, between 1985 and 2007, suggests that household income, household location, and gender are consistently associated with levels of school attainment as well as educational inequality (figure 5.6). Worldwide, for example, people from the top expenditure quintile have about 4.0 more years of formal education than people from the bottom quintile; people from rural areas have about 2.0 years less formal education than people from urban areas, and men have about 0.5 year more education than women. Between 1985 and 2007 there was a reduction of about 0.5 year in the difference in school attainment between people from the top and bottom expenditure quintiles. At this pace, it would take more than 100 years to achieve educational equality by income level.[6]

The difference in educational attainment in urban and rural areas also narrowed only slightly during this 22-year period. People from urban areas are likely to have 2.0 more years of education than their rural counterparts, down from 2.5 in 1985. Urban-rural differences in attainment decreased at

Figure 5.6: Sources of Global Disparity in Educational Attainment among the 26–29 Cohort, 1985–2007

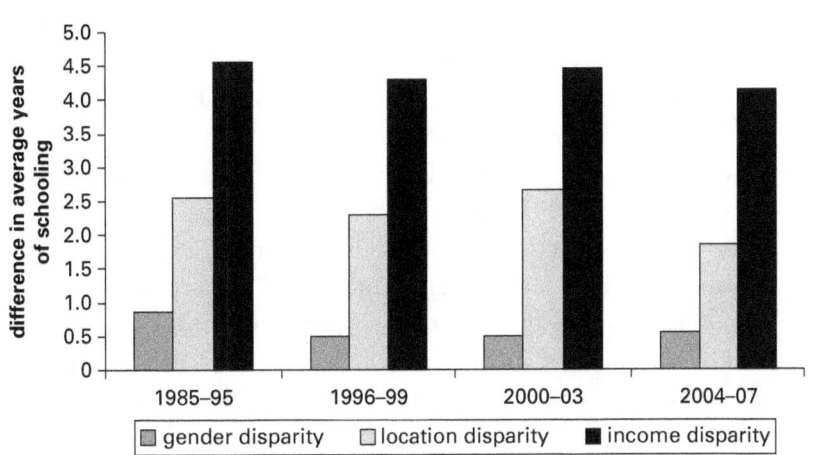

Source: Estimated by Porta (2011) using data from the Demographic and Health Surveys, Multiple Indicator Cluster Surveys, and Living Standards Measurement Studies for 1985–2007.

a faster rate than did differences in income, suggesting that efforts at increasing education access in rural areas have borne some success. Nevertheless, it would take more than 100 years to achieve location parity. As for gender-related disparities, the 0.5-year difference in educational attainment between men and women remained stagnant between 1985 and 2007.

This analysis refers to adults 26–29—people who most likely did not participate in the expansion of coverage resulting from global initiatives such as Education for All or the Millennium Development Goals. If global educational equity is examined for a younger cohort, the results are somewhat better, but they, too, indicate the need to implement the same policies to address inequality.

Educational Inequality and Internal Efficiency in the Education Sector

The examination of educational inequality through the Gini coefficient can be complemented with information on disparities in indicators of educational efficiency between boys and girls, urban and rural populations, and between nonpoor and poor households.

Analysis of some key indicators of internal efficiency from about 50 countries reveals several findings (figure 5.7):

- Net intake rates for the first grade of primary school are similar, regardless of gender, location, or household expenditures.
- Net attendance rates for primary school are affected by income and location. Net attendance rates of students from households in the top income quintile are about 10 percentage points higher than those of children from households in the bottom quintile. Urban children have net attendance rates that are about 5 percentage points higher than those of rural students.
- Net secondary attendance rates show even more marked income and location disparities. Attendance rates are 15 percentage points higher for urban dwellers than for rural dwellers, and children from households in the highest income quintile have rates of attendance that are 29 percentage points higher than children from households in the bottom quintile.
- Net attendance rates for postsecondary school show similar patterns: urban dwellers and children from higher-income households have

Chapter 5: Analyzing Education Inequality with ADePT Edu

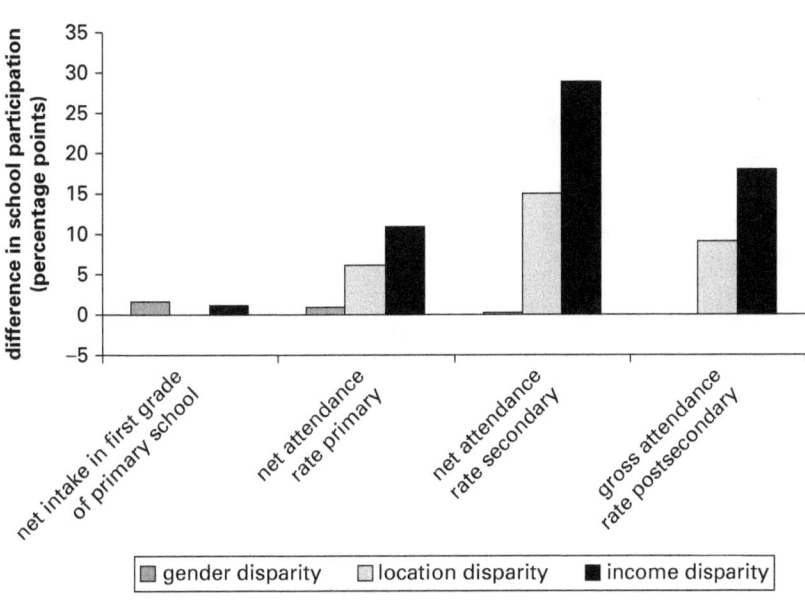

Figure 5.7: Sources of Global Disparity in School Participation among the 15–19 Cohort, by Education Level

Source: Estimated by Porta (2011) using data from the Demographic and Health Surveys, Multiple Indicator Cluster Surveys, and Living Standards Measurement Studies for 1985–2007.

much higher rates of attendance than rural dwellers and children from poorer households.
- Men and women have equal access to education at the postsecondary level.

Disparity in School Participation

In analyzing out-of-school children, it is very important to distinguish three main subcategories: children who enter school but later drop out, children who are not currently in school but are expected eventually to enroll (late entry), and children who have never been in school (figure 5.8).[7]

Children from higher-income households have higher dropout rates than children from lower-income households; these children are also more likely to enter school late.[8] For children who have never been to school, the trend is reversed: the proportion of children who have never been to school is

Figure 5.8: Sources of Global Disparity among Out-of-School Children

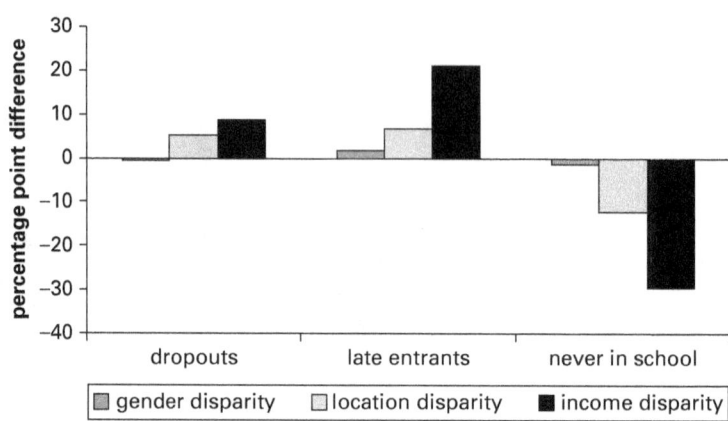

Source: Estimated by Porta (2011) using data from the Demographic and Health Surveys, Multiple Indicator Cluster Surveys, and Living Standards Measurement Studies, latest year available per country 1985–2007.

30 percentage points higher among children from households in the bottom quintile than it is among children from the top quintile.

Disparity in School Progression

Access to school is only part of the educational inequality picture. Educational inequality is drastically reduced if most—if not all—children progress from primary to secondary education. In the most advanced countries, the rate of transition from primary to secondary education approaches 100 percent.

Disparity in the primary to secondary education transition rate fosters income inequality, because there is a direct link between salaries and school attainment. Students who finish high school generally command higher salaries than those who finish only primary school (Psacharopoulos and Patrinos 2002).

Figure 5.9 shows primary and secondary completion rates for the 15–19 cohort, as well as the transition rate from primary to secondary. The inequalities in primary completion rates are glaring. Completion rates of children from families in the top quintile are 35 percentage points higher than those of children from the lowest quintile. The primary

Figure 5.9: Sources of Global Disparity in School Progression among the 15–19 Cohort

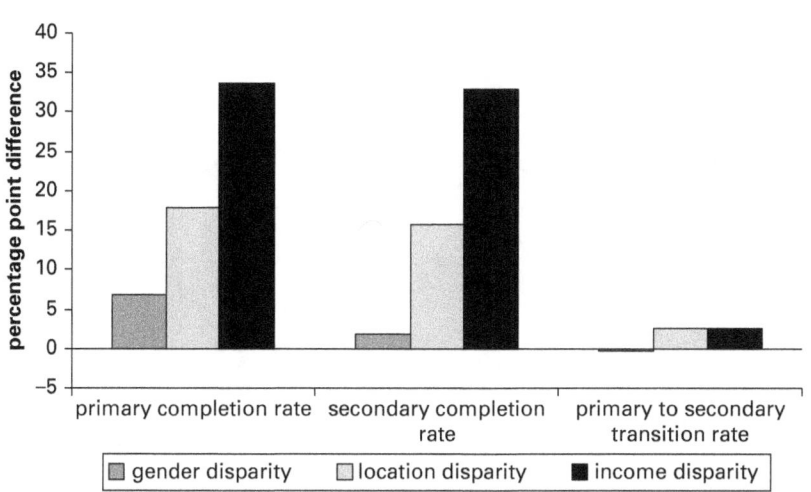

Source: Estimated by Porta (2011) using data from the Demographic and Health Surveys, Multiple Indicator Cluster Surveys, and Living Standards Measurement Studies for 1985–2007.

school completion rate is 18 percentage points higher in urban areas than in rural areas. It is about 7 percentage points higher for boys than for girls.

Differences in the transition rate to secondary school are negligible. This is an extremely interesting finding because it suggests that inequality in the completion of primary or secondary school is more closely related to inequality among students who do not drop out during primary or secondary school than it is to inequality in the transition from primary to secondary. As secondary enrollment rates in most developing countries are significantly lower than primary rates, these results suggest that policies and programs oriented toward inequality in completion rates should pay attention to income and location differences, as the problem with secondary enrollment is unrelated to inequalities in the transition rates.

Disparity in the Number of Years of Schooling

School attainment—defined as the total number of years of formal schooling received by a person—is a powerful indicator of educational access. Differences in school attainment across groups in a society are a powerful indicator of educational inequality.

Figure 5.10: Sources of Global Disparity in School Attainment among the 15–19 Cohort

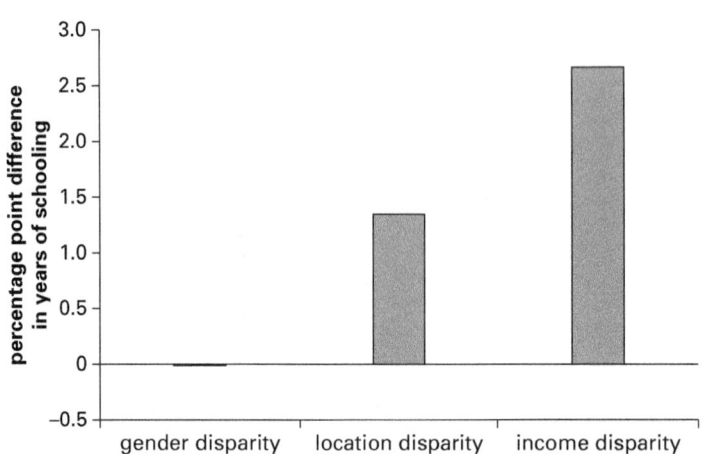

Source: Estimated by Porta (2011) using data from the Demographic and Health Surveys, Multiple Indicator Cluster Surveys, and Living Standards Measurement Studies for 1985–2007.

Figure 5.10 shows the disparities in school attainment between boys and girls, urban and rural dwellers, and children from the top and bottom income quintiles. The results show the following:

- Gender differences do not exist for the sample of 50 countries as a whole.[9]
- Urban dwellers have 1.5 more years of schooling, on average, than do rural dwellers.
- People from the top income quintile have 2.6 more years of schooling, on average, than do people from the bottom income quintile.

Educational Inequality across Regions

This section examines the association between education inequality and gender, location, and income across regions. The regional trends are supplemented with examples from individual countries, to illustrate the relevance of inequality to specific educational policies and programs.

Chapter 5: Analyzing Education Inequality with ADePT Edu

Regional Disparity in School Participation

Participation in the educational system is a clear indicator of educational access. School participation by children at an appropriate age reflects a country's commitment to the internal efficiency of the educational system; the reasons for not attending school shed light on a country's efforts to provide an adequate number of teachers and facilities at a reasonable distance from students' homes. School participation rates capture children who are not in school, a reverse indicator of school participation that can be extremely useful for identifying policy interventions. The net attendance ratio provides a strong signal about a country's commitment to ensure educational access to everyone, because it measures the proportion of school-age children actually attending school. In the case of postsecondary education, where age is not as constraining as it is at the primary or secondary level, the gross attendance ratio is used in the analysis.

Primary School Attendance

Figure 5.11 shows disparities in net primary attendance rates across regions by gender, location, and income. The largest disparities are in South Asia and Sub-Saharan Africa, where the net attendance rate among the poorest households is almost 20 percentage points lower than the attendance rate among the least poor households. The net attendance rate among urban students is 12 percentage points higher than among rural students in Sub-Saharan Africa and 5 percentage points higher in South Asia. Disparity in other regions in the world are small.

The disparities in Sub-Saharan Africa hide wide disparities across countries. In Benin, for example, inequalities are wider than the average for the region (figure 5.12). School participation is slightly unequal, with boys, urban dwellers, and children from higher-income households more likely to attend school. The net attendance rate among rural children (57.8 percent) is 15.8 percentage points lower than participation among urban children (73.6 percent). This large difference indicates the need to broaden rural education coverage. Income-related differences are also large: the net attendance rate among children from the top income quintile (82.3 percent) is 40.4 percentage points higher than participation among children from the bottom quintile (41.9 percent). A similar pattern is observed for secondary and postsecondary education. The example of Benin shows that although

Assessing Sector Performance and Inequality in Education

Figure 5.11: Sources of Global Disparity in Net Primary Attendance Rates, by Region

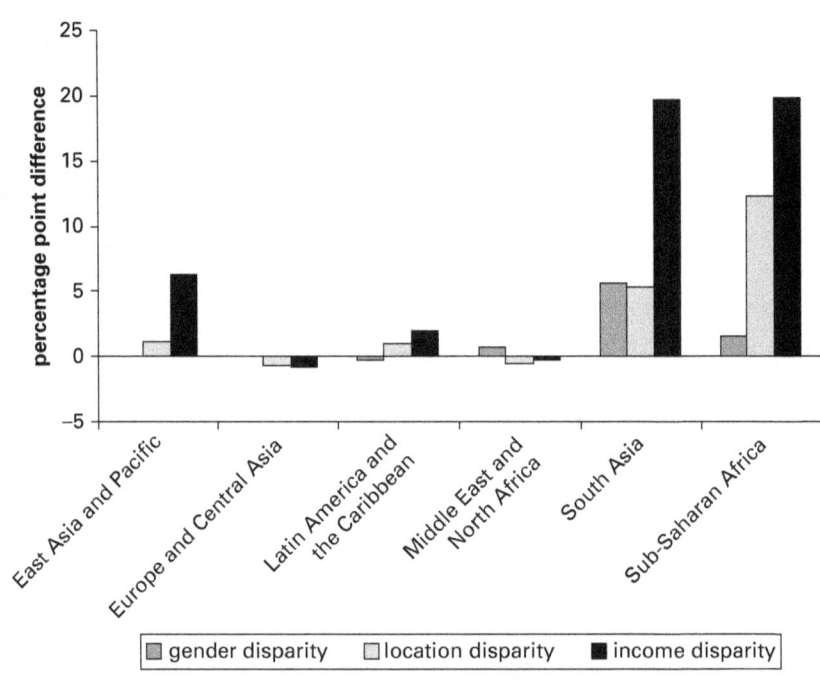

Source: Estimated by Porta (2011) using data from the Demographic and Health Surveys, Multiple Indicator Cluster Surveys, and Living Standards Measurement Studies for 1985–2007.

Figure 5.12: Net Primary Attendance Ratios in Benin, 2006

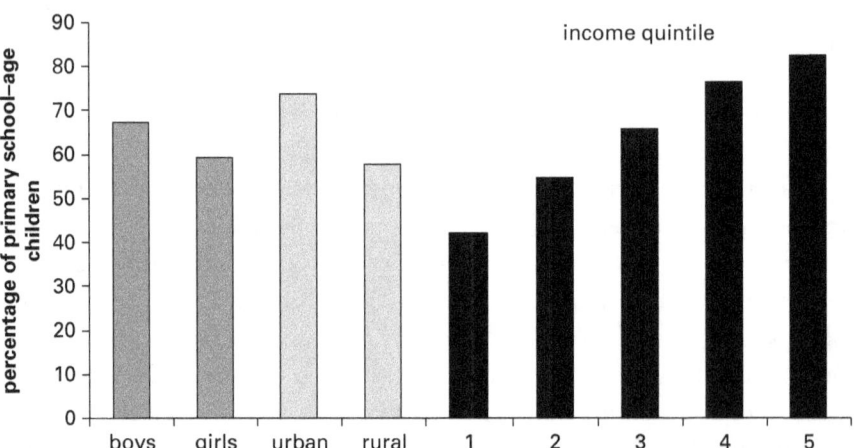

Source: Estimated by Porta (2011) using data from the Benin Demographic and Health Survey 2006 (INSAE and Macro International 2007).

Chapter 5: Analyzing Education Inequality with ADePT Edu

gender and location disparities may seem small at the regional level, they may be large at the country level.

Secondary School Attendance

Net attendance rates for secondary school are very important in low- and middle-income countries, many of which have moved toward universal primary education but lack the resources to accommodate vast numbers of students in secondary education. Analysis of the net attendance rate in secondary education may yield insight into the progress of educational inequality in the process of expanding access to secondary education.

At the secondary level, gender is a significant source of disparity only in South Asia, where more boys attend school than girls (figure 5.13). (In Latin America and the Caribbean, more girls attend secondary school

Figure 5.13: Sources of Disparity in Net Secondary Attendance Rates, by Region

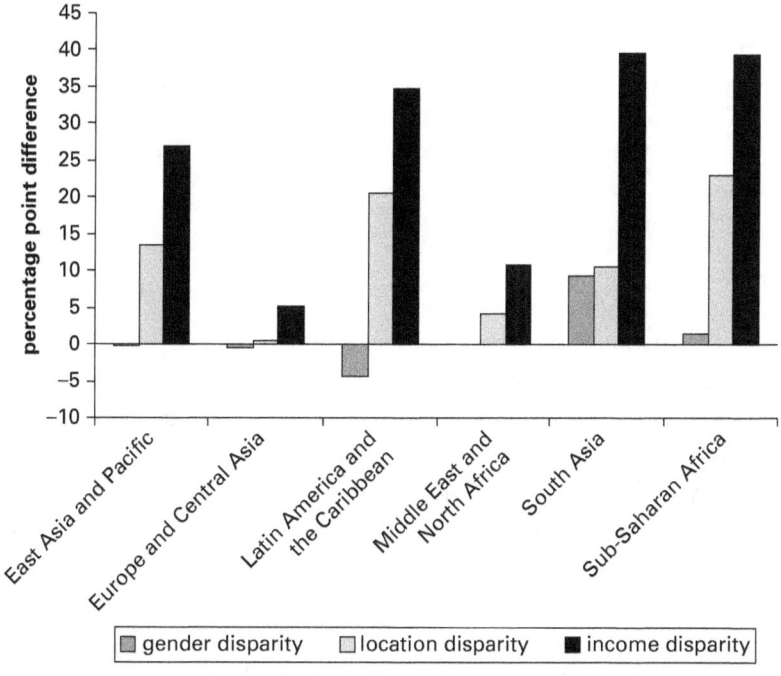

Source: Estimated by Porta (2011) using data from the Demographic and Health Surveys, Multiple Indicator Cluster Surveys, and Living Standards Measurement Studies for 1985–2007.

159

Assessing Sector Performance and Inequality in Education

than boys.) Urban students have much higher net secondary attendance rates than rural students. This finding is not surprising given that countries face significant difficulties serving rural students of secondary age because of the lack of population density and because of economies of scales in school infrastructure and the higher costs of transportation and lodging. In addition, poverty tends to be higher in rural areas, forcing youth to enter the labor market.

The largest disparities in net secondary attendance rate are associated with income. Children from households in the lowest income quintile have net attendance rates that are 27 percentage points lower than students from households in the top income quintile in East Asia and Pacific, about 35 percentage points lower in Latin America and the Caribbean, and nearly 40 percentage points lower in South Asia and Sub-Saharan Africa.

Postsecondary Attendance

More girls than boys attend postsecondary education in East Asia and Pacific, Europe and Central Asia, and Latin America and the Caribbean (figure 5.14).[10] In the Middle East and North Africa, South Asia, and Sub-Saharan Africa, more boys than girls attend postsecondary education. Urban students have gross attendance rates for postsecondary that are about 10–15 percentage points higher than those of rural students in all regions except Sub-Saharan Africa, where the disparity is about 5 percentage points.

Net Primary Intake Rate

Educational inequality in school progression can be analyzed by observing differences in the net intake rate, defined as the proportion of children of official age for entry into the first grade that enter first grade on time. Generally, poorer children and children in rural areas enter school at a later age than children who are less poor and children in urban areas. Such a discrepancy reflects lower access to school—school is often too distant for young children in rural areas—as well as inadequate preschool coverage in poorer areas. Both factors result in lower educational opportunities for a large number of children.

Figure 5.15 shows the disparities in the net intake rate in the first grade of primary school. Gender disparities are relatively small across all regions. As

Figure 5.14: Sources of Disparity in Gross Postsecondary Attendance Rates, by Region

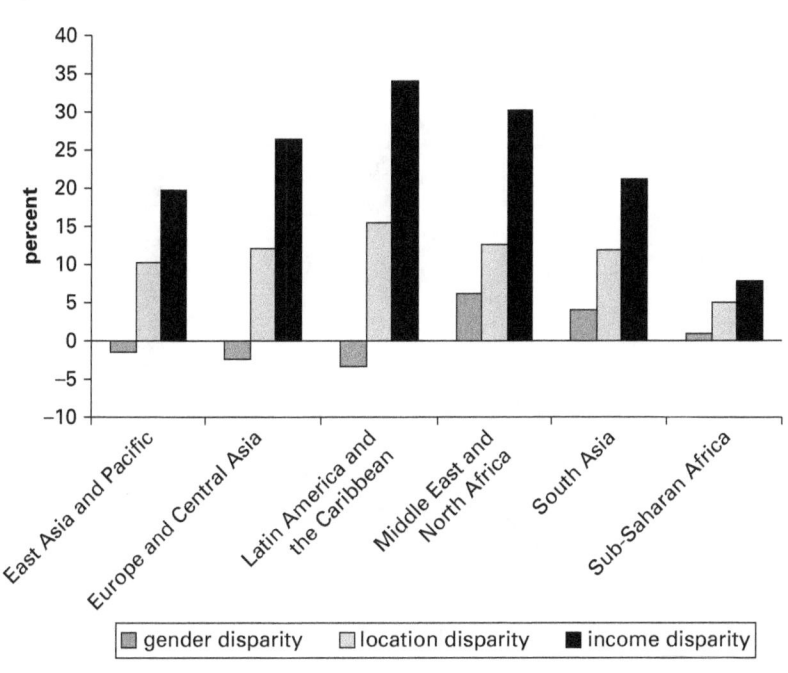

Source: Estimated by Porta (2011) using data from the Demographic and Health Surveys, Multiple Indicator Cluster Surveys, and Living Standards Measurement Studies for 1985–2007.

net intake rates are generally in the 30–40 percent range for most developing countries, a 5 percentage point difference between two groups is significant, albeit not overly large. There is no obvious pattern in urban-rural intake: in East Asia and Pacific, the Middle East and North Africa, and Sub-Saharan Africa, the net intake rate favors boys over girls, but the percentage point difference between the two is modest (less than 5 points in the worst case). In Europe and Central Asia and in Latin America and the Caribbean, the net intake rate for the first grade favors girls over boys by a very small margin. In South Asia the net intake rate is higher in rural areas and among students from lower-income households, but these results should be interpreted with caution, as they are based on data from just two countries.

Out-of-School Children

Another aspect of education inequality relates to children of school age who are not in school. ADePT Edu classifies these children into three

Assessing Sector Performance and Inequality in Education

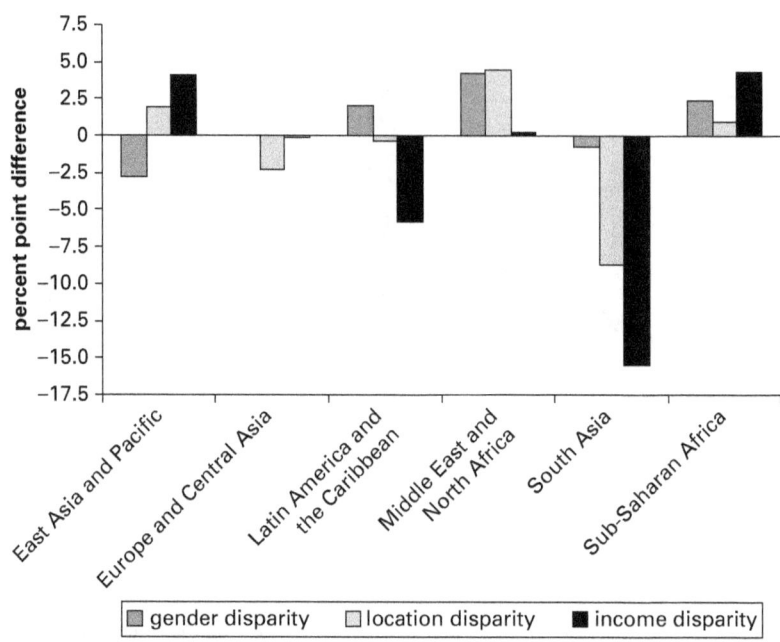

Figure 5.15: Sources of Disparity in Net Intake Rate for First Grade of Primary School, by Region

Source: Estimated by Porta (2011) using data from the Demographic and Health Surveys, Multiple Indicator Cluster Surveys, and Living Standards Measurement Studies for 1985–2007.

categories: children who have never been to school; children who are not yet in school because they are late for entry for any reason, such as sickness or a family situation; and children who are no longer in school because they dropped out. The implications for policy and inequality are different for each of these reasons. For children who have never been to school or who are late for entry, the policy prescriptions may include reducing the distance to school by building more schools, increasing preschool coverage to encourage households to enter children into the system, and ensuring that schools are safe. As Pritchett (2004) notes, however, the reason for never having been to school usually has little to do with the supply of schools. Policies oriented toward reducing the dropout rate may include ensuring that teachers show up to teach, preventing disillusionment among students, and reexamining the education curriculum for relevance.

At the regional level, disparities in the percentage of out-of-school children are explained largely by differences in income (figure 5.16). In general, lower rates of out-of-school children are observed for boys,

Chapter 5: Analyzing Education Inequality with ADePT Edu

Figure 5.16: Sources of Disparity in Children Out of Primary School, by Region

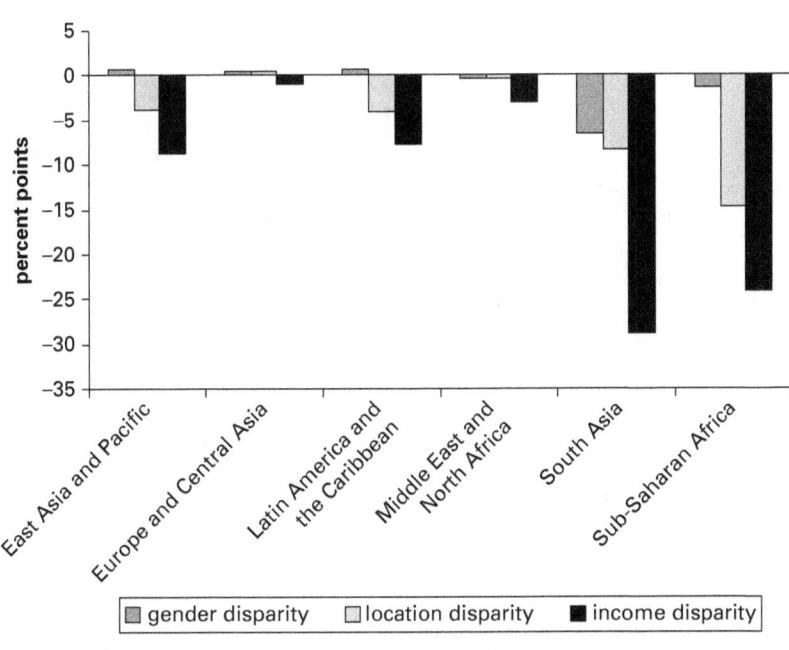

Source: Estimated by Porta (2011) using data from the Demographic and Health Surveys, Multiple Indicator Cluster Surveys, and Living Standards Measurement Studies for 1985–2007.

urban areas, and higher-income households. The largest disparity is in South Asia, where the proportion of out-of-school children is 5.7 percent in the top income quintile and 34.6 percent in the bottom quintile, a difference of 28 percentage points. This difference is also large in Sub-Saharan Africa (24 percentage points). Income also affects the percentage of children out of school in other regions, but the differential is much smaller.

The association between low income and lower access to education is reinforced by the regional data on dropouts. In Latin America and the Caribbean, the Middle East and North Africa, and South Asia, the dropout rate in the bottom income expenditure quintile is 15 percentage points higher than the rate in the top quintile (figure 5.17). In contrast, in Europe and Central Asia the dropout rate is higher among children from higher-income households.

Differences in income also explain most of the regional disparities in the proportion of out-of-school children who are expected to enter school at a

Figure 5.17: Sources of Disparity in Dropout Rates, by Region

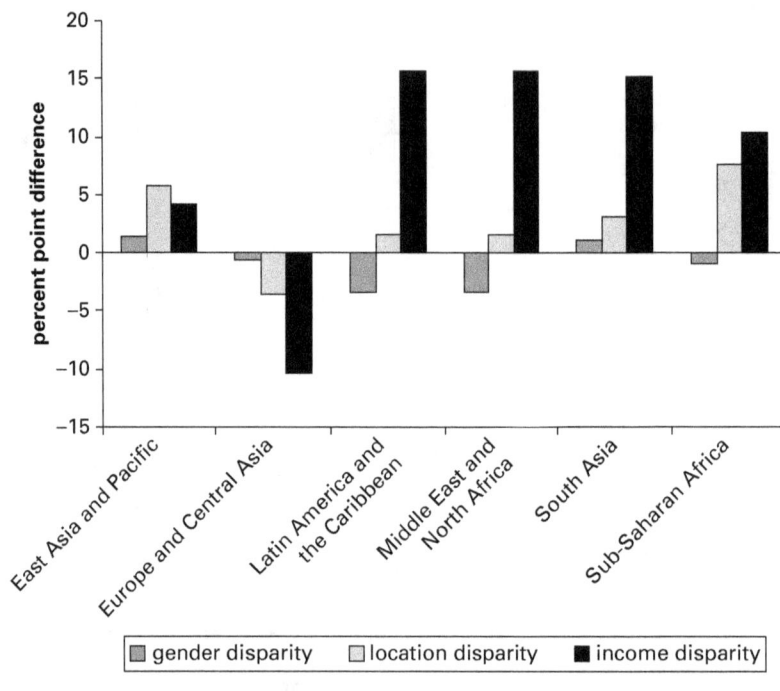

Source: Estimated by Porta (2011) using data from the Demographic and Health Surveys, Multiple Indicator Cluster Surveys, and Living Standards Measurement Studies for 1985–2007.

later age (figure 5.18). Across all six regions, poorer children enter school at a later age than children from less poor households, with that difference ranging from 15 to 25 percentage points. In Europe and Central Asia, and to a lesser extent Sub-Saharan Africa, late entry is also more prevalent among rural children.

Across regions, the percentage of children who are classified as never in school is much higher among children from the bottom income quintile, with differences of 15–30 percentage points (figure 5.19).

Regional Disparity in School Progression

This section describes regional disparities in school completion, the transition from primary to secondary levels, and school attainment. These disparities reflect the need to address education inequality in Sub-Saharan Africa

Figure 5.18: Sources of Disparity in Late Entry among Out-of-School Children, by Region

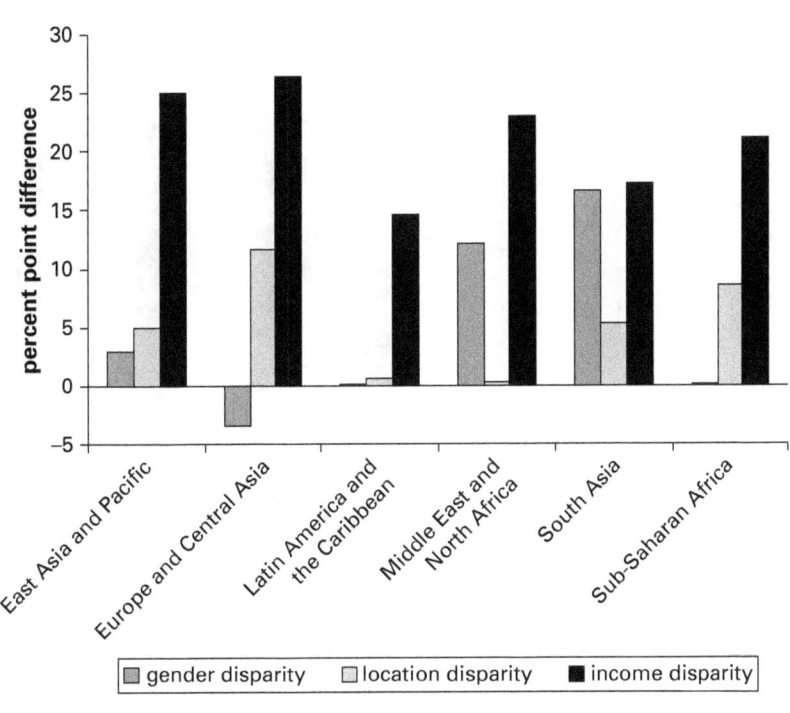

Source: Estimated by Porta (2011) using data from the Demographic and Health Surveys, Multiple Indicator Cluster Surveys, and Living Standards Measurement Studies for 1985–2007.

and South Asia, where some of these disparities are larger than they are in other regions.

Primary Completion Rates

Income disparity has a large impact on primary completion rates in all regions except Europe and Central Asia (figure 5.20). In Sub-Saharan Africa, the primary completion rate for students from the top expenditure quintile is 55 percentage points higher than the rate for students from the bottom quintile. In all regions except the Middle East and North Africa and Europe and Central Asia, the difference in primary completion rates between children from the top and bottom expenditure quintiles is more than 30 percentage points. Across regions differentials in income are the most important source of disparities in primary completion rates.

Assessing Sector Performance and Inequality in Education

Figure 5.19: Sources of Disparity among Out-of-School Children Who Never Attended School, by Region

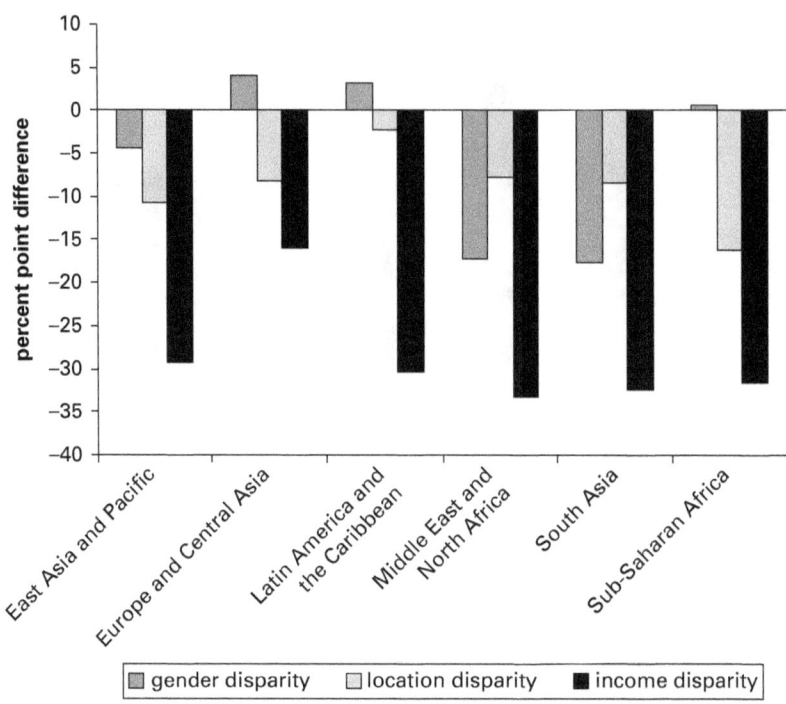

Source: Estimated by Porta (2011) using data from the Demographic and Health Surveys, Multiple Indicator Cluster Surveys, and Living Standards Measurement Studies for 1985–2007.

Secondary Completion Rates

The regional evidence shows a similar pattern at the secondary level, but the disparities are larger, because secondary enrollment is almost always lower among poorer children, who often need to enter the labor force to help their households (figure 5.21). The impact of income is substantially higher in Latin America and the Caribbean, South Asia, and Sub-Saharan Africa than in other regions. Also important in these regions are disparities between urban and rural children. All three regions need to be more active in targeting programs and policies for improving access to secondary education by the poor.

Data on completion rates indicate that the effect of income on school entry is much greater at the secondary than the primary level (figure 5.22). In India the proportion of children who complete secondary school is about

Figure 5.20: Sources of Disparity in Primary Completion Rates, by Region

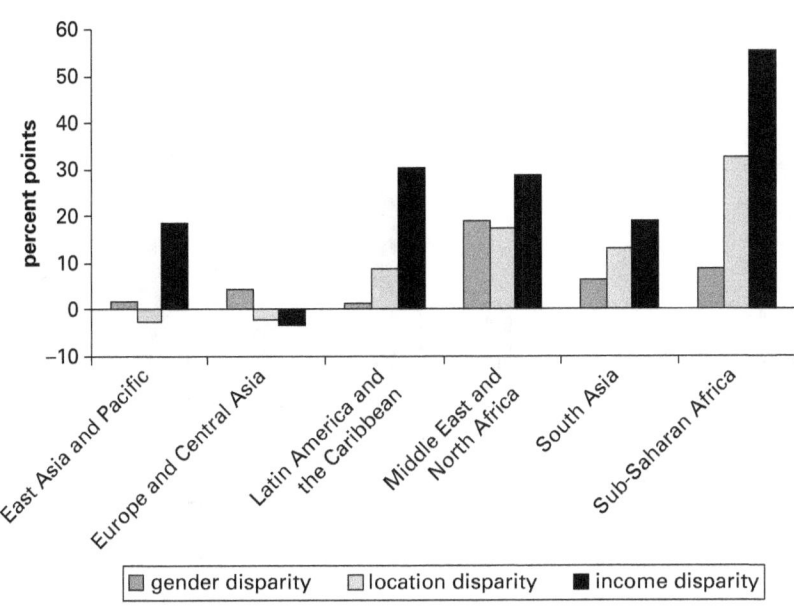

Source: Estimated by Porta (2011) using data from the Demographic and Health Surveys, Multiple Indicator Cluster Surveys, and Living Standards Measurement Studies for 1985–2007.

10 percent in the bottom quintile and about 65 percent in the top quintile. The relationship between secondary completion rate and income is positive: as income increases, the completion rate increases as well. This pattern suggests the need to target programs for the poor and to develop sliding formulas to take into account the positive relationship between income and access to secondary education.

Primary to Secondary Transition Rate

Income is a major source of inequality in the transition to secondary school in Latin America and the Caribbean, the Middle East and North Africa, and South Asia. In the Middle East and North Africa and Sub-Saharan Africa, rural areas are at a significant disadvantage relative to urban areas (figure 5.23)

Regional Disparity in School Attainment

Educational inequality is also reflected in the number of years of formal education attained by 15- to 19-year-olds. Income differentials have the

Assessing Sector Performance and Inequality in Education

Figure 5.21: Sources of Disparity in Secondary Completion Rates, by Region

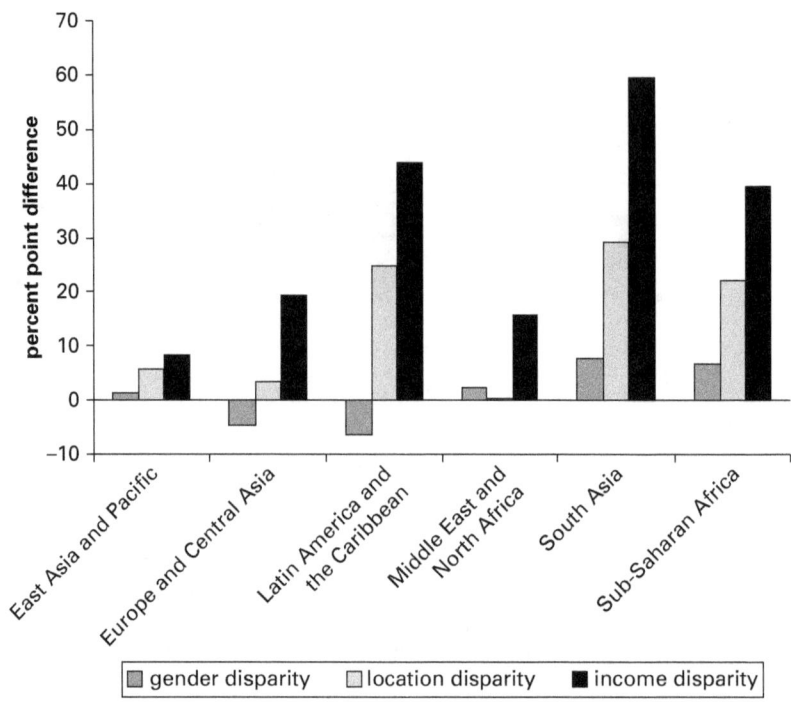

Source: Estimated by Porta (2011) using data from the Demographic and Health Surveys, Multiple Indicator Cluster Surveys, and Living Standards Measurement Studies for 1985–2007.

Figure 5.22: Primary and Secondary Completion Rates in India, 2005

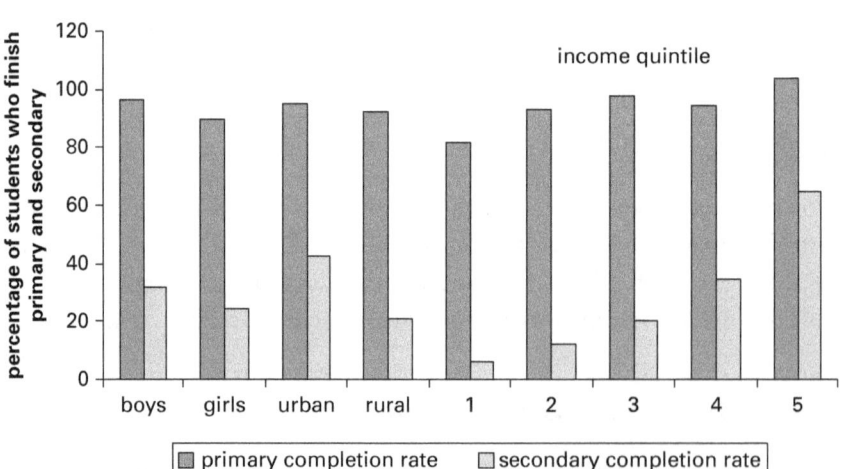

Source: Estimated by Porta (2011) using data from the 2005 Demographic and Health Survey of India (IIPS 2007).

Chapter 5: Analyzing Education Inequality with ADePT Edu

Figure 5.23: Sources of Disparity in Primary to Secondary Transition Rates, by Region

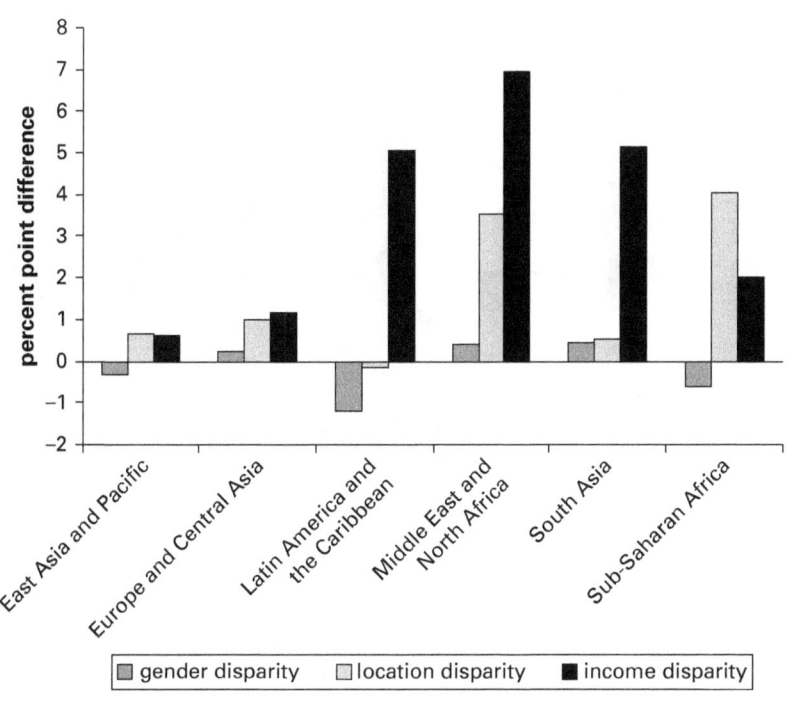

Source: Estimated by Porta (2011) using data from the Demographic and Health Surveys, Multiple Indicator Cluster Surveys, and Living Standards Measurement Studies for 1985–2007.

greatest impact on the average total years of schooling of people 15–19 (figure 5.24). Urban residents have more education than rural residents in all regions except Europe and Central Asia, but the difference attributed to location is only about one year of schooling. Gender is not a significant source of disparity (although regional averages may hide significant intraregional variations). The strong impact of poverty on years of schooling across all regions calls for policy interventions aimed at overcoming the income barrier and increasing educational access to and attainment by the poor.

Analyzing the number of years of education among people 25–45 is a good way to assess education inequality. People in this age range are most likely finished with their formal education and are most likely to be in the labor market. Assessing their total years of education is thus a good way to capture the effect of inequality. Figure 5.25 shows the Gini coefficient for school attainment by region. It shows that Europe and Central Asia is the

Figure 5.24: Sources of Disparity in Total Years of Schooling, by Region

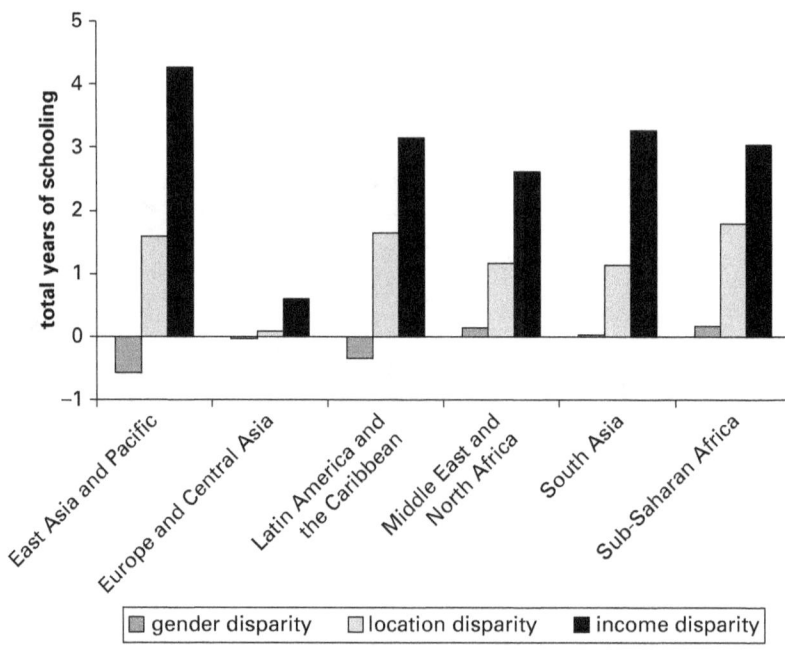

Source: Estimated by Porta (2011) using data from the Demographic and Health Surveys, Multiple Indicator Cluster Surveys, and Living Standards Measurement Studies for 1985–2007.

Figure 5.25: Gini Coefficient of School Attainment, by Region

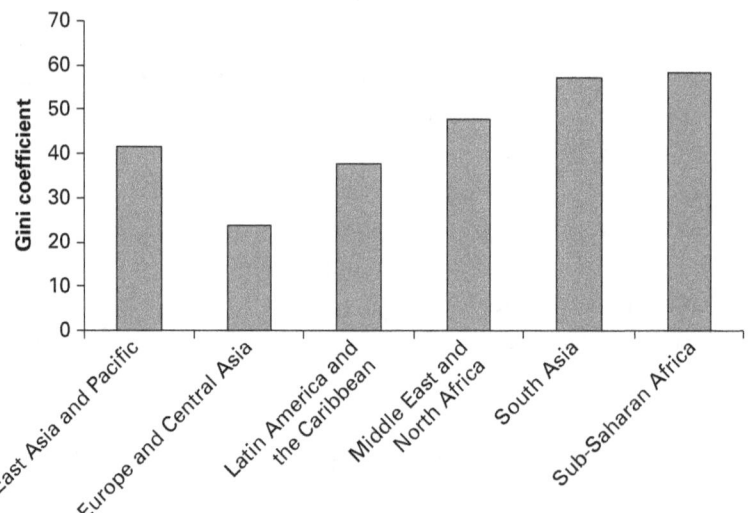

Source: Estimated by Porta (2011) using data from the Demographic and Health Surveys, Multiple Indicator Cluster Surveys, and Living Standards Measurement Studies for 1985–2007.

most equitable region, followed by Latin America and the Caribbean, East Asia and Pacific, the Middle East and North Africa, South Asia, and Sub-Saharan Africa.

Concluding Comments

Analysis using ADePT Edu reveals the relationships between inequality in education on the one hand and income, location, and gender on the other. It shows that gender differences are modest in most countries for most indicators. In countries where gender disparities are still large and favor boys, policies must be implemented to increase girls' access to learning; policies should also be in place to ensure equality in countries where boys are being left behind.

Across regions, households from the top expenditure quintile have much better educational indicators than households from the bottom expenditure quintile. Poverty, the data clearly suggest, is a significant barrier to educational equality in most countries in the ADePT Edu database.

Urban-rural disparities are larger in Sub-Saharan Africa and smaller in Europe and Central Asia than in the rest of the world. However, policies that favor access in rural areas may not be appropriate, for several reasons. First, a dichotomous variable such as urban/rural may hide continuities in urbanization that may render comparisons by location uninformative for policy. Second, access to education does not mean access to school infrastructure but rather access to quality education. Taken together the distinction in urban-rural inequalities should serve as a baseline for further analysis to study hidden variations and identify the critical points.

The main findings on inequality and school participation, school progression, and school attainment can be summarized as follows:

- Net intake rates for the first grade of primary school are fairly equal across income levels, location, and gender.
- Net attendance rates for primary school are affected by income and location. Children from households in the highest expenditure quintile have net attendance rates that are about 10 percentage points higher than those of children from the lowest expenditure quintile. Urban children have net attendance rates that are about 5 percentage points higher than those of rural children.

- Secondary attendance rates are 15 percentage points higher in urban areas than in rural areas. Children from households in the highest expenditure quintile have rates of attendance that are 29 percentage points higher than those of children from the lowest expenditure quintile.
- Gender differences are very low, but the evidence may need to be fleshed out, as between-country variations may cancel out at the regional level. In some countries girls are ahead of boys; in other countries boys are ahead of girls. In both cases education policy should take corrective action.

The main findings on school progression can be summarized as follows:

- 99.0 percent of children from the top expenditure quintile and just 65.3 percent from the bottom quintile complete primary school, a difference of about 34 percentage points.
- 94.1 percent of urban children and 76.2 percent of rural children finish primary school, a difference of about 18 percentage points.
- 85.6 percent of boys and 78.8 percent of girls complete primary school, a difference of 7 percentage points.
- The transition from primary to secondary school is about the same regardless of income, gender, or location. This is an extremely interesting finding because it suggests that inequality in the completion of primary or secondary school is more related to inequality among children *within* primary and *within* secondary school, than to inequality reflected in the dropouts, that is, during the transition from primary to secondary school.

The main findings on school attainment can be summarized as follows:

- For the world as a whole, people in the highest expenditure quintile have about four more years of formal education than do people in the lowest expenditure quintile. Urban residents have about two years' more formal education than do rural residents, and men have about half a year more education than do women.
- Regions and countries with high degrees of income inequality tend to have high levels of educational inequality.
- Regions and countries with low net attendance ratios in primary school tend to have high levels of educational inequality.

- Regions and countries with low rates of primary school completion tend to have high levels of educational inequality.

The ADePT Edu results can be treated as benchmarks for education indicators and educational inequality. Their consistency with international indicators and their systematic approach to data presentation make them useful tools for tracking performance in the education sector.

Notes

1. The household survey profiles analyzed in this chapter were produced by Emilio Porta (2011). This dataset is available as an EdStat data query.
2. Household surveys generally use expenditures as a proxy for income. To facilitate reading, the term *income* is used interchangeably with *household expenditures per capita* throughout the chapter. The percentage point difference between the top and bottom expenditure quintiles is referred to as *income disparity* throughout the rest of this chapter.
3. In comparing the differentials associated with income with the differentials associated with dichotomous variables such as urban/rural, one has to be careful about interpreting the results. As Luis Crouch noted in his review of an earlier draft of this chapter, urban/rural is a dichotomous variable, whereas income is a continuous variable. Comparing the top and bottom income quintiles is equivalent to comparing extremes in a continuous variable, which tends to exaggerate the impact of income as opposed to location. It may be, for example, that if one defined the 40th income percentile as nonpoor and all households below it as poor, the difference attributed to income would not be as large as in the case in which the nonpoor are defined as households in the top 2 percent of income. If urban/rural locations were continuous—expressed in distance to the center of town, for example—and households were divided into quintiles, differences between urban and rural locations would be larger.
4. For education the Lorenz curve is applied to the population 25–45, under the assumption that most people in this age group are in the labor force and have already received as much formal education as they will receive.
5. In the case of income, for example, complete inequality would mean that a single person captures 100 percent of all income and the rest of

the population receives none; the Gini coefficient would then be equal to 1. Conversely, a completely equal society would be one in which every person received the same amount of income. In this case, the Gini coefficient would be 0. In the case of education, perfect inequality means that all the education is received by a single person; perfect equality means that every person in the country has exactly the same number of years of education.
6. These figures refer only to the gap in years, not to inequality within each category, as in the case of the Gini coefficient. The Gini coefficient is akin to a coefficient of variation (that is, for a given variance, the Gini is lower if the mean is higher). Thus, the absolute gap between rich and poor may be constant or even growing, but if the mean years of school attainment for both groups are increasing faster than the gap, the Gini coefficient will decrease and inequality will be reduced.
7. The percentages of out-of-school children were estimated using the UNESCO methodology described in box 4.1 in chapter 4.
8. This finding requires further analysis. Anecdotal evidence suggests it may reflect the move from public to private school.
9. Gender is still an issue in many countries (including countries in which girls have more education than boys). The policies that produced gender equality and gender inequality in school attainment need to be analyzed.
10. Here the gross attendance rate is used instead of the net attendance rate because in developing countries many people study part time for many years. As a result, many postsecondary students are older than the official age for postsecondary education.

References

Arcia, Gustavo, Harry Anthony Patrinos, Emilio Porta, and Kevin Macdonald. 2011. "School Autonomy and Accountability: System Assessment for Benchmarking Education for Results, Regulatory and Institutional Framework." World Bank, Human Development Network, Washington, DC.

Bourguignon, François. 2006. "Distribution, Equity and Development." In *Equity and Development*, ed. Gudrun Kochendörfer-Lucius and Boris Pleskovic, 39–45. Washington, DC: World Bank.

Bourguignon, François, and Sébastien Dessus. 2007. "Equity and Development: Political Economy Considerations." In *No Growth without Equity? Inequality, Interests and Competition in Mexico*, ed. Santiago Levy and Michael Walton, 45–70. Washington, DC: World Bank.

Hanushek, Eric, and Ludger Wößmann. 2007. *Education Quality and Economic Growth*. Washington, DC: World Bank.

IIPS (International Institute for Population Sciences) and Macro International. 2007. *National Family Health Survey (NFHS-3), 2005–06: India: Volume I*. Mumbai, India: IIPS.

INSAE (Institut National de la Statistique et de l'Analyse Économique) and Macro International. 2007. *Enquête Démographique et de Santé (EDSB-III) - Bénin 2006*. Calverton, MD: INSAE and Macro International.

Mankiw, N. Gregory, David Romer, and David Weil. 1992. "A Contribution to the Empirics of Economic Growth." *Quarterly Journal of Economics* 107 (2): 407–37.

Porta, Emilio. 2011. "A Data Set for Estimating Global Indicators of Education Inequality." World Bank, Human Development Network, Washington, DC.

Pritchett, Lant. 2004. "Towards a New Consensus for Addressing the Global Challenge of the Lack of Education." Working Paper 43, Center for Global Development, Washington, DC.

Psacharopoulos, George, and Harry Anthony Patrinos. 2002. "Returns to Investment in Education: A Further Update." Policy Research Working Paper 2881, World Bank, Washington, DC.

Ravallion, Martin. 2006. "Should Poor People Care about Inequality?" In *Equity and Development*, ed. Gudrun Kochendörfer-Lucius and Boris Pleskovic, 89–101. Washington, DC: World Bank.

Stevens, Philip, and Martin Weale. 2004. "Education and Economic Growth." In *International Handbook on the Economics of Education*, ed. G. Johnes and Jill Johnes, 164–88. Camberley: Edward Elgar.

Thomas, Vinod, Yan Wang, and Xibo Fan. 2001. "Measuring Education Inequality. Gini Coefficients of Education." Policy Research Working Paper 2525, World Bank, Washington, DC.

World Bank. 2005. *World Development Report 2006: Equity and Development*. Washington, DC: World Bank.

Bibliography

Abdul Wahab, Mohammed. 1980. "Income and Expenditure Surveys in Developing Countries: Sample Design and Execution." LSMS (Living Standards Measurement Study Surveys) Working Paper 9, World Bank, Washington, DC.

Arcia, Gustavo. 2003. "The Incidence of Public Education Spending in Nicaragua: The Impact of the Education for All/Fast Track Initiative." Consulting report submitted to the World Bank, Washington, DC.

Arcia, Gustavo, Harry Anthony Patrinos, Emilio Porta, and Kevin Macdonald. 2011. "School Autonomy and Accountability." System Assessment for Benchmarking Education for Results, Regulatory and Institutional Framework. World Bank, Human Development Network, Washington, DC.

Barrera-Osorio, Felipe, Tazeen Fasih, and Harry Patrinos, with Lucrecia Santibañez. 2009. *Decentralized Decision-Making in Schools: The Theory and Evidence on School-Based Management*. Washington, DC: World Bank.

Bourguignon, François. 2006. "Distribution, Equity and Development." In *Equity and Development*, ed. Gudrun Kochendörfer-Lucius and Boris Pleskovic, 29–38. Washington, DC: World Bank.

Bourguignon, François, and Sébastien Dessus. 2007. "Equity and Development: Political Economy Considerations." In *No Growth without Equity? Inequality, Interests and Competition in Mexico*, ed. Santiago Levy and Michael Walton, 45–70. Washington, DC: World Bank.

Bibliography

Bruns, Barbara, Deon Filmer, and Harry Anthony Patrinos. 2011. *Making Schools Work: New Evidence on Accountability Reforms.* Washington, DC: World Bank.

Cassidy, Tom. 2005. *Education Management Information System (EMIS) Development in Latin America and the Caribbean: Lessons and Challenges.* Washington, DC: Inter-American Development Bank.

Crouch, Luis. 1997. "Sustainable EMIS: Who Is Accountable?" In *From Planning to Action: Government Initiatives for Improving School-Level Practices*, ed. David Chapman, Lars Mählck, and Anna Smulders, 211–39. Paris: UNESCO International Institute for Educational Planning.

Das, Jishnu. 2004. "Equity in Educational Expenditures: Can Government Subsidies Help?" Working Paper 3249, World Bank, Development Research Group, Washington, DC.

Deaton, Angus. 1997. *The Analysis of Household Surveys: A Microeconometric Approach.* Washington, DC: World Bank.

EPDC (Education Policy and Data Center). 2009. "How (Well) Is Education Measured in Household Surveys? A Comparative Analysis of the Education Modules in 30 Household Surveys from 1996–2005." IHSN (International Household Survey Network) Working Paper 002, World Bank, Washington, DC.

Filmer, Deon, and Lant Pritchett. 2001. "Estimating Wealth Effects without Expenditure Data—or Tears: An Application to Educational Enrollments in States of India." *Demography* 38 (1): 115–32.

Filmer, Deon, and Marta Rubio-Codina. 2011. "Information for Accountability." In *Making Schools Work: New Evidence on Accountability Reforms*, ed. Barbara Bruns, Deon Filmer, and Harry Anthony Patrinos. Washington, DC: World Bank.

Glewwe, Paul, and Michael Levin. 2005. "Presenting Simple Descriptive Statistics from Household Survey Data." In *Household Sample Surveys in Developing and Transition Countries.* New York: United Nations.

Grosh, Margaret, and Paul Glewwe. 1995. "A Guide to Living Standards Measurement Study Surveys and Their Data Sets." LSMS (Living Standards Measurement Study Surveys) Working Paper 120, World Bank, Washington, DC.

Hanushek, Eric, and Lutger Wößmann, 2007. *Education Quality and Economic Growth.* Washington, DC: World Bank.

IHSN (International Household Survey Network). 2011. "Harmonizing and Improving Survey Methods." January. http://www.surveynetwork.org/home/index.php?q=activities/harmonization/rationale.

IIPS (International Institute for Population Sciences) and Macro International. 2007. *National Family Health Survey (NFHS-3), 2005–06: India: Volume I*. Mumbai, India: IIPS.

Ilon, Lynn, and Peter Mock. 1991. "School Attributes, Household Characteristics, and the Demand for Schooling: A Case Study of Rural Peru." *International Review of Education* 37 (4): 429–51. DOI: 10.1007/BF00597620.

INSAE (Institut National de la Statistique et de l'Analyse Économique) and Macro International. 2007. *Enquête Démographique et de Santé (EDSB-III) - Bénin 2006*. Calverton, MD: INSAE and Macro International.

Kasprzyk, Daniel. 2005. "Measurement Error in Household Surveys: Sources and Measurement." In *Household Sample Surveys in Developing and Transition Countries*. New York: United Nations.

Keogh, Erica. 2005. "Developing a Framework for Budgeting for Household Surveys in Developing Countries." In *Household Sample Surveys in Developing and Transition Countries*, 279–300. New York: United Nations.

Kitamura, Yuto, and Yasushi Hirosato. 2009. "An Analytical Framework of Educational Development and Reform in Developing Countries: Interaction among Actors in the Context of Decentralization." In *The Political Economy of Educational Reforms and Capacity Development in Southeast Asia*, ed. Y. Hirosato and Y. Kitamura, 41–54. Berlin: Springer.

Klassen, Stephen. 2006. "What Is Equity?" In *Equity and Development*, ed. Gudrun Kochendörfer-Lucius and Boris Pleskovic. Washington, DC: World Bank.

Lepkowski, James. 2005. "Non-Observation Error in Household Surveys in Developing Countries." In *Household Sample Surveys in Developing and Transition Countries*. New York: United Nations.

Mankiw, N. Gregory, David Romer, and David Weil. 1992. "A Contribution to the Empirics of Economic Growth." *Quarterly Journal of Economics* 107 (2): 407–37.

OECD (Organisation for Economic Co-operation and Development). 2010. *The High Cost of Low Educational Performance: The Long-Run Economic Impact of Improving PISA Outcomes*. Paris: Program for International Student Assessment.

Patrinos, Harry, and Emmanuel Skoufias. 2007. *Economic Opportunities for Indigenous Peoples in Latin America*. Washington, DC: World Bank.

Porta, Emilio. 2011. "A Data Set for Estimating Global Indicators of Education Inequality." World Bank, Human Development Network, Washington, DC.

Bibliography

Porta, Emilio, and Jennifer Klein. 2010. "Increasing Education Data Availability for Knowledge Generation." Background paper for the Education Sector Strategy 2020, World Bank, Washington, DC.

Porta, Emilio, and José R. Laguna. 2007a. "Educational Equity in Central America: A Pending Issue for the Public Agenda." Academy for Educational Development, Washington, DC.

———. 2007b. "Equidad de la educación en Guatemala Centroamérica." Academy for Educational Development, Guatemala City, Guatemala.

Pritchett, Lant. 2004. "Towards a New Consensus for Addressing the Global Challenge of the Lack of Education." Working Paper 43, Center for Global Development, Washington, DC.

Psacharopoulos, George, and Harry Anthony Patrinos. 2002. "Returns to Investment in Education: A Further Update." Policy Research Working Paper 2881, World Bank, Washington, DC.

Ravallion, Martin. 2006. "Should Poor People Care about Inequality?" In *Equity and Development*, ed. Gudrun Kochendörfer-Lucius and Boris Pleskovic, 89–101. Washington, DC: World Bank.

Rutstein, Shea O., and Kiersten Johnson. 2004. "The DHS Wealth Index. DHS Comparative Reports 6." ORC Macro, Calverton, MD.

Scott, Kinnon, Diane Steele, and Tilahun Temesgen. 2005. "Living Standards Measurement Study Surveys." In *Household Sample Surveys in Developing and Transition Countries*, 523–56. New York: United Nations.

Stevens, Philip, and Martin Weale. 2004. "Education and Economic Growth." In *International Handbook on the Economics of Education*, ed. G. Johnes and Jill Johnes, 164–88. Camberley: Edward Elgar.

Strauss, John, and Duncan Thomas, 1995. "Human Resources: Empirical Modeling of Household and Family Decisions." In *Handbook of Development Economics* (vol. 3A), ed. J. Behrman and T. N. Srinivasan. Amsterdam: North Holland Press.

———. 2005. "Human Resources: Empirical Modeling of Household and Family Decisions." In *Handbook of Development Economics*, III, ed. J. Behrman and T. N. Srinivasan. Amsterdam: Elsevier Science.

Stukel, Diana Maria, and Yassamin Feroz-Zada. 2010. "Measuring Educational Participation: Analysis of Data Quality and Methodology Based on Ten Studies." Technical Paper 04, UNESCO Institute of Statistics, Montreal.

Sulliman, E. D., and S. E. El-Kogali. 2002. "Why Are the Children Out of School? Factors Affecting Children's Education in Egypt." Paper presented at the Ninth Economic Research Forum, Sharjah, United Arab Emirates, October 26–28.

UIS (UNESCO Institute for Statistics). 2005. *Global Education Digest 2005: Comparing Education Statistics across the World.* Montreal: UNESCO Institute for Statistics.

UN (United Nations). 2010. *The Millennium Development Goals Report 2010.* New York: United Nations.

UNESCO (United Nations Education, Scientific and Cultural Organization). 2010. "Use of Cohort Analysis Models for Assessing Educational Internal Efficiency." Technical Note, Paris.

UNESCO (United Nations Education, Scientific and Cultural Organization), and UNICEF (United Nations Children's Fund). 2005. *Children Out of School: Measuring Exclusion from Primary Education.* Montreal: UNESCO Institute for Statistics.

Vaasen, Martin, Mamadou Thiam, and Than Lê. "The Demographic and Health Surveys." In *Household Sample Surveys in Developing and Transition Countries*, 495–522. New York: United Nations.

World Bank. 2003. *World Development Report 2004: Making Services Work for Poor People.* Washington, DC: World Bank.

———. 2005. *World Development Report 2006: Equity and Development.* Washington, DC: World Bank.

———. 2010. *ADePT Version 4.1 Technical User's Guide.* Washington, DC: World Bank.

Yansaneh, Ibrahim S. 2005. "An Analysis of Cost Issues for Surveys in Developing and Transition Countries." In *Household Sample Surveys in Developing and Transition Countries*, 253–66. New York: United Nations.

About the Authors

Emilio Porta is a senior education specialist in the Human Development Network at the World Bank, Washington, DC

Gustavo Arcia is a senior economist at Analítica LLC, Miami, FL

Kevin Macdonald is an economist in the Human Development Network at the World Bank, Washington, DC

Sergiy Radyakin is an economist in the Development Research Group at the World Bank, Washington, DC

Michael Lokshin is an adviser in the Development Research Group at the World Bank, Washington, DC

Index

Boxes, figures, notes, and tables are indicated by *b*, *f*, *n*, and *t*, respectively.

A

ADePT Edu software, 1–3
  batch mode operation, 75–76
  common task performance, 55, 57
  complex survey design, 62
  compound fields, 51–53, 52*f*
  computation process, 37–42
  computational engine and output viewer selection, 69, 71, 72*f*
  data loading, 42–44, 43*f*–44*f*
  debug mode, 78–80, 79*f*
  education graphs, 132–35, 132*f*–139*f*
  education inequality assessment, 9–12, 118, 141–74
  error, warning, and notification messages, 85–87, 85*f*–86*f*
  Gini coefficient and Theil index techniques, 118
  global filter, 39
  hardware requirements, 33, 34*t*
  household survey analysis, 22, 24, 25*t*
  installation and setup, 34–35, 36*f*, 78
  licensing agreement acceptance, 35, 35*f*
  main screen, 40*f*–41*f*
  missing values recoding, 39
  module selection, 39*f*
  Original Data Report table, 87
  project management applications, 72–74, 73*f*
  reporting option, 55, 56*f*
  results replication, 74
  school-household data access, 5–12
  settings adjustments, 67–69, 68*f*–70*f*
  simulation analysis, 66–67
  software requirements, 33–34, 34*t*
  Start Menu, 38*f*
  starting and closing, 37
  system requirements, 33–34, 34*t*
  table of contents, 84*f*
  tables and graphs generation, 53–55, 54*f*–55*f*, 57–62, 57*f*, 62*f*
  troubleshooting, 78–80
  updates, 76–77, 77*f*
  variables specification, 44–51, 45*f*, 46*t*, 48*f*, 49, 50*f*, 50*t*, 51*f*, 64–66, 65*f*

Index

adult population, school attainment tables, 111, 113–18, 113f
  grade completion data, 114, 115f
  inequality in years of schooling, 114, 117f, 118
  percentage of age group, 113
age-based attendance, percentage of student-age population, school participation indicator tables, 99, 99f–101f
age-earning profile and education levels, 135, 138f–139f
attendance data
  education attainment inequality and, 146–47, 147f, 152–54, 153f–154f, 171–72, 174n10
  household survey analysis, 26–27
  regional disparities in
    postsecondary attendance, 160–61, 161f
    primary school, 157–59, 158f
    secondary school, 159–60, 159f
average years of schooling by age group, 113–14

B
batch mode operation, 75–76
birth dates, lack of, in household surveys, 28
Boolean expression, tables and graphics generation, 58–61

C
categorical variables, 44–51, 45f, 46t, 48f, 49, 50f, 50t, 51f
Central America, educational inequality assessment in, 11
completed education tab, 49
completion rate
  education inequality assessment, 143–44, 147–49, 148f
  primary school, 106
  regional disparities in, 165–67, 167f–168f
  secondary school, 107–8
compound fields, 51–53, 52f
computational engine selection, 69, 71, 72f
continuous variables, 44–51
contradictory values, in household surveys, 29
current school year quadrant, 47–51

D
datasets tab, 43f, 49–51
debug mode, 78–80, 79f
Demographic and Health Survey (DHS), 17–22, 24, 25t
  attendance and enrollment data in, 26–27
  EdData module, 21
  MEASURE DHS Project, 19–22
  non-educational data in, 27–28
  questionnaire content summary, 20–21, 20t
  Wealth Index, 21–22
disabled variables, ADePT, 49–50, 51f
dropout rate
  primary school, 105–6
  regional disparities, 163–64, 164f
  secondary school, 107
  by single grade (primary school), 111, 112f
dummy variables, 45–51

E
earning inequalities
  age-earning profile and education levels, 135, 138f–139f
  labor market outcome tables, 121–23, 122f
  school enrollment rates and, 134–35, 134f
economic independence indicators, 129–30, 130f
Edstat
  ADePT Edu software platform and, 2–3, 12
  Household Survey module, educational inequality assessment, 11–12
  website, 7–8
education expenditure tables, 118–21, 120f, 172, 174n2
Education for All (EFA) initiative, 152
education inequality assessment
  ADePT Edu software tools, 9–12, 141–74

Index

changes over time, 150–52, 151f
Gini coefficient. *See under* Gini coefficient
global indicators, 144–56, 151f, 155f–156f
household survey data, 12, 16–17
income inequality and school attainment, 145–46, 146f
internal efficiency in education and, 152–54, 153f
regional disparities. *See under* regional disparities
reporting function, 143–44
school attainment measurements, 114, 117f, 118
education levels
age-earning profile, 135, 138f–139f
earnings based on, 127, 128f
in household surveys, 27
labor market outcomes and, 135, 139f
rate of return for years of schooling, 130–31
school attendance ratios and out of school, by level, 88–93, 89f
Education Management Information Systems (EMIS), 6
education policy and ADePT Edu software platform, 1–3
Education Policy and Data Center
Educational Attainment Model, 8
Enrollment Rates Model, 9
Education Projections modules, 7–9
education sector performance, household survey data, 16–17
educational indicators
availability and quality of, 6–12
education inequality assessment, 10–12
global availability of data, 7–8, 8f
percentage of countries reporting data, 6, 7f
variation in, 16–17
EFA (Education for All) initiative, 152
EMIS (Education Management Information Systems), 6
enable only common variables checkpoint, 49–51
enrollment data
ADePT Edu graphs, 132–35, 132f–135f
household survey analysis, 26–27
overestimation errors, 139n4
equity, education inequality assessment and concept of, 141–42

F
frequencies, tables of, 61–62

G
gender disparities, educational inequality and, 141–43, 150–72, 174n9
Gini coefficient
computational algorithm, 140n5
earning inequalities, 121–23, 122f
education inequality assessment, 144–46, 145f–146f, 174n5
internal efficiency in education sector, 152–54, 153f
years of schooling by age, 118, 174n6
school attainment, 170–71, 170f
attendance ratios and, 146–47, 147f
primary completion rate and, 147–49, 148f
global filter, tables generation, ADePT Edu software, 57–61, 57f
global indicators
education inequality assessment, 144–56, 151f
educational attainment disparities, 155–56, 155f–156f
school participation disparities, 152–54, 153f–154f
school progression disparities, 154–55, 155f
grade completion, adult population, proportion of, 114, 115f–116f
graphics generation, 53–55, 54f–55f
education graphs, 132–39, 132f–139f
output graphs, generation and interpretation, 81–140, 82t, 84f–87f, 89f, 94f, 96f, 99f–101f, 104f, 109f, 113f, 115f–117f, 120f, 122f, 124f, 126f, 128f, 130f–139f
gross attendance rate, school participation indicator tables
postsecondary education, 93
primary school, 88, 90
secondary school, 91

Index

gross intake rate to grade 1
  net intake rate *vs.*, 94–95
  school participation indicator tables, 93–94, 94f

H

Highly Indebted Poor Countries (HIPC), educational inequality assessment, 11–12
household ID field, 45–51, 51f
household survey data, 15–16
  advantages and limitations, 26–29
  age, timing, and duration of, 27–28
  availability and quality of, 5–6
  DHS, 19–22
  education levels, 27
  education sector performance, 16–17
  educational inequality assessment and, 12, 16–17, 150–52, 151f
  enrollment *vs.* attendance, 26–27
  expenditures on education, 119–21, 120f, 174n2
  guidelines for using, 22, 24, 25t
  LSMS, 18–19
  main household surveys, 17–18
  MICS, 22–23
  missing and contradictory values, 29
  poverty quintiles and poverty groups, 28–29
  standard errors, 28

I

if-condition tab, 53–54, 57–61, 58f, 60f–61f
IHSN 2011 (International Household Survey Network), 15–17
IIASA/VID (International Institute for Applied Systems Analysis/Vienna Institute of Demography) Educational Attainment Model, 8
income quintiles
  educational attainment inequality and, 145–46, 145f–146f174n3, 174n56
  school enrollment rates and, 134–35, 134f
indicator tables, 81–82, 82t
intake rates
  education inequality assessment, 152–54, 153f, 171–72
  regional disparities in, 160–62, 162f
  school participation indicators, 93–95, 94f
internal efficiency in education sector, education inequality assessment, 152–54, 153f
International Household Survey Network (IHSN 2011), 15–17
International Institute for Applied Systems Analysis/Vienna Institute of Demography (IIASA/VID) Educational Attainment Model, 8
International Standard Classification of Education (ISCED), educational level classifications, 27

L

labor market outcome tables, 121–31
  earning inequalities, 121–23, 122f
  earnings by education level, 127, 128f
  economic independence, 129, 130f
  education levels and, 135, 139f
  returns on education, 129–31, 131f
  sector-based employment indicators, 125, 126f, 127
  youth employment, 123–25, 124f
labor market tab, 49, 50f, 50t, 51
language change in ADePT Edu software, 67–69, 68f
Living Standards Measurement Study (LSMS), 17–19, 19t, 21, 28–29
Lorenz curve
  education inequality assessment, 144–46, 145f, 174n4
  educational attainment, Nicaragua, 135, 138f–139f
LSMS (Living Standards Measurement Study), 17–19, 19t, 21, 28–29

M

main form variables, 46–47, 46t, 48f, 49, 50f, 50t, 51
MDGs. *See* Millennium Development Goals
MEASURE DHS Project, 19–22
MICS (Multiple Indicator Cluster Survey), 18, 20, 22–24, 23t, 25t

Index

Millennium Development Goals
(MDGs), 152
ADePT Edu software development, 5–6
data availability for, 7–8, 8f
Mincer earnings function, 129–30, 140n6
missing values
compound field, 52–53, 52f
defined, in ADePT Edu software,
62–64, 64f
in household surveys, 29
Multiple Indicator Cluster Survey (MICS),
18, 20, 22–24, 23t, 25t

N

NBS (Numerics by Stata), 69, 71, 72f
net attendance rate, school participation
indicator tables
primary school, 90
secondary school, 92
net enrollment rate (NER+)/adjusted net
attendance rate (NAR+), 26–27
Nicaragua
enrollment rates, 132–35, 132f–136f
survival rates, 133–39
Numerics by Stata (NBS), 69, 71, 72f

O

observations subsample, tables generation,
ADePT Edu software, 57–61
on-time percentage, school participation
indicator tables
primary education, 95–97, 96f
by single grade, 98
Original Data Report table, 87, 87f
out-of-school children, proportion of
ADePT Edu graphs, 134–35,
136f–137f, 174n7
global disparities in, 153–54, 154f
school participation indicator tables
dropout classification, by level, 103
late entry, by education level, 103
never in school percentage, 102–3,
102f
primary school, 90–91
reasons, 99–100, 99f–101f
secondary school, 92
typology of out of school, 100–103,
101f–102f

UNESCO method for estimating, 101b
output tables and graphs, 81–140, 82t,
84f–87f, 89f, 104f, 109f, 112f, 113f,
115f–117f, 120f, 122f, 124f, 126f,
128f, 130f–139f
contents table, 83, 84f
information tables, 83
notifications table, 83
original data report table, 87
school participation indicator tables,
88–103, 89f, 94f, 96f, 99f–102f
output viewer selection, ADePT Edu
software, 69, 71, 72f
over-age percentage, school participation
indicator tables
grade 1 students older than official
grade 1 age, 94–95, 94f
primary school, 97
by single grade, 98

P

parameter inputs, ADePT Edu software
specification, 45–51, 45f
participation indicators. *See also* school
participation indicator tables
primary school. *See under* primary school
secondary school. *See under* secondary
school
single grade, 98
postsecondary education
education attainment inequality and
attendance rates, 152–53
educational expenditure indicators, 121
gross attendance rate, 93
regional disparities in attendance,
160–61, 161f
repetition rate, 108
poverty quintiles/poverty groups
educational attainment inequality and
extreme poverty correlation,
149–50, 149f
in household surveys, 28–29
income inequality and school attainment
and, 145–46, 145f–146f
primary school
education attainment inequality
attendance ratios, 146–47, 147f,
152–53, 153f

189

Index

primary school (*continued*)
  completion rate, 147–49, 148*f*
  education inequality assessment in, 143–44
  educational expenditure indicators, 119–21, 120*f*
  participation indicators
    gross attendance rate, 88, 90
    net attendance rate, 90
    on-time percentage, 95–97, 96*f*
    out-of-school children, proportion of, 90–91
    over-age percentage, 97
    under-age percentage, 97
  progression indicators, 105–6, 110–11
  regional disparities in
    attendance rate, 157–59, 158*f*
    completion rates, 165–67, 167*f*–168*f*
    net primary intake, 160–62, 162*f*
    transition to secondary school, 167, 169, 169*f*
    transition rate to secondary school, 108, 164–67, 169, 169*f*, 172
Project Appraisal Documents, 9
project management applications
  ADePT Edu software, 72–74, 73*f*
  ADePT project files, different computer, 74
promotion rate
  primary school, 105
  secondary school, 107
  by single grade (primary school), 110
Public Expenditure Database, 9

R

rate of return for years of schooling, 129–31, 131*f*
recoding of variables, 65–66, 65*f*
regional disparities
  education inequality assessment, 156–71
    net primary intake, 160–62, 162*f*
    out-of-school children, 161–66, 163*f*–166*f*
    postsecondary attendance, 160–61, 161*f*
    primary completion rates, 165–67, 167*f*–168*f*
    primary school attendance, 157–59, 158*f*

primary-to-secondary transition rate, 167
school progression indicators, 164–67
secondary completion rates, 166–67, 168*f*
secondary school attendance, 159–60, 159*f*
primary school. *See under* primary school
school attainment, 167–71, 168*f*–170*f*
secondary school. *See under* secondary school
repetition rate
  postsecondary school, 108
  primary school, 105
  secondary school, 107
  by single grade (primary school), 110
reporting option
  ADePT Edu software, 55, 56*f*
  education inequality assessment, 143–44
results replication, ADePT Edu software, 74
returns on education indicators, 129–31, 131*f*

S

school attainment
  ADePT graphs, 132–35, 136*f*
  attendance inequality and, 146–47, 147*f*
  changes over time in, 150–52, 151*f*
  education inequality assessment, 143–44
  Gini coefficient. *See under* Gini coefficient
  global disparities in, 155–56, 155*f*–156*f*
  income inequality and, 145–46, 145*f*–146*f*
  primary school completion rate and, 147–49, 148*f*
  regional disparity in, 167–71
school attainment tables, 111–18
  adult population, 111, 113–18, 113*f*
  grade completion data, 114, 115*f*–116*f*
  inequality in years of schooling, 114, 117*f*, 118
  percentage of age group, 113
  average years of schooling by age, 113–14

Index

Gini coefficient for years of schooling by age, 118
Theil index for years of schooling by age, 118
school data and ADePT Edu software development, 5–12
school participation indicator tables, 88–103, 89f, 94f, 96f, 99f–101f
   education inequality assessment, 143–44
   global disparities in participation, 152–54, 153f–154f
   gross attendance rate
      postsecondary education, 93
      primary school, 88, 90
      secondary school, 91
   gross intake rate, to grade 1, 93–94, 94f
   net attendance rate
      primary school, 90
      secondary school, 92
   net intake rate, gross intake rate, 94–95
   on-time percentage
      primary education, 95–97, 96f
      by single grade, 98
   out-of-school children. *See under* out-of-school children, proportion of
   over-age percentage
      grade 1 students older than official grade 1 age, 94–95, 94f
      primary school, 97
      by single grade, 98
   percentage of student-age population, attendance by age, 99, 99f–101f
   school attendance ratios and out of school, by level, 88–93, 89f
   survival rate to grade 5, 94–95, 94f
   under-age percentage
      primary school, 97
      by single grade, 98
school progression tables, 103–11, 104f, 109f, 112f
   completion rate
      primary school, 106
      secondary school, 107–8
   dropout rate
      primary school, 105–6
      secondary school, 107
   education inequality assessment, 143–44
   global disparities in, 154–55, 155f
   promotion rate
      primary school, 105
      secondary school, 106
   regional disparities, 164–67, 165f–166f
   repetition rate
      postsecondary education, 108
      primary school, 105
      secondary school, 107
   transition rate, primary to secondary, 108
secondary school
   education attainment inequality and attendance rates, 152–53, 153f
   educational expenditure indicators, 119, 120f, 121
   participation indicators
      gross attendance rate, 91
      net attendance rate, 92
      out-of-school children, proportion of, 92
   primary school transition to, 108, 164–67, 169, 169f, 172
   progression indicators, 107–8, 111, 112f
   regional disparities
      attendance rates, 159–60, 159f, 172
      completion rates, 166–68, 167f–168f
      primary school transition to, 108, 164–67, 169, 169f, 172
sector-based employment indicators, 125, 126f, 127
settings adjustments, ADePT Edu software, 67–69, 68f–70f
simulations, ADePT Edu software applications, 66–67
single grade participation indicators, 98
single grade progression indicators
   primary school, 108–11, 109f
   secondary education, 111, 112f
Social Protection module, 51–53
SPSS (.sav) datasets
   ADePT Edu data loading, 42–44, 43f–44f
   education inequality assessment, 10

Index

standard errors
    ADePT tables generation, 61–62, 139n2
    in household surveys, 28
Stata (.dta) applications
    ADePT Edu data loading, 42–44, 44f
    education inequality assessment, 10
    if-conditions in, 58–61
    standard errors in, 61–62, 139n2
Sub-Saharan Africa
    education inequality assessment in, 9
    income inequality and school attainment in, 145–46, 145f–146f
survey design, ADePT Edu software applications, 62
Survey Settings button, 47–51
survival rate to grade 5
    ADePT Edu graphs, 133–34, 134f
    school participation indicator tables, 94–95, 94f

T

tables generation, 53–55, 54f–55f
    output tables, generation and interpretation, 81–140, 82t, 84f–87f, 89f, 94f, 96f, 99f–101f, 104f, 109f, 112f, 113f, 115f–117f, 120f, 122f, 124f, 126f, 128f, 130f–139f
    standard errors and tables of frequencies, 61–62
    subsample of observations, 57–61
Theil index
    earning inequalities, 122f, 123
    education inequality assessment, years of schooling by age, 118
transition rate, primary to secondary school, 108, 164–67, 169f, 172
troubleshooting, 78–80

U

under-age percentage, school participation indicator tables
    primary school, 97
    by single grade, 98
UNESCO Institute for Statistics (UIS), 7
    education inequality assessment tools, 10
    enrollment measurements, 26–27
    out-of-school children, estimating proportion of, 101b
United Nations Children's Fund (UNICEF), 18, 22
updates to ADePT Edu software, 76–77, 77f
U.S. Agency for International Development (USAID), 17–18

V

variables specification, 44–51, 45f, 46–47, 46t, 48f, 49, 50f, 50t, 51, 64–66, 65f
variables tab
    compound fields, 52–53, 52f
    variables specification, 46–47, 46t, 48f, 49, 50f, 50t, 51, 64–66, 65f

W

Wealth Index (DHS), 21–22
World Bank
    ADePT Edu software development, 1, 5–6
    Edstat website and, 7–8
    education inequality assessment tools, 10
    Education Projects Database, 9
    Living Standards Measurement Study (LSMS), 17–19

Y

youth employment indicators, 123–25, 124f

ECO-AUDIT
Environmental Benefits Statement

The World Bank is committed to preserving endangered forests and natural resources. The Office of the Publisher has chosen to print *Assessing Sector Performance and Inequality in Education* on recycled paper with 50 percent postconsumer fiber in accordance with the recommended standards for paper usage set by the Green Press Initiative, a nonprofit program supporting publishers in using fiber that is not sourced from endangered forests. For more information, visit www.greenpressinitiative.org.

Saved:
- 5 trees
- 2 million Btu of total energy
- 446 lb. of net greenhouse gases
- 2,008 gal. of waste water
- 127 lb. of solid waste